by Rachel Carley

Illustrations by
Ray Skibinski
and Ed Lam

A ROUNDTABLE PRESS BOOK

A HENRY HOLT REFERENCE BOOK
Henry Holt and Company / New York

The Visual Dictionary of American Domestic Architecture

A HENRY HOLT REFERENCE BOOK

Henry Holt and Company, Inc.
Publishers since 1866
115 West 18th Street
New York, New York 10011

Henry Holt ® is a registered
trademark of Henry Holt and Company, Inc.

Published in Canada by Fitzhenry & Whiteside Ltd.,
195 Allstate Parkway, Markham, Ontario L3R 4T8.

Library of Congress Cataloging-in-Publication Data
Carley, Rachel.
The visual dictionary of American domestic architecture / Rachel
Carley ; illustrated by Ray Skibinski. — 1st ed.
p.   cm.
Includes index.
1. Architecture, Domestic—United States—Dictionaries.
2. Architecture—United States—Dictionaries.   I. Title.
NA7205.C27   1994   94-20071
728'.0973—dc20   CIP

ISBN 0-8050-2646-0

Henry Holt books are available for special promotions and premiums.
For details contact: Director, Special Markets.

A ROUNDTABLE PRESS BOOK
Directors: Marsha Melnick, Susan E. Meyer
Executive Editor: Amy T. Jonak
Editors: William L. Broecker, Marisa Bulzone, Sue Heinemann
Editorial Assistants: Megan Keiler, Alexis Wilson
Architectural Consultant: Andrew Scott Dolkart
Designer: Betty Binns
Design/Production Associates: Leslie Goldman, Laura Smyth
Illustrators: Ray Skibinski, chapters 1, 2, 5, 7, 8
            Ed Lam, chapters 3, 4, 6, 9, 10, 11, 12

Printed in the United States of America
All first editions are printed on acid-free paper. ∞

10   9   8   7   6   5   4   3   2

Contents

Acknowledgments

Each of the more than 500 labeled illustrations in *The Visual Dictionary of American Domestic Architecture* was drawn specifically for this volume. Gathering the research materials on which these pictures were based was an extensive undertaking, and it would not have been possible without the generosity and help of numerous individuals, libraries, museums, and preservation organizations across the country.

I am grateful for the advice and expertise shared by Andrew Scott Dolkart of the Columbia University School of Architecture. I also thank the following: the staff of the American Indian Archaeological Institute in Washington, Connecticut, and the Museum of the American Indian in New York City; Jonathan Fricker, Director of the Division of Historic Preservation, Baton Rouge; the staff of the Missouri Historical Society; Phoebe Hopkins of the Berks County Conservancy in Pennsylvania; the library staff of the Museum of New Mexico in Santa Fe; and Hope and Kenneth LeVan of Oley, Pennsylvania, who gave me a memorable tour of early Germanic buildings in that state and provided measured drawings of their own home.

The periodical and rare book collections of Avery Architectural Library at Columbia University were an invaluable resource for this project. I am also grateful to the library and archives of the American Institute of Architects in Washington, D.C., which houses the George P. Lindsay Collection published in the White Pine Monograph Series. (Many of these monographs have been reprinted in a multi-volume series, *The Architectural Treasures of Early America*, published by the National Historical Society of Harrisburg, Pennsylvania.)

I am indebted to the scholarship of numerous architectural historians whose original research and published work were of great help: Abbott Lowell Cummings for his work on the postmedieval architecture of colonial Massachussetts; Andrew Scott Dolkart for his research on the Greek Revival; Robert Easton and Peter Nabokov for their extensive study of Native American architecture; Ronald Haase for his documentation of the Cracker architecture of Florida; Thomas Hubka for his theory on the connected farm buildings of Maine; Sarah Landau for her theory on the origins of the Stick Style; Albert Manucy for his research on the early architecture of St. Augustine, Florida; William McMillen for his research on early Dutch and English Colonial building technology; Charles Peterson for his documentation of the French houses of the Illinois Country; Robert St. George and Robert F. Trent for their research and fieldwork in 17th-century New England building; John Michael Vlach for his study on the origins of the shotgun house; and William Woys Weaver for his research on early Germanic buildings in Pennsylvania.

Finally, I extend my sincere thanks to Marsha Melnick, Susan Meyer, and the entire staff of Roundtable Press, and especially to Ray Skibinski and Ed Lam, two talented and remarkably patient illustrators, who often did double duty as architects.

Introduction

When I was approached with the idea of a dictionary of American architecture, my first reaction was, "How do you *define* architecture?" There is, of course, an accepted vocabulary of terms for the various elements of a building, but by breaking anything down into individual parts out of context, you risk obscuring the broader picture. With these concerns in mind, *The Visual Dictionary of American Domestic Architecture* evolved as an illustrated reference guide to American building that defines terminology through the universal language of pictures, but also attempts to explain architectural types and styles within the framework of the social, historical, geographic, climactic, and ethnic influences that shaped them.

To help narrow down the subject, this book is concerned exclusively with domestic building, which answered its own distinctive needs and purposes independent of civic, religious, and commercial architecture. Beginning with the indigenous dwelling types of Native American groups and working up to the 1990s, styles and types are presented chronologically, grouped by chapters according to the names and periods by which they are generally recognized.

In reality, of course, buildings don't fall so neatly into categories, and what emerges is a fascinating timeline of both continuity and contrasts. From the beginning of European settlement until the post-Revolutionary period, the prevailing tastes in American architectural styles—which were extremely fashion-conscious—closely mirrored changing trends in England, albeit 20 years or so behind. That, however, is only part of the picture. Isolated by politics, religion, and language, many settlements, such as those established by the French in the Mississippi Valley and by the Spanish in Florida and the Southwest, had their own distinctly individual character. These colonies may have been on the same continent as colonies founded contemporaneously by English, Dutch, and Germanic immigrants, but for all intents and purposes they were foreign countries to one another.

As communication and transportation improved, and as territories changed hands, building styles and traditions were absorbed to some degree from one culture to another. From the start, however, while one thing was happening, something else was always going on. Currents in architecture overlapped, incorporating features from one style that was going out with those of another style coming in. Moreover, the houses built by one economic class were entirely different from those of another. This was as true in the 1600s as it was in the Victorian era, when it was just as common to spend thousands of dollars on imported marble as it was to order gingerbread trim from a catalog—and it remains true today.

In an effort to present a comprehensive picture of changing currents and trends, *The Visual Dictionary of American Domestic Architecture* illustrates both high-style and vernacular buildings, exploring urban, rural, and regional variations. Each chapter not only offers several exterior views, but also tries to present the many elements that are integral to defining and identifying a particular style or type, including floor plans, interior architectural features, and characteristic details, as well as barns, garages, and other outbuildings. Also included throughout the volume are diagrams that explain the underpinnings or "anatomy" of building structures. Among these anatomies are structural systems distinctive to a particular group, such as the anchorbent frame of the Dutch colonists, along with innovations such as the balloon frame, which precipitated major changes in the development of American architecture.

The idea behind this multilayered approach is that it is not enough to show *what* something looked like: This visual dictionary seeks to put enough pieces together to explain *why* it looked that way. In order not to repeat what has already been accomplished by other architectural reference books, I have made an effort to present buildings and elements that are representative of their period but have not been published frequently before.

The majority of the illustrations are based on designs and advertisements published in contemporary journals. Many of the Victorian buildings, for example, come from the pages of *American Architect and Building News*, begun in 1876 as the first magazine in America devoted to architectural design. Others derive from popular plan books of the late 19th and early 20th centuries. Still others are based on the photographs and measured drawings of the Historic American Buildings Survey (HABS), a government-sponsored program that has documented thousands of historic buildings since 1933 (many now demolished). This kind of research has made it possible to show a single element in great detail, such as both sides of the same door, and it has yielded many surprises, ranging from the startling graphic interior paint patterns used by German Colonial settlers to a garage designed in 1916 as a miniature Swiss chalet.

The Visual Dictionary of American Domestic Architecture is designed to be both a reference book and a field guide, intended for students, architects, and anybody curious about the buildings they see in their own neighborhoods. No single book can offer a definitive analysis of a subject as complex as American architecture, but I hope that through simple labeled illustrations, this dictionary will answer questions, clarify terms, and invite readers to explore. In the end, there is no better way to learn about buildings than to look at them.

The Visual

Dictionary of

American

Domestic

Architecture

Chapter One
Native American Dwellings

At the time of European colonization in the 16th and 17th centuries, there were some 300 native groups in North America. While Native American shelters differed significantly across the continent, three broad types can be identified: pole- and sapling-framed dwellings, more substantial gable-roofed timber and plank houses, and "earth" homes made primarily of mud, clay, or stone. Many of these indigenous building types date back thousands of years; some are still used today.

Quite naturally, Native American building evolved in direct response to climate, local materials, and hunting and farming patterns, as well as to social and religious organization. Wood structures prevailed in the forested areas of the East, the Great Lakes, California, and the Northwest Coast. Peoples of the Southwest and lower Mississippi recognized the advantage of mud plaster made from local clay or adobe (sun-dried earth and straw), which absorbs heat during the day and holds it in at night. In the Deep South, cool open-air shelters developed, raised off the ground to provide protection from snakes and flooding. All groups adapted their homes to changing seasons, using shade arbors in hot weather, and erecting windbreaks of planks, thatch, or adobe and adding warm interior liners for winter months.

On the Great Plains, the portable hide-covered tipi served the seminomadic buffalo-hunting tribes, who used dogs, and later horses, to transport the dismantled framing poles to new hunting grounds. Painted tipi patterns held mystical meanings, which might also affect the siting of a dwelling. The Plains Indians, for example, revered the circle as a symbol of the nest, and the Navajo hogan always faces east, toward the rising sun.

Pole and Sapling Frame

ALGONQUIAN WIGWAM (NORTHEAST AND GREAT LAKES)

FRAME

BARK TIE DETAIL

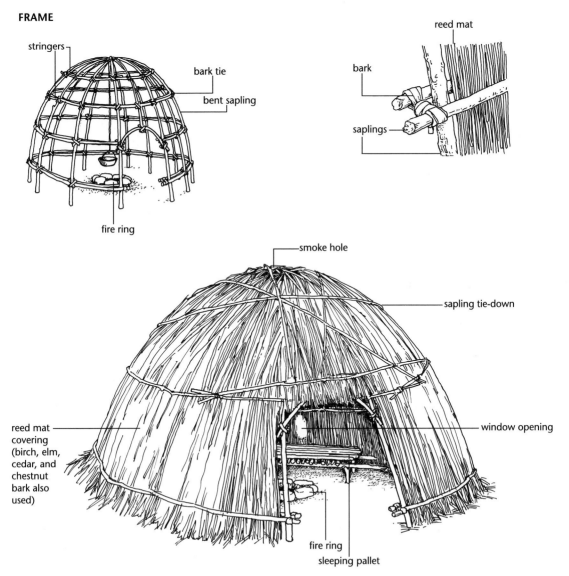

stringers

bark tie

bent sapling

fire ring

reed mat

bark

saplings

smoke hole

sapling tie-down

window opening

reed mat covering (birch, elm, cedar, and chestnut bark also used)

fire ring

sleeping pallet

Pole and Sapling Frame

IROQUOIS LONGHOUSE
(NORTHEAST AND GREAT LAKES)

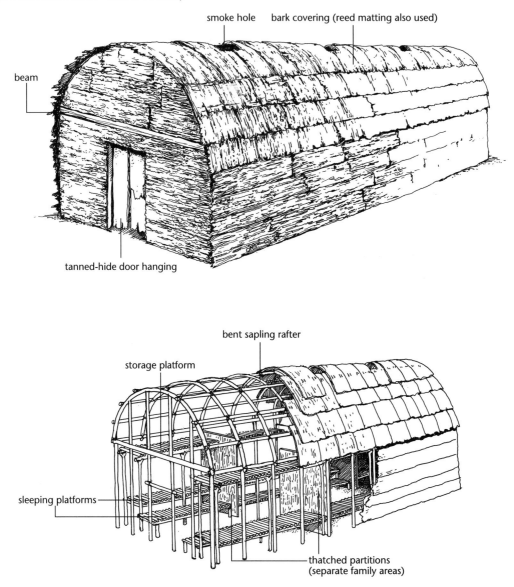

smoke hole   bark covering (reed matting also used)

beam

tanned-hide door hanging

bent sapling rafter

storage platform

sleeping platforms

thatched partitions
(separate family areas)

Most Native Americans lived communally, as shown in this 16th-century engraving after a 1585 drawing by John White. The Algonquian village of Pomeiooc, in what is now North Carolina, consisted of barrel-roofed structures ranging from forty to one hundred feet long, and each housing several families. Reed mat coverings could be rolled up or removed for ventilation. During hunting and fishing seasons, the Algonquians traveled away from their villages, setting up camp with smaller, temporary wigwams.

Pole and Sapling Frame

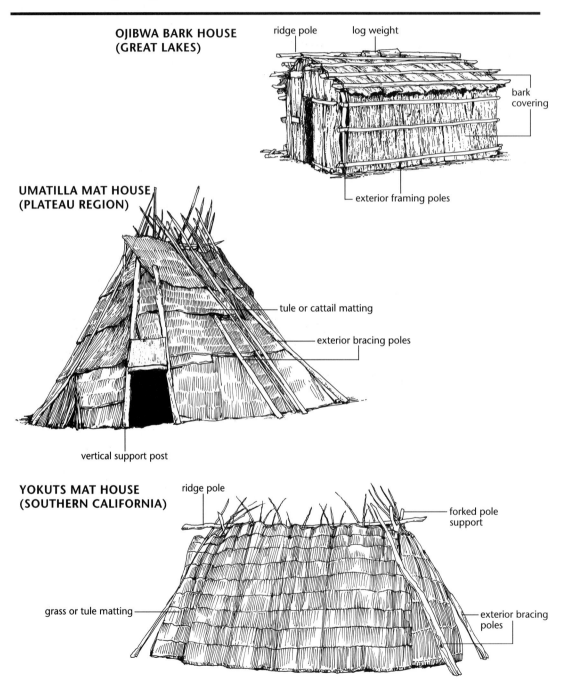

OJIBWA BARK HOUSE (GREAT LAKES)

ridge pole

log weight

bark covering

exterior framing poles

UMATILLA MAT HOUSE (PLATEAU REGION)

tule or cattail matting

exterior bracing poles

vertical support post

YOKUTS MAT HOUSE (SOUTHERN CALIFORNIA)

ridge pole

forked pole support

grass or tule matting

exterior bracing poles

Pole and Sapling Frame

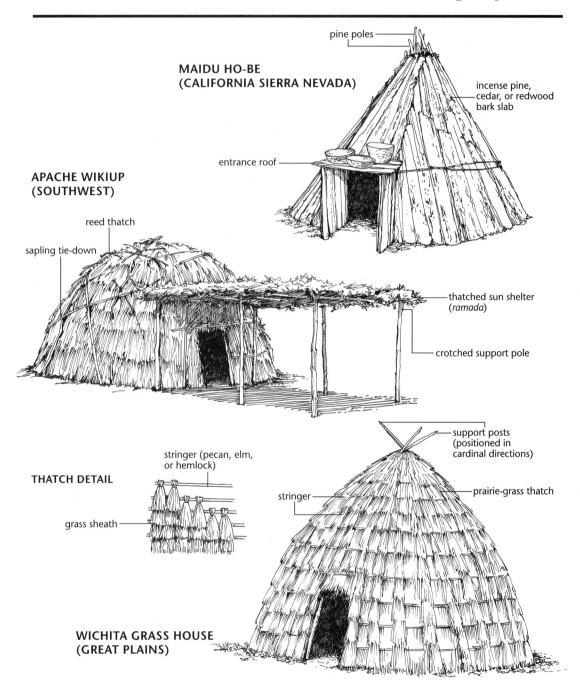

pine poles

MAIDU HO-BE
(CALIFORNIA SIERRA NEVADA)

incense pine, cedar, or redwood bark slab

entrance roof

APACHE WIKIUP
(SOUTHWEST)

reed thatch

sapling tie-down

thatched sun shelter (*ramada*)

crotched support pole

support posts (positioned in cardinal directions)

stringer (pecan, elm, or hemlock)

THATCH DETAIL

stringer

prairie-grass thatch

grass sheath

WICHITA GRASS HOUSE
(GREAT PLAINS)

Pole and Sapling Frame

TIPI (GREAT PLAINS AND SOUTHWEST)

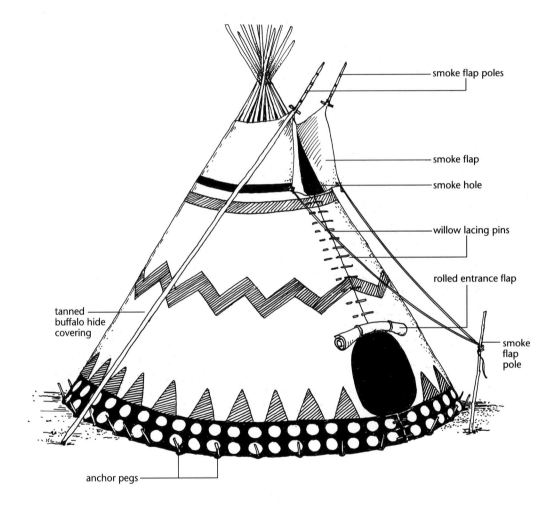

smoke flap poles

smoke flap

smoke hole

willow lacing pins

rolled entrance flap

tanned buffalo hide covering

smoke flap pole

anchor pegs

Anatomy of a Tipi

The tipi was the portable shelter of the Plains Indians, including the Cree, Blackfeet, Crow, and Cheyenne. This tentlike dwelling consisted of a basic frame of either three or four poles (of red cedar or lodgepole pine) that were positioned in cardinal directions and tilted to brace against prevailing winds, producing an oval, rather than a round, plan. Intermediate poles were laid over the frame, followed by a hide covering. When it was time to move to a new hunting ground, the disassembled parts were packed onto a drag, or travois, pulled by dogs. After horses were introduced to North America by the Spanish in the 1500s, tipis doubled in size, as these animals could pull a heavier load.

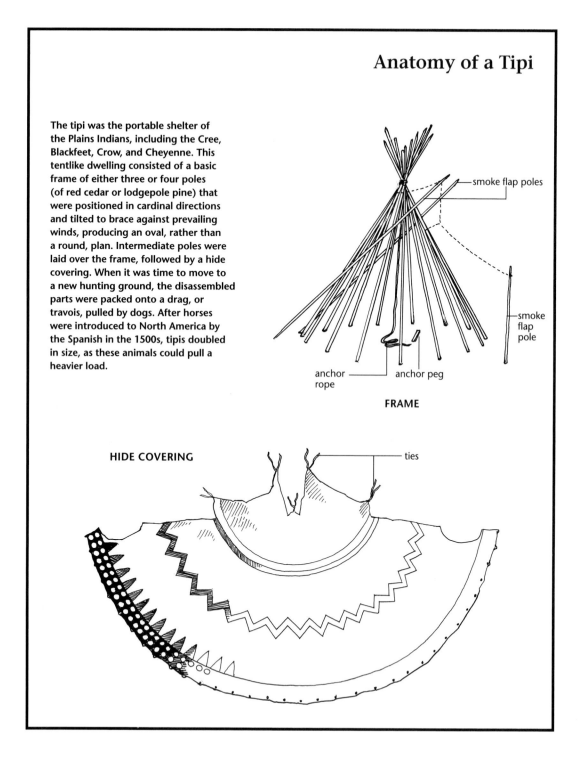

smoke flap poles

smoke flap pole

anchor rope

anchor peg

FRAME

HIDE COVERING

ties

Gable Roof

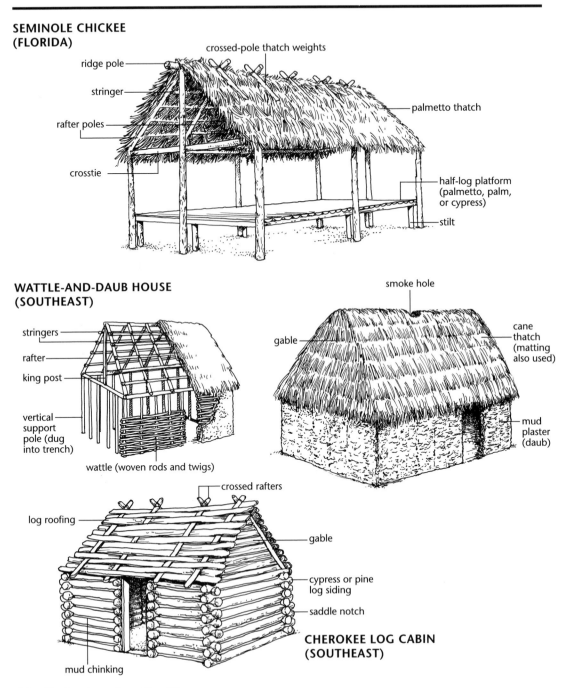

**SEMINOLE CHICKEE
(FLORIDA)**

crossed-pole thatch weights

ridge pole

stringer

rafter poles

crosstie

palmetto thatch

half-log platform
(palmetto, palm,
or cypress)

stilt

**WATTLE-AND-DAUB HOUSE
(SOUTHEAST)**

smoke hole

stringers

rafter

king post

vertical
support
pole (dug
into trench)

wattle (woven rods and twigs)

gable

cane
thatch
(matting
also used)

mud
plaster
(daub)

crossed rafters

log roofing

gable

cypress or pine
log siding

saddle notch

**CHEROKEE LOG CABIN
(SOUTHEAST)**

mud chinking

Gable Roof

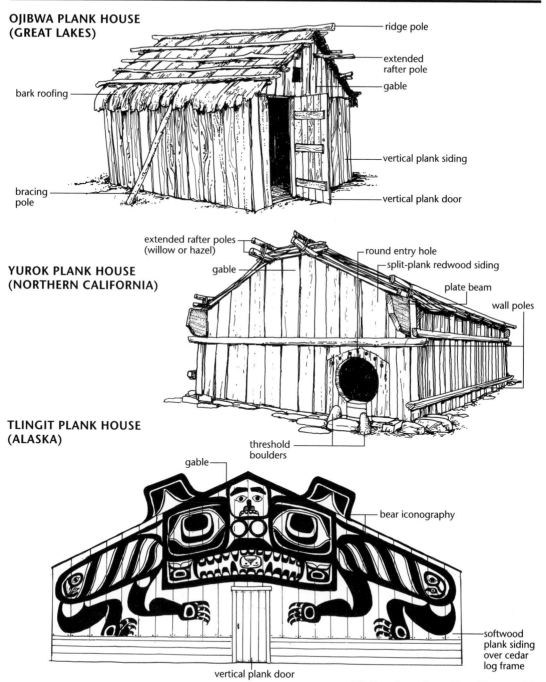

OJIBWA PLANK HOUSE (GREAT LAKES)

ridge pole

extended rafter pole

gable

bark roofing

vertical plank siding

bracing pole

vertical plank door

YUROK PLANK HOUSE (NORTHERN CALIFORNIA)

extended rafter poles (willow or hazel)

gable

round entry hole

split-plank redwood siding

plate beam

wall poles

TLINGIT PLANK HOUSE (ALASKA)

threshold boulders

gable

bear iconography

softwood plank siding over cedar log frame

vertical plank door

Earth Wall

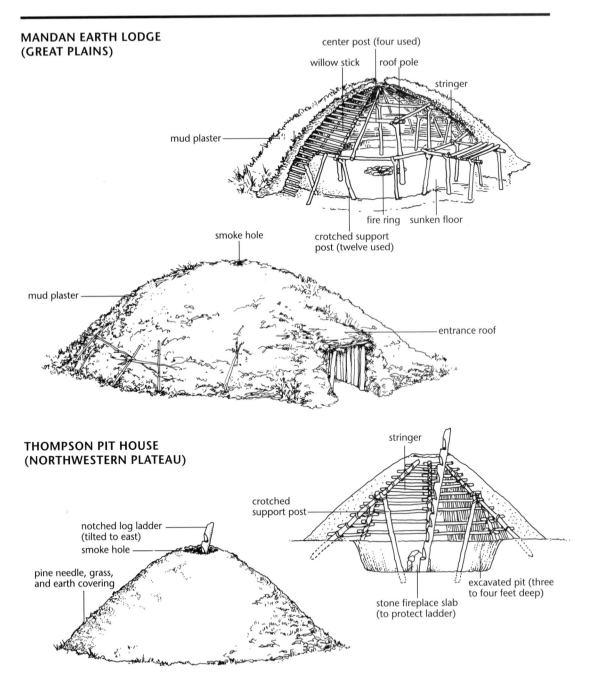

**MANDAN EARTH LODGE
(GREAT PLAINS)**

center post (four used)

willow stick   roof pole

stringer

mud plaster

fire ring   sunken floor

crotched support
post (twelve used)

smoke hole

mud plaster

entrance roof

**THOMPSON PIT HOUSE
(NORTHWESTERN PLATEAU)**

stringer

crotched
support post

notched log ladder
(tilted to east)

smoke hole

pine needle, grass,
and earth covering

stone fireplace slab
(to protect ladder)

excavated pit (three
to four feet deep)

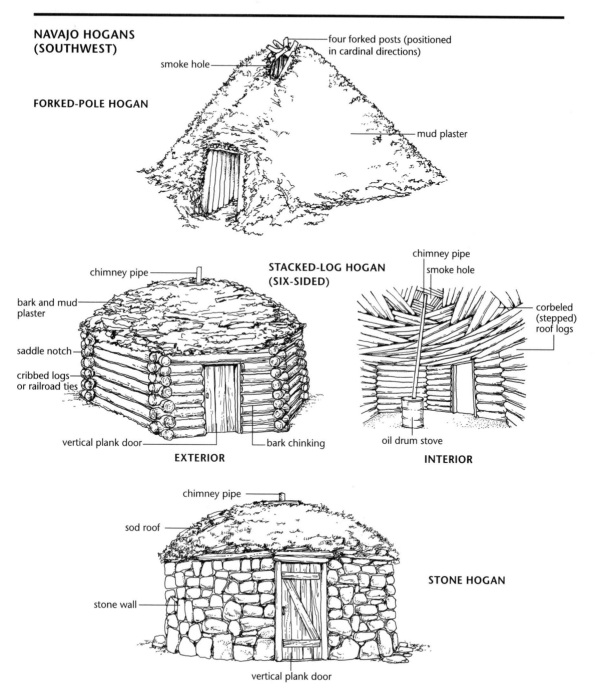

**NAVAJO HOGANS
(SOUTHWEST)**

FORKED-POLE HOGAN

four forked posts (positioned in cardinal directions)

smoke hole

mud plaster

**STACKED-LOG HOGAN
(SIX-SIDED)**

chimney pipe

bark and mud plaster

saddle notch

cribbed logs or railroad ties

vertical plank door

bark chinking

EXTERIOR

chimney pipe

smoke hole

corbeled (stepped) roof logs

oil drum stove

INTERIOR

chimney pipe

sod roof

stone wall

STONE HOGAN

vertical plank door

Earth Wall

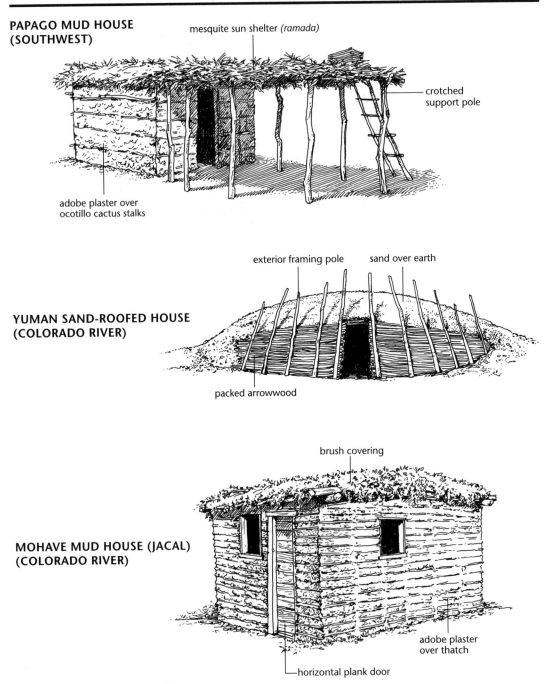

PAPAGO MUD HOUSE (SOUTHWEST)

mesquite sun shelter *(ramada)*

crotched support pole

adobe plaster over ocotillo cactus stalks

YUMAN SAND-ROOFED HOUSE (COLORADO RIVER)

exterior framing pole

sand over earth

packed arrowwood

MOHAVE MUD HOUSE (JACAL) (COLORADO RIVER)

brush covering

adobe plaster over thatch

horizontal plank door

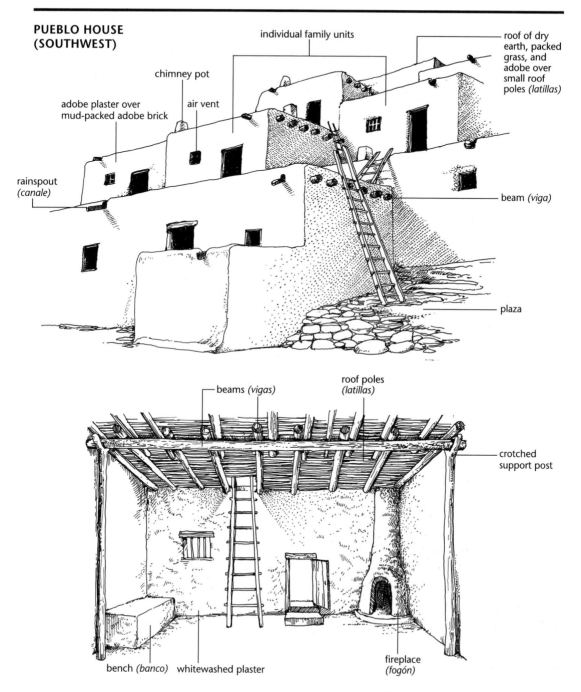

**PUEBLO HOUSE
(SOUTHWEST)**

individual family units

roof of dry earth, packed grass, and adobe over small roof poles (latillas)

chimney pot

air vent

adobe plaster over mud-packed adobe brick

rainspout (canale)

beam (viga)

plaza

beams (vigas)

roof poles (latillas)

crotched support post

bench (banco)   whitewashed plaster

fireplace (fogón)

Chapter Two
Continental Influences

The first Europeans to establish a strong identity in America were the Spanish, who founded the earliest permanent colonial settlement at St. Augustine, in the territory they called Florida, in 1565. Spanish colonization—which lasted until 1821—produced a string of military outposts and missions from Florida to Virginia, into Louisiana, and from the Southwest territories into California.

In the North, enterprising Dutch fur traders arrived in the Hudson River Valley in 1610 and founded the colony of New Netherland in 1621. The term "Dutch Colonial" actually refers to an amalgam of building traditions brought to the region between the Connecticut and Delaware rivers by a broad range of immigrants, including the Dutch, Flemish, Swedes, French Huguenots, Walloons, and Prussians.

In the 1680s, a climate of religious tolerance began drawing German and Swiss settlers from the Lower Rhine palatinate to the Pennsylvania colony, as well as to areas of Virginia, Maryland, Delaware, and North Carolina. While many assimilated into the English culture already established (see Chapter Three), small separatist sects, including the Moravians, Amish, Dunkers, Schwenkfelders, and Mennonites, held on to a strong Germanic identity clearly evident in regional architecture.

French colonists first made their mark in 1682, when La Salle descended the Mississippi River. Consisting largely of trading posts dependent on Quebec, the upper region of the Mississippi Valley was known as the Illinois Country. In 1718 this became part of the Louisiana Territory, where the Acadians (French Canadians from Nova Scotia) and the Creoles (descendants of West Indian, French, and Spanish settlers) blended their own architectural vocabulary into a distinctive regional style.

PLANK HOUSE (CASA DE TABLAS)
(FLORIDA TERRITORY)

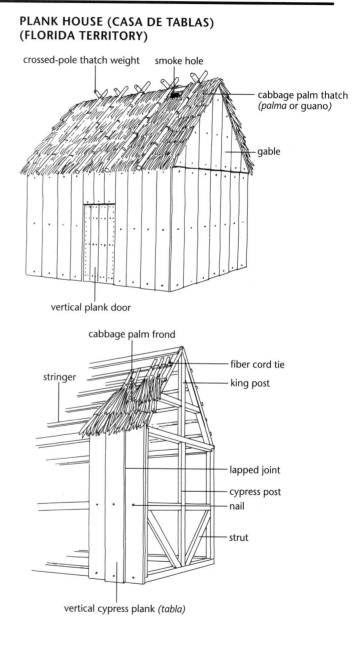

crossed-pole thatch weight

smoke hole

cabbage palm thatch
(*palma* or guano)

gable

vertical plank door

cabbage palm frond

stringer

fiber cord tie

king post

lapped joint

cypress post

nail

strut

vertical cypress plank (*tabla*)

The largest settlements in the Spanish Southeast grew around such military outposts as Pensacola and St. Augustine, Florida, which were built on a European grid plan. Walled houses fronted directly on the street; a door through the wall provided access to an enclosed yard, where one entered the house through a side or rear loggia, or roofed gallery. Along with hanging street balconies and galleries, these practical outdoor rooms usually faced southeast, to catch prevailing summer breezes and the warmth of the low winter sun. Many early homes in St. Augustine were built of coquina, an indigenous limestone made of shell aggregate the Spanish discovered on nearby Anastasia Island in 1583. Coated with tabby, a cement made of oyster shells and lime, coquina proved a durable and waterproof type of masonry.

In the Southwest the prevailing building material was the local clay adobe, mud mixed with a chopped straw binder and used as plaster or sun-dried in bricks. Here the Spanish concept of the enclosed household found expression in large, self-contained ranchos and haciendas. One of the most distinctive features of Spanish architecture in this region is the *fogón*, a bell-shaped corner fireplace.

Anatomy of Tabby Wall Construction

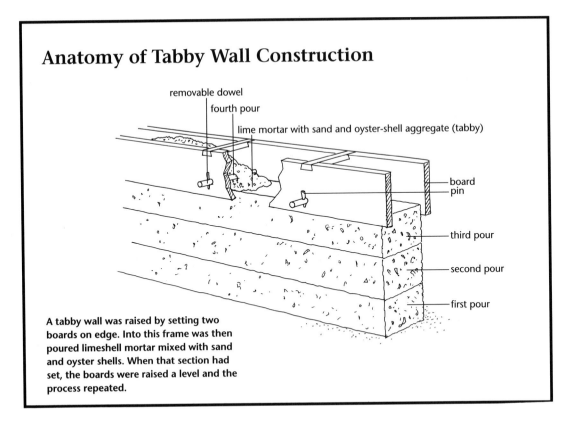

removable dowel

fourth pour

lime mortar with sand and oyster-shell aggregate (tabby)

board
pin

third pour

second pour

first pour

A tabby wall was raised by setting two boards on edge. Into this frame was then poured limeshell mortar mixed with sand and oyster shells. When that section had set, the boards were raised a level and the process repeated.

FLAT-ROOFED HOUSE (AZOTEA) (FLORIDA TERRITORY)

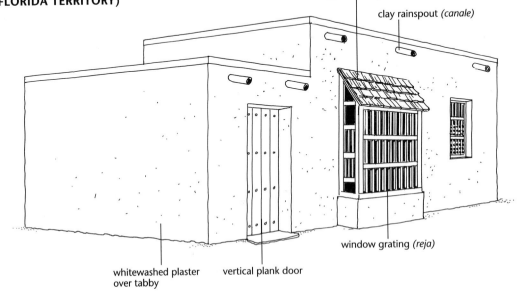

cypress shingles

clay rainspout (canale)

window grating (reja)

whitewashed plaster over tabby

vertical plank door

STREET HOUSE
(FLORIDA TERRITORY)

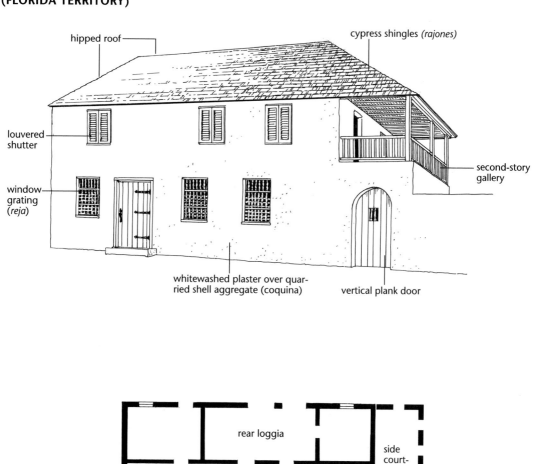

hipped roof

cypress shingles (rajones)

louvered shutter

second-story gallery

window grating (reja)

whitewashed plaster over quarried shell aggregate (coquina)

vertical plank door

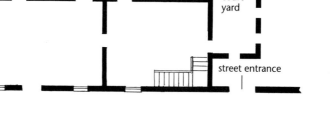

rear loggia

side court-yard

street entrance

Spanish Colonial

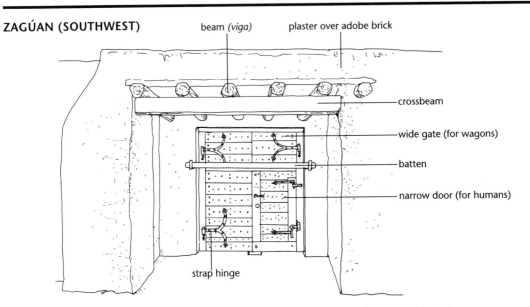

beam *(viga)*

plaster over adobe brick

crossbeam

wide gate (for wagons)

batten

narrow door (for humans)

strap hinge

HACIENDA PLAN

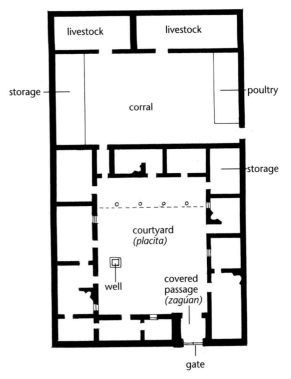

livestock

livestock

storage

poultry

corral

storage

courtyard
(placita)

well

covered
passage
(zagúan)

gate

Surrounded by a windowless adobe wall, the large fortresslike hacienda of the Southwest housed not only numerous members of the extended Spanish family, but also farmhands and livestock. Arranged contiguously, household rooms opened onto a front court-yard, called a *placita*. A back court-yard served as a corral, where barns, storerooms, and animal sheds were located. A massive front gate opened into a covered passage, or *zagúan*, wide enough for a wagon to pass through.

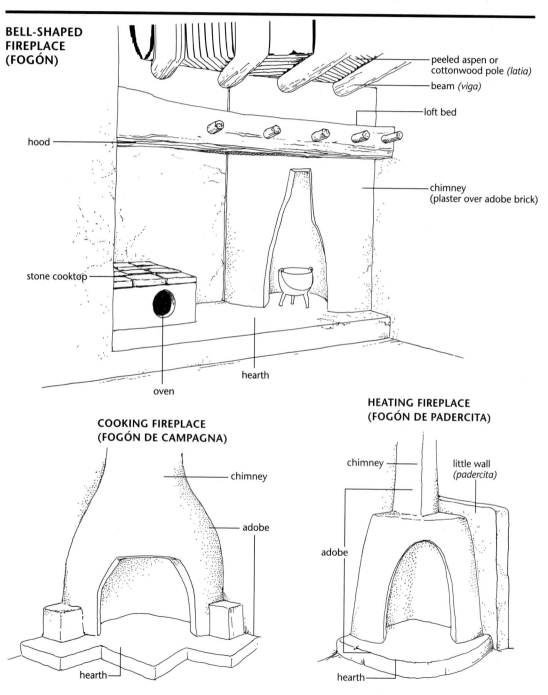

BELL-SHAPED FIREPLACE (FOGÓN)

peeled aspen or cottonwood pole *(latia)*

beam *(viga)*

loft bed

hood

chimney (plaster over adobe brick)

stone cooktop

oven

hearth

COOKING FIREPLACE (FOGÓN DE CAMPAGNA)

chimney

adobe

hearth

HEATING FIREPLACE (FOGÓN DE PADERCITA)

chimney

little wall *(padercita)*

adobe

hearth

Spanish Colonial

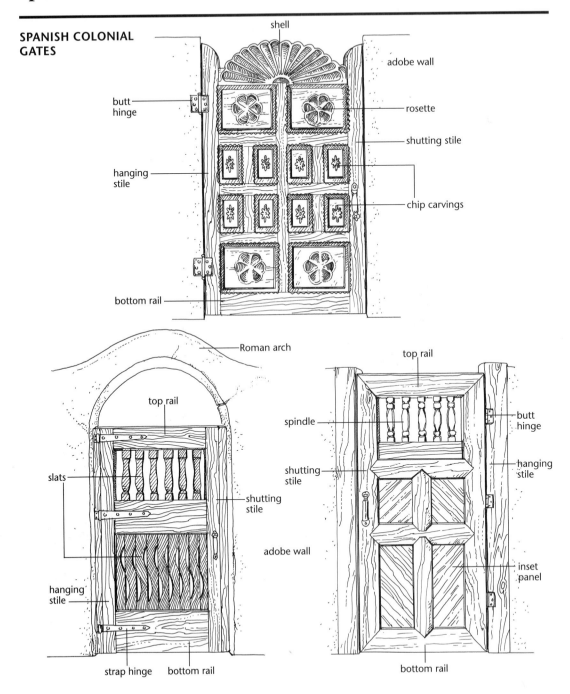

shell

adobe wall

butt
hinge

rosette

shutting stile

hanging
stile

chip carvings

bottom rail

Roman arch

top rail

top rail

spindle

butt
hinge

slats

hanging
stile

shutting
stile

shutting
stile

hanging
stile

adobe wall

strap hinge   bottom rail

inset
panel

bottom rail

Dutch Colonial

URBAN HOUSE (NEW AMSTERDAM)

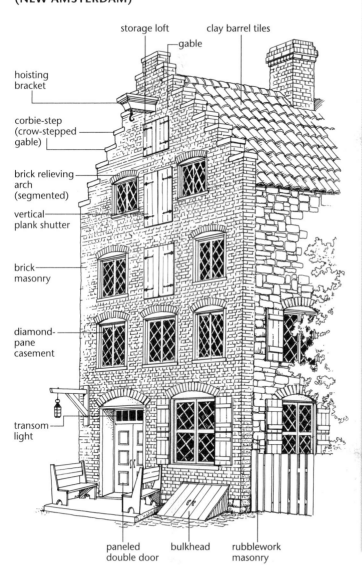

storage loft

gable

clay barrel tiles

hoisting bracket

corbie-step (crow-stepped gable)

brick relieving arch (segmented)

vertical plank shutter

brick masonry

diamond-pane casement

transom light

paneled double door

bulkhead

rubblework masonry

Architecture in the Dutch colony was defined by distinctive regional characteristics that lingered in more isolated areas for at least a century after the British gained control in 1664. The principal house type of the two commercial centers, New Amsterdam (New York) and Fort Orange (Albany), was the narrow town house, which faced gable end to the street and often included a storefront and a storage loft. In these urban areas, law required a brick veneer over the timber frame for fire protection. Stone houses were more prevalent in the lower Hudson Valley, while the clapboarded Flemish farmhouse with flared roof eaves was local to southern New York, Long Island, and northern New Jersey.

A notable feature of early Dutch buildings was a hooded fireplace (with no jambs, or side walls), fitted with a cloth mantel skirt to keep smoke in. The Dutch also introduced the distinctive anchorbent framing and the wide aisle barn, with doors on the gable ends, to the New World.

Dutch Colonial

BRICK HOUSE (ALBANY)

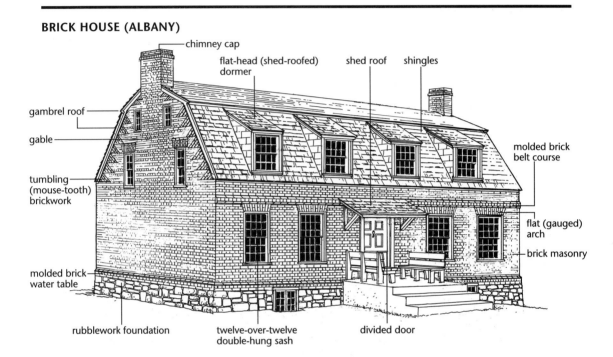

- chimney cap
- flat-head (shed-roofed) dormer
- shed roof
- shingles
- gambrel roof
- gable
- tumbling (mouse-tooth) brickwork
- molded brick belt course
- flat (gauged) arch
- brick masonry
- molded brick water table
- rubblework foundation
- twelve-over-twelve double-hung sash
- divided door

JAMBLESS (SIDELESS) FIREPLACE

- anchor beam
- mantel
- hood
- corbel brace (*korbeel*)
- whitewash over plaster
- post
- cloth skirt
- tile facing
- cast-iron fireback
- hearthstone

FLEMISH FARMHOUSE
(NEW JERSEY & LONG ISLAND)

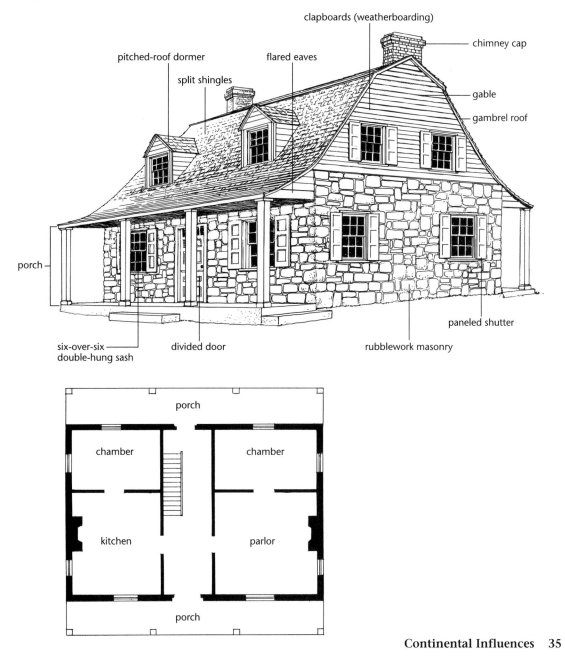

clapboards (weatherboarding)

chimney cap

pitched-roof dormer

flared eaves

gable

split shingles

gambrel roof

porch

paneled shutter

six-over-six
double-hung sash

divided door

rubblework masonry

porch

chamber

chamber

kitchen

parlor

porch

Dutch Colonial

**STONE HOUSE
(HUDSON VALLEY)**

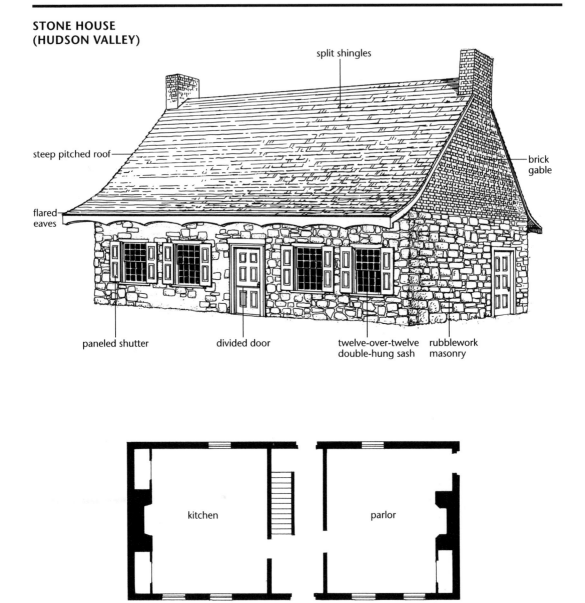

split shingles

steep pitched roof

brick gable

flared eaves

paneled shutter   divided door   twelve-over-twelve double-hung sash   rubblework masonry

kitchen

parlor

Dutch Colonial

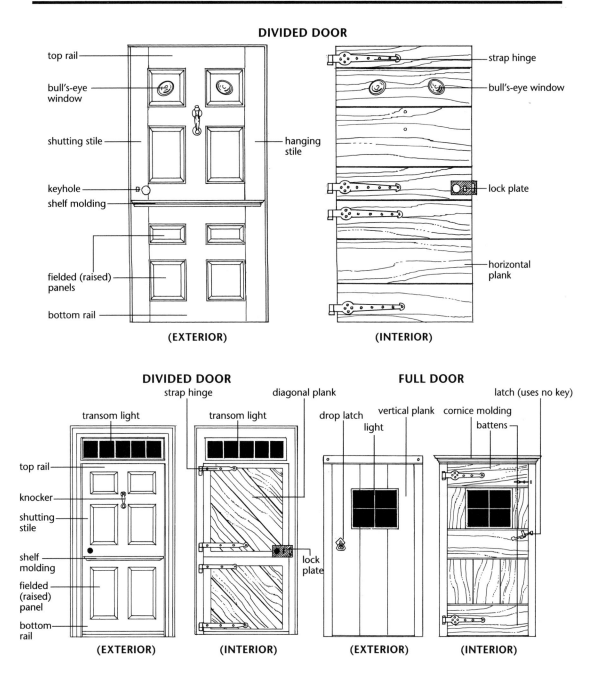

DIVIDED DOOR

top rail

bull's-eye window

shutting stile

hanging stile

keyhole

shelf molding

fielded (raised) panels

bottom rail

(EXTERIOR)

strap hinge

bull's-eye window

lock plate

horizontal plank

(INTERIOR)

DIVIDED DOOR

transom light

strap hinge

transom light

diagonal plank

top rail

knocker

shutting stile

shelf molding

fielded (raised) panel

bottom rail

lock plate

(EXTERIOR)

(INTERIOR)

FULL DOOR

drop latch

light

vertical plank

cornice molding

latch (uses no key)

battens

(EXTERIOR)

(INTERIOR)

Anatomy of a Dutch Anchorbent Frame

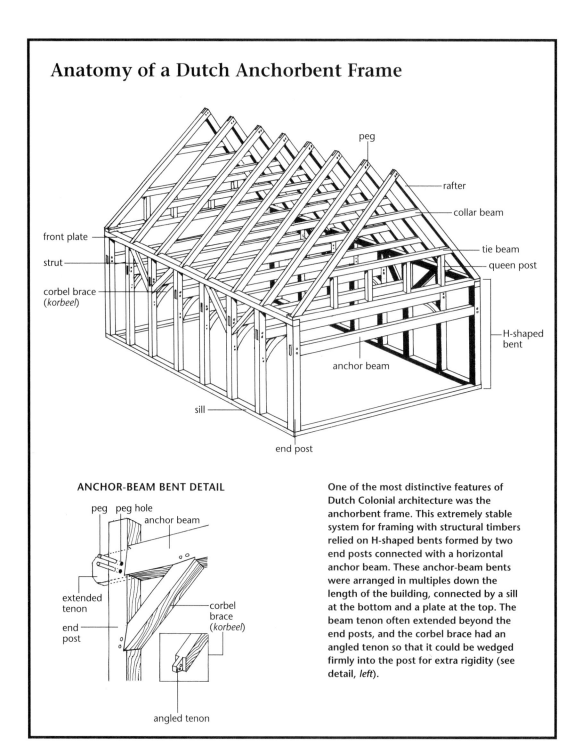

peg

rafter

collar beam

front plate

tie beam

strut

queen post

corbel brace
(*korbeel*)

H-shaped
bent

anchor beam

sill

end post

ANCHOR-BEAM BENT DETAIL

peg   peg hole

anchor beam

extended
tenon

corbel
brace
(*korbeel*)

end
post

angled tenon

One of the most distinctive features of Dutch Colonial architecture was the anchorbent frame. This extremely stable system for framing with structural timbers relied on H-shaped bents formed by two end posts connected with a horizontal anchor beam. These anchor-beam bents were arranged in multiples down the length of the building, connected by a sill at the bottom and a plate at the top. The beam tenon often extended beyond the end posts, and the corbel brace had an angled tenon so that it could be wedged firmly into the post for extra rigidity (see detail, *left*).

AISLE BARN

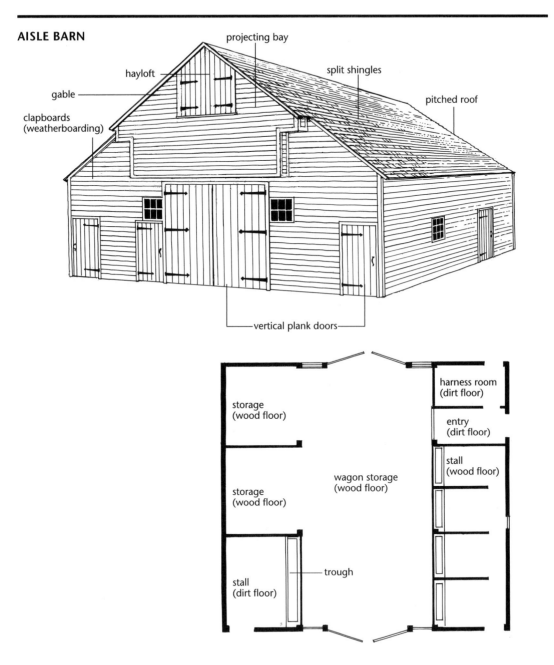

projecting bay

hayloft

gable

clapboards
(weatherboarding)

split shingles

pitched roof

vertical plank doors

storage
(wood floor)

harness room
(dirt floor)

entry
(dirt floor)

stall
(wood floor)

storage
(wood floor)

wagon storage
(wood floor)

stall
(dirt floor)

trough

German/Swiss Colonial

TRIPARTITE HOUSE

Germanic housing in the colonies was typically well built and designed for efficiency. One of the earliest Germanic building types in Pennsylvania was the tripartite house, which reflected the Old World tradition of combining a house, a threshing area, and a stable under the same roof. For convenience, a springhouse was often incorporated directly into a dwelling, which might also include an attic meat-smoking room, or *Rauchkammer*, connected to the chimney stack. Particularly practical building types were the bank house and bank barn, built into a ground slope to provide cool lower-level storage rooms.

The majority of early Germanic houses in America were simple, well-built log dwellings, although it is mostly the stone buildings that have survived. Stone, considered a status symbol, was favored primarily by the rural gentry. The typical Germanic plan was an asymmetrical three-room layout, placing the kitchen (*Kich,* in Pennsylvania German) on the main level, usually to the right of the chimney. To the left was the stove room (*Schtupp*), with a sleeping chamber (*Kammer*) in the rear. By the mid-1700s, many Germanic settlers had adopted the Georgian center-hall plan (page 76).

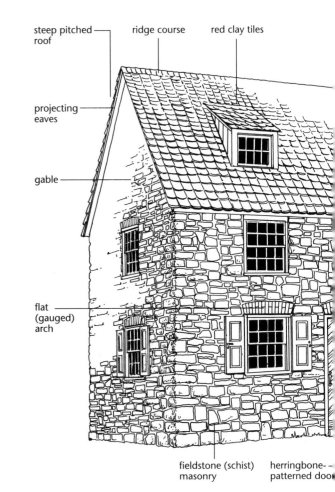

steep pitched roof — ridge course — red clay tiles

projecting eaves

gable

flat (gauged) arch

fieldstone (schist) masonry

herringbone-patterned door

German/Swiss Colonial

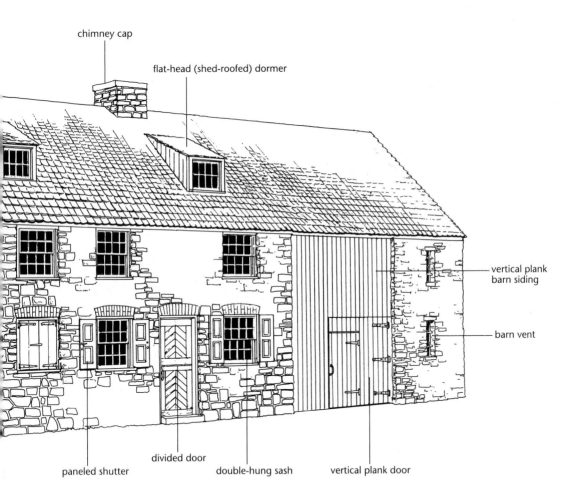

chimney cap

flat-head (shed-roofed) dormer

vertical plank barn siding

barn vent

paneled shutter

divided door

double-hung sash

vertical plank door

German/Swiss Colonial

LOG HOUSE

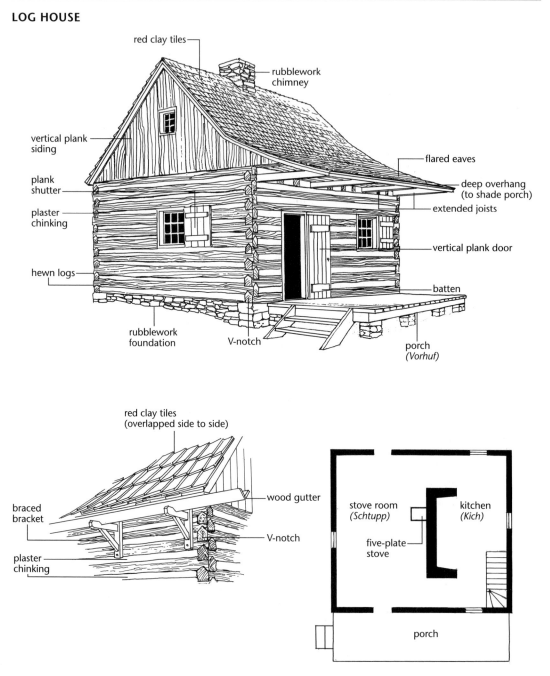

red clay tiles

rubblework chimney

vertical plank siding

flared eaves

deep overhang (to shade porch)

plank shutter

extended joists

plaster chinking

vertical plank door

hewn logs

batten

rubblework foundation

V-notch

porch (Vorhuf)

red clay tiles (overlapped side to side)

wood gutter

braced bracket

V-notch

plaster chinking

stove room (Schtupp)

kitchen (Kich)

five-plate stove

porch

SWISS BANK HOUSE

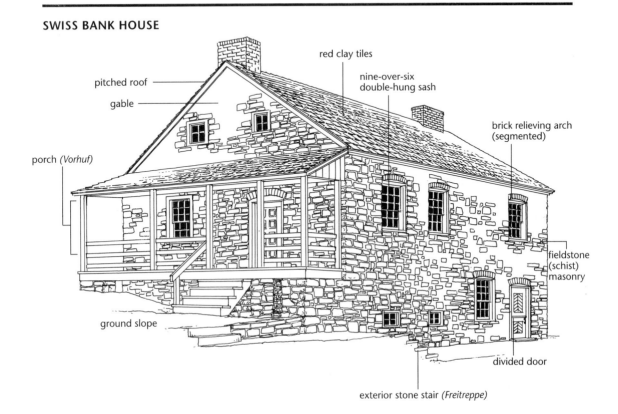

pitched roof

gable

porch *(Vorhuf)*

red clay tiles

nine-over-six double-hung sash

brick relieving arch (segmented)

fieldstone (schist) masonry

ground slope

divided door

exterior stone stair *(Freitreppe)*

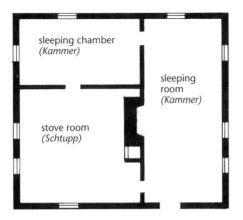

sleeping chamber *(Kammer)*

sleeping room *(Kammer)*

stove room *(Schtupp)*

The Swiss bank house was typically built with the gable end set into the ground slope. The kitchen was located on the lower level, with a rear room dug into the earth. Many of the Swiss settlers were distillers and stored their brews in this cool space.

German/Swiss Colonial

GERMANIC FIREPLACE

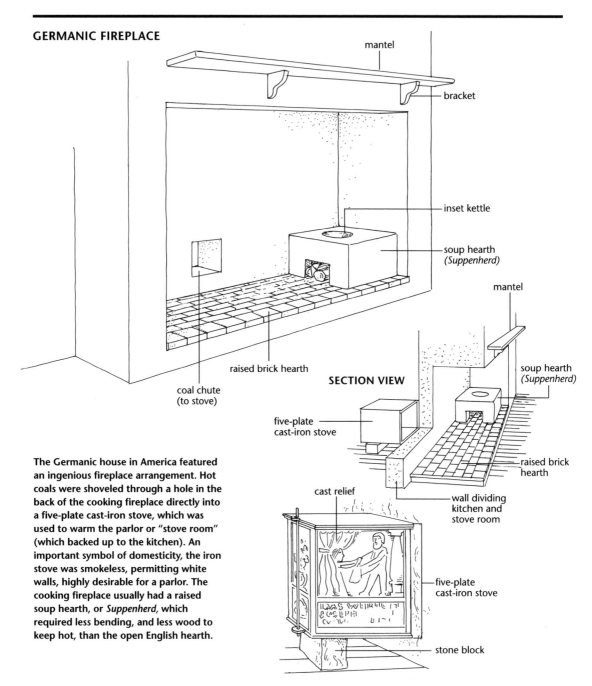

mantel

bracket

inset kettle

soup hearth
(Suppenherd)

raised brick hearth

coal chute
(to stove)

mantel

soup hearth
(Suppenherd)

SECTION VIEW

five-plate
cast-iron stove

raised brick
hearth

cast relief

wall dividing
kitchen and
stove room

five-plate
cast-iron stove

stone block

The Germanic house in America featured an ingenious fireplace arrangement. Hot coals were shoveled through a hole in the back of the cooking fireplace directly into a five-plate cast-iron stove, which was used to warm the parlor or "stove room" (which backed up to the kitchen). An important symbol of domesticity, the iron stove was smokeless, permitting white walls, highly desirable for a parlor. The cooking fireplace usually had a raised soup hearth, or *Suppenherd,* which required less bending, and less wood to keep hot, than the open English hearth.

German/Swiss Colonial

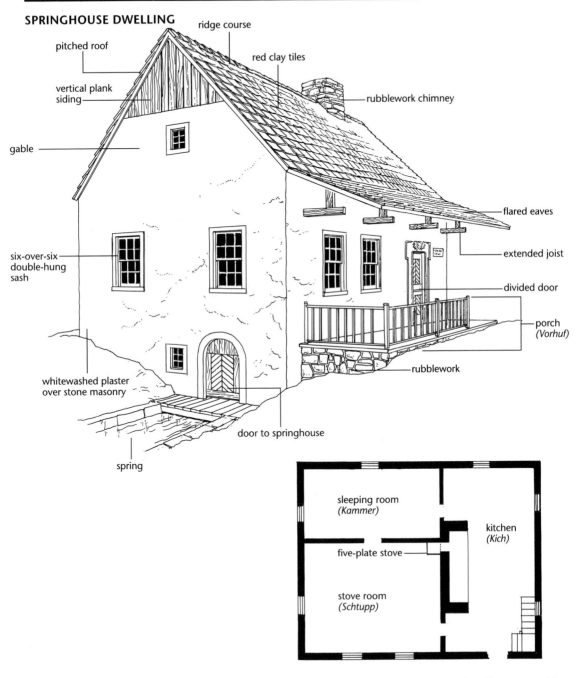

SPRINGHOUSE DWELLING

- ridge course
- pitched roof
- red clay tiles
- vertical plank siding
- rubblework chimney
- gable
- flared eaves
- six-over-six double-hung sash
- extended joist
- divided door
- porch *(Vorhuf)*
- whitewashed plaster over stone masonry
- rubblework
- door to springhouse
- spring

- sleeping room *(Kammer)*
- kitchen *(Kich)*
- five-plate stove
- stove room *(Schtupp)*

Continental Influences 45

Anatomy of a Germanic Roof Frame

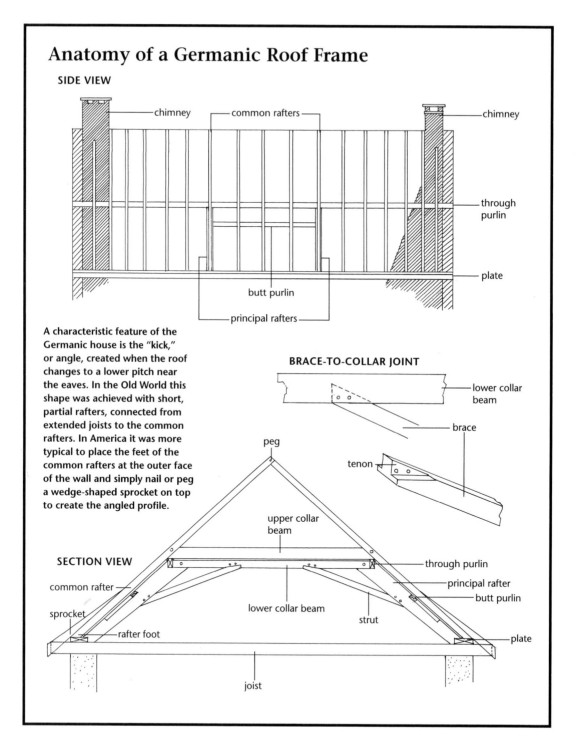

SIDE VIEW

chimney

common rafters

chimney

through purlin

plate

butt purlin

principal rafters

A characteristic feature of the Germanic house is the "kick," or angle, created when the roof changes to a lower pitch near the eaves. In the Old World this shape was achieved with short, partial rafters, connected from extended joists to the common rafters. In America it was more typical to place the feet of the common rafters at the outer face of the wall and simply nail or peg a wedge-shaped sprocket on top to create the angled profile.

BRACE-TO-COLLAR JOINT

lower collar beam

brace

tenon

peg

upper collar beam

SECTION VIEW

through purlin

principal rafter

common rafter

butt purlin

sprocket

lower collar beam

strut

rafter foot

plate

joist

CENTER-HALL HOUSE

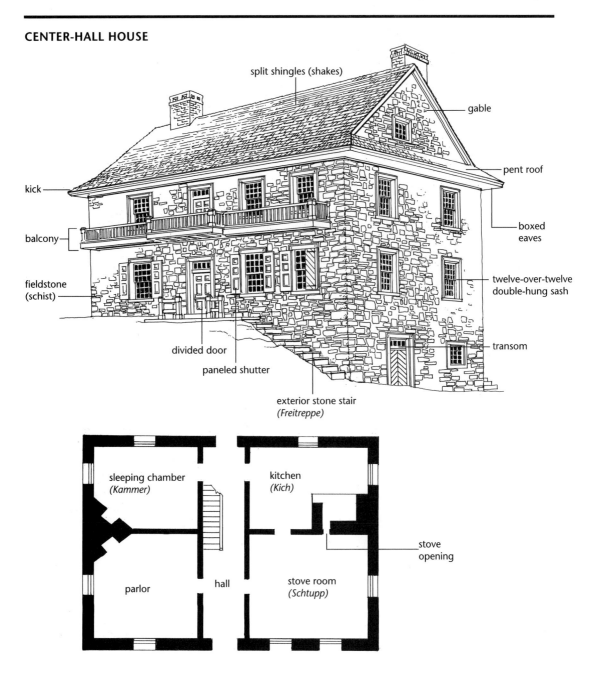

split shingles (shakes)

gable

pent roof

kick

boxed eaves

balcony

fieldstone (schist)

twelve-over-twelve double-hung sash

transom

divided door

paneled shutter

exterior stone stair (*Freitreppe*)

sleeping chamber (*Kammer*)

kitchen (*Kich*)

stove opening

parlor

hall

stove room (*Schtupp*)

German/Swiss Colonial

PAINTED WALL PATTERNS

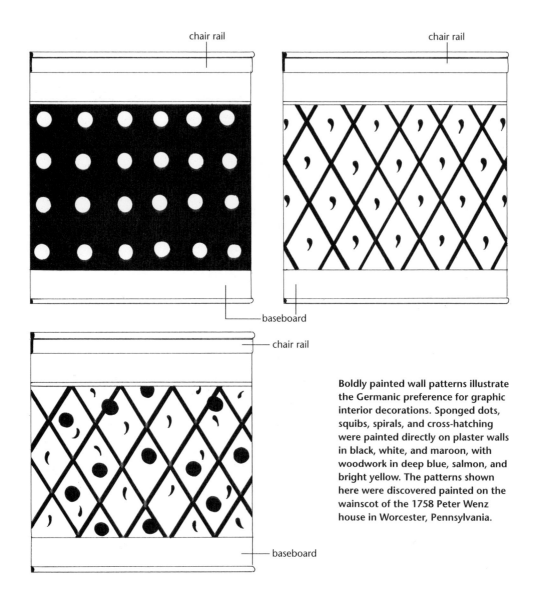

chair rail

chair rail

baseboard

chair rail

baseboard

Boldly painted wall patterns illustrate the Germanic preference for graphic interior decorations. Sponged dots, squibs, spirals, and cross-hatching were painted directly on plaster walls in black, white, and maroon, with woodwork in deep blue, salmon, and bright yellow. The patterns shown here were discovered painted on the wainscot of the 1758 Peter Wenz house in Worcester, Pennsylvania.

BAKE OVEN

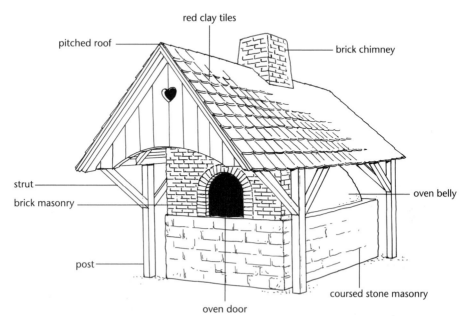

red clay tiles

pitched roof

brick chimney

strut

brick masonry

post

oven door

oven belly

coursed stone masonry

Few Germanic households were without a bake oven, often a separate outbuilding that might be incorporated into a larger smokehouse, washhouse, or summer kitchen. The outdoor oven was considered safer than its indoor counterpart, and its larger hearth permitted greater baking yields—as many as a dozen loaves of bread and even more pies at a time. The overhanging roof often shaded cooling shelves.

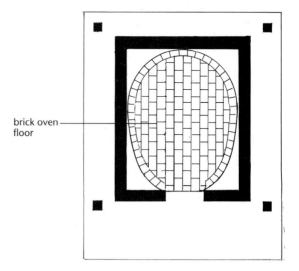

brick oven floor

German/Swiss Colonial

BANK BARN (FRONT VIEW)

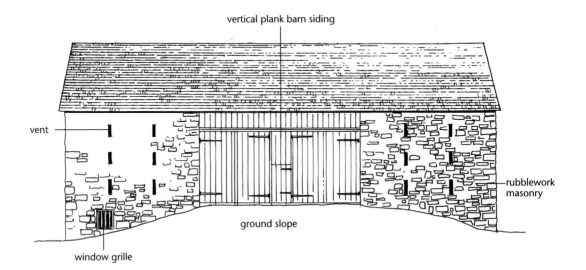

vertical plank barn siding

vent

window grille

ground slope

rubblework masonry

UPPER LEVEL

hay mow

threshing floor

granary

hay mow

hay chute

hay chute

BANK BARN (REAR VIEW)

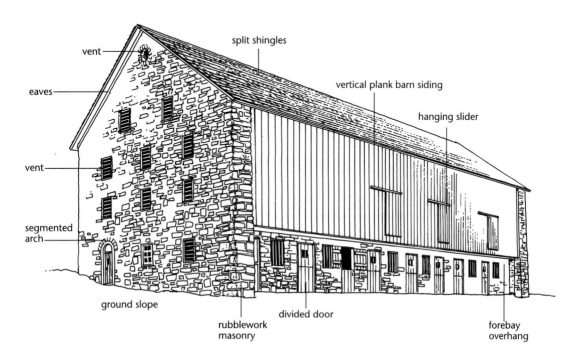

vent

eaves

vent

segmented arch

split shingles

vertical plank barn siding

hanging slider

ground slope

rubblework masonry

divided door

forebay overhang

LOWER LEVEL

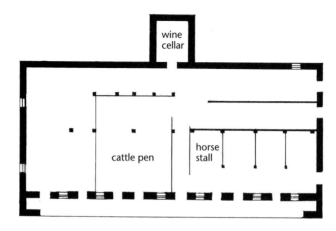

wine cellar

cattle pen

horse stall

French Colonial

The early houses of both the Illinois Country and the Louisiana Territory shared two distinct characteristics: the steep hipped Norman pavilion roof and the four-sided porch (*galerie*), which gave the roof a second (broken) pitch partway down. One basic house type, the *maison de poteaux-en-terre*, was built on upright posts driven into the ground; the other, the *maison de poteaux-sur-solle*, had a massive timber frame built directly on a sill. Both types used a fill of either stones and lime mortar (*pierrotage*) or a mud plaster bound with grass or Spanish moss (*bousillage*). The exterior was usually plastered.

The early French plan was a two-room, center-chimney layout. As houses grew larger, this evolved into a single or double row of rooms placed end to end with interior chimneys located at the gable ends. Rooms opened directly out onto the porch—there were seldom interior halls—by means of full-length casements. In the bayou areas of Louisiana, the house was typically raised as much as two feet to keep out moisture; riverside plantation houses were raised about seven feet. The kitchen was in a separate building.

MAISON DE POTEAUX-EN-TERRE

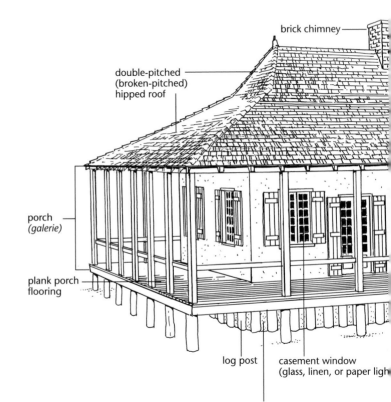

brick chimney

double-pitched
(broken-pitched)
hipped roof

porch
(*galerie*)

plank porch
flooring

log post

casement window
(glass, linen, or paper light)

stones and lime mortar (*pierrotage*)
or mud and grass plaster (*bousillage*)

decorative finial
(*épi*)

plank shutter

split cypress shingles

rafter tails

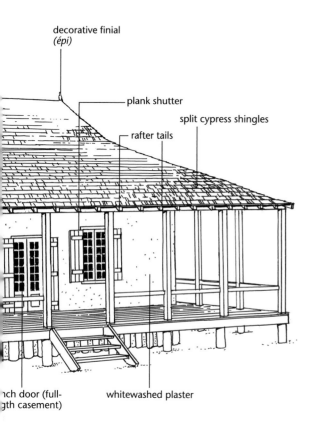

ch door (full-
gth casement)

whitewashed plaster

fill of stones and lime mortar
(*pierrotage*) or mud and
grass plaster (*bousillage*)

post (red cedar,
cypress, or
mulberry)

post hewn flat
above ground line

whole post below
ground line

vertical post set in
one-foot-deep
trench

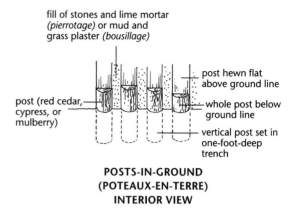

**POSTS-IN-GROUND
(POTEAUX-EN-TERRE)
INTERIOR VIEW**

Possibly derived from the Caribbean or the Gulf of
Mexico, the *poteaux-en-terre* building method was
the most common in the French territories. This
technique did not involve true framing; instead,
logs (mulberry or rot-resistant cedar or cypress)
were placed upright at three- or four-inch intervals
in a one-foot-deep trench. The trench was then
backfilled, and the uprights, which were hewn flat
above the ground, were secured at the tops with a
plate for additional stability.

French Colonial

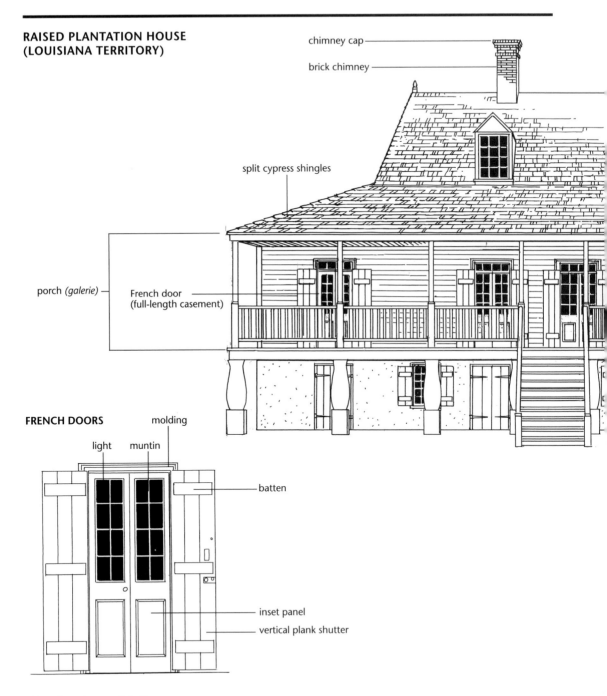

**RAISED PLANTATION HOUSE
(LOUISIANA TERRITORY)**

chimney cap

brick chimney

split cypress shingles

porch *(galerie)*

French door
(full-length casement)

FRENCH DOORS

molding

light

muntin

batten

inset panel

vertical plank shutter

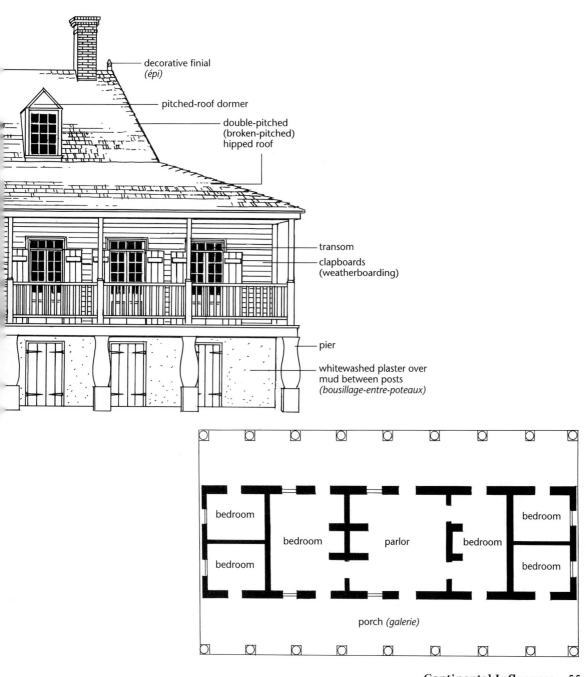

decorative finial
(*épi*)

pitched-roof dormer

double-pitched
(broken-pitched)
hipped roof

transom

clapboards
(weatherboarding)

pier

whitewashed plaster over
mud between posts
(*bousillage-entre-poteaux*)

bedroom

bedroom

bedroom

parlor

bedroom

bedroom

bedroom

porch (*galerie*)

Anatomy of a Norman Truss

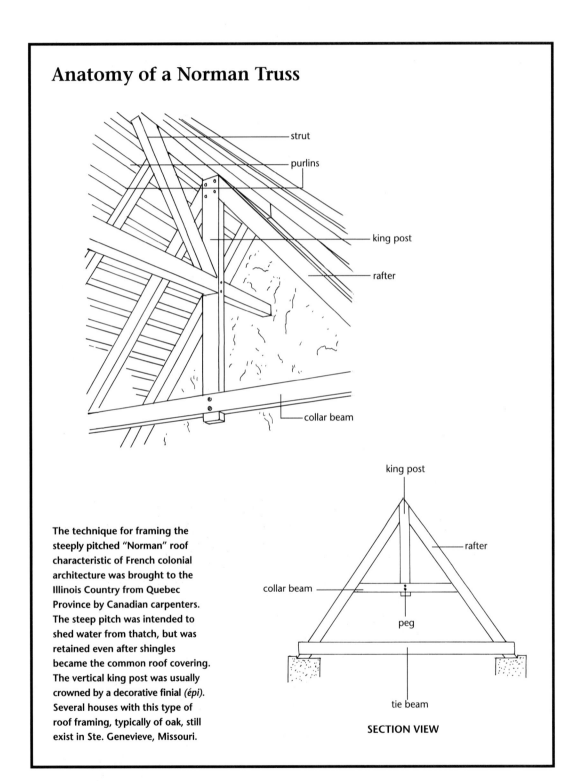

strut

purlins

king post

rafter

collar beam

The technique for framing the steeply pitched "Norman" roof characteristic of French colonial architecture was brought to the Illinois Country from Quebec Province by Canadian carpenters. The steep pitch was intended to shed water from thatch, but was retained even after shingles became the common roof covering. The vertical king post was usually crowned by a decorative finial *(épi)*. Several houses with this type of roof framing, typically of oak, still exist in Ste. Genevieve, Missouri.

king post

rafter

collar beam

peg

tie beam

SECTION VIEW

French Colonial

MAISON DE POTEAUX-SUR-SOLLE

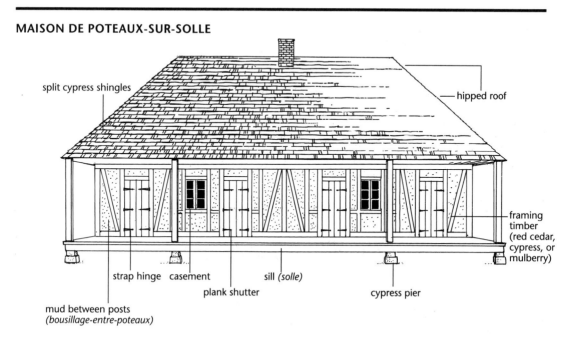

split cypress shingles

hipped roof

framing timber (red cedar, cypress, or mulberry)

strap hinge   casement

plank shutter

sill *(solle)*

cypress pier

mud between posts *(bousillage-entre-poteaux)*

DOOR HARDWARE

RAM'S HORN HINGE

INTERIOR LATCHES

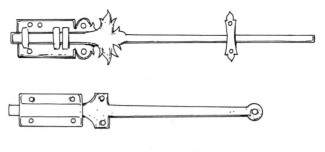

Among the distinctive hardware used in the French Colonial period was the ram's horn hinge *(left)*. Long interior latches *(above)* were necessary to secure the tops of French and double paneled doors. A shorter version of the same latch was used for the door bottoms.

French Colonial

RAISED HOUSE
(LOUISIANA TERRITORY)

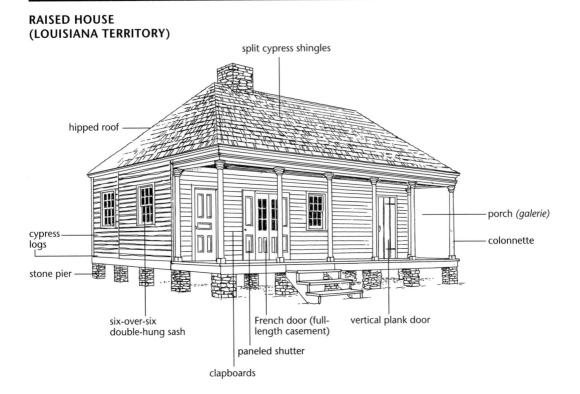

split cypress shingles

hipped roof

porch (galerie)

colonnette

cypress logs

stone pier

six-over-six double-hung sash

French door (full-length casement)

vertical plank door

paneled shutter

clapboards

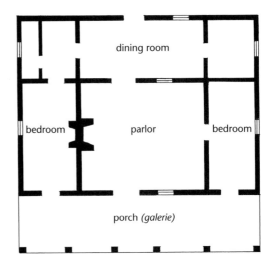

dining room

bedroom

parlor

bedroom

porch (galerie)

LOG HOUSE
(ILLINOIS COUNTRY)

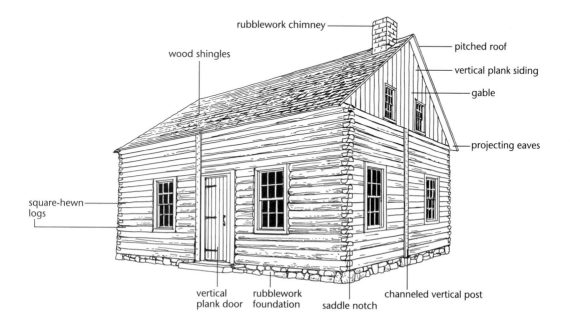

rubblework chimney

wood shingles

pitched roof

vertical plank siding

gable

projecting eaves

square-hewn
logs

vertical
plank door

rubblework
foundation

saddle notch

channeled vertical post

CHANNELED POST DETAIL

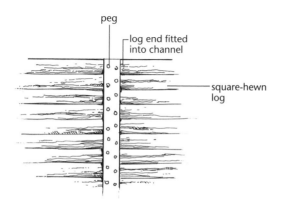

peg

log end fitted
into channel

square-hewn
log

French Colonial log construction featured an unusual system in which one end of a log was notched at the building corners and the other end was set in a vertical post placed at or near the center of each wall. A three-inch-deep channel ran along both sides of the post; each end of a log was hewed to fit the channel and pegged into place. This made it possible to build longer walls out of the shorter logs typically available in the northern Mississippi Valley.

French Colonial

BARN

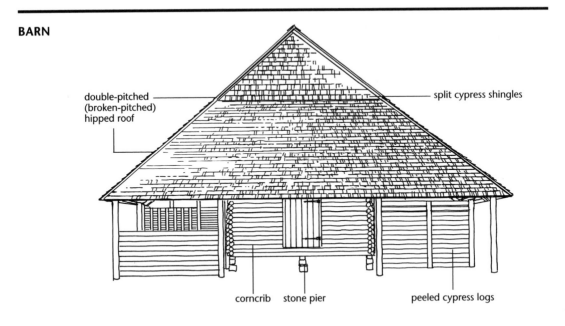

double-pitched (broken-pitched) hipped roof

split cypress shingles

corncrib   stone pier

peeled cypress logs

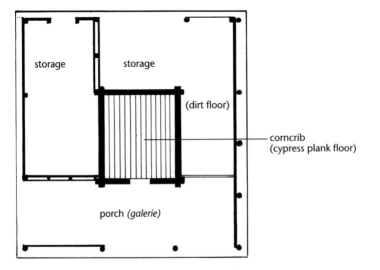

storage   storage

(dirt floor)

corncrib (cypress plank floor)

porch (*galerie*)

PIGEONNIER

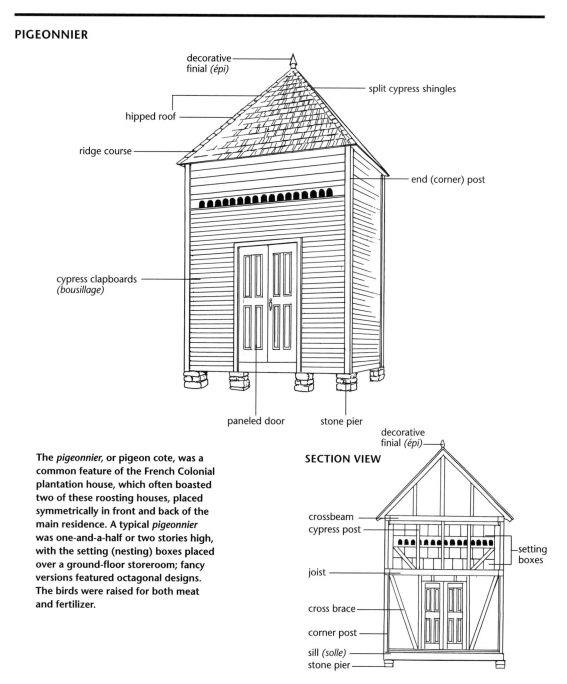

decorative finial (épi)

split cypress shingles

hipped roof

ridge course

end (corner) post

cypress clapboards (bousillage)

paneled door   stone pier

The *pigeonnier,* or pigeon cote, was a common feature of the French Colonial plantation house, which often boasted two of these roosting houses, placed symmetrically in front and back of the main residence. A typical *pigeonnier* was one-and-a-half or two stories high, with the setting (nesting) boxes placed over a ground-floor storeroom; fancy versions featured octagonal designs. The birds were raised for both meat and fertilizer.

SECTION VIEW

decorative finial (épi)

crossbeam
cypress post

setting boxes

joist

cross brace

corner post

sill (solle)
stone pier

Chapter Three
Early English Colonial

Establishing their first settlements in Jamestown, Virginia, in 1607, and Plymouth, Massachusetts, in 1620, some half a million colonists had emigrated to America from England, Scotland, and Ireland by the end of the 17th century. With them came a thoroughly British pattern of social and cultural values that soon traversed the Atlantic seaboard.

Building characteristics varied from colony to colony and town to town. However, a broad distinction can be drawn between the New England village, which comprised individual houses grouped around a town green, and the isolated southern plantation, a self-sufficient enterprise supported by slave labor and complete with a forge, carpentry shop, and perhaps a brickyard. New England settlers were primarily middle-class yeoman families. Most came from a single area of England (East Anglia), and they continued a well-entrenched tradition of heavytimber-framed buildings. Settlers of the Virginia tidewater region and farther south came from more diverse areas and included a significant number of bricklayers and masons. Lime, used for mortar, was also readily available in the South, so masonry construction was more typical.

Until about 1700, all early English Colonial houses shared a distinct postmedieval character, most noticeable in steep pitched roofs (a holdover originally designed to support thatch), immense stacked chimneys, and small casement windows. The plan was typically a one-room, all-purpose "fireroom," or "hall," used for cooking, eating, and sleeping, or a two-room layout with a central chimney dividing the hall and parlor or kitchen. Additional sleeping chambers were located above.

VILLAGE HOUSE (NEW ENGLAND)

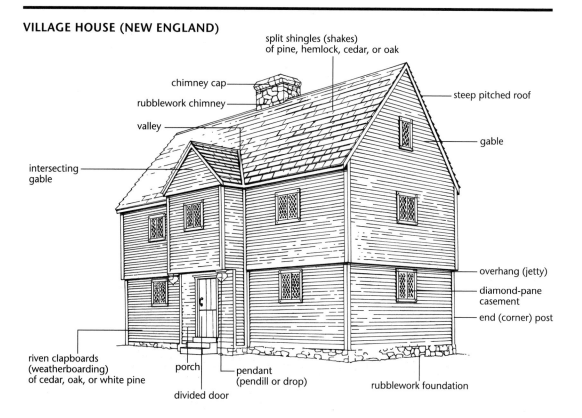

split shingles (shakes)
of pine, hemlock, cedar, or oak

chimney cap

rubblework chimney

valley

intersecting gable

steep pitched roof

gable

overhang (jetty)

diamond-pane casement

end (corner) post

riven clapboards (weatherboarding) of cedar, oak, or white pine

porch

pendant (pendill or drop)

divided door

rubblework foundation

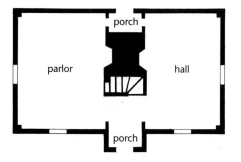

porch

parlor

hall

porch

A mark of late Elizabethan architecture, the overhang, or jetty, was a feature of early Colonial houses throughout the 1600s, primarily in towns and cities. In England it may have been used to provide shelter over street-level market stalls, but in America the shallower overhang—four to six inches deep—was apparently a purely decorative holdover.

Early English Colonial

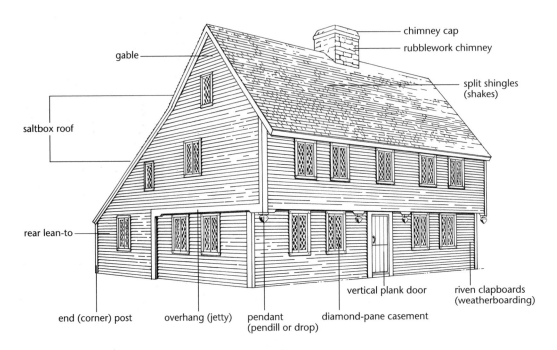

chimney cap

rubblework chimney

gable

split shingles
(shakes)

saltbox roof

rear lean-to

end (corner) post

overhang (jetty)

pendant
(pendill or drop)

diamond-pane casement

vertical plank door

riven clapboards
(weatherboarding)

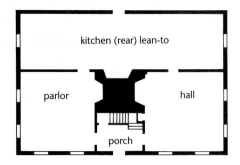

kitchen (rear) lean-to

parlor

hall

porch

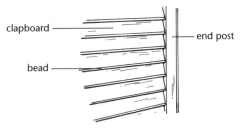

CLAPBOARD DETAIL

clapboard

bead

end post

PENDANTS

Common during the second half of the 17th century, wood pendants (also called pendills or drops) were used to finish the lower ends of the front second-story posts that framed an overhang. Purely decorative, pendants offered a place for the woodcarver to try out different designs. The overhang and pendants seldom, if ever, appeared on the rear of a structure. These oak examples survive from late 17th-century houses in Connecticut and Massachusetts.

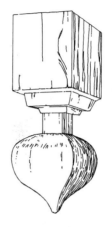

tenon

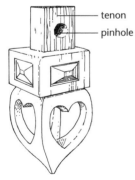

tenon

pinhole

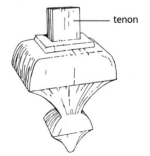

tenon

Early English Colonial

STONE-ENDER (RHODE ISLAND)

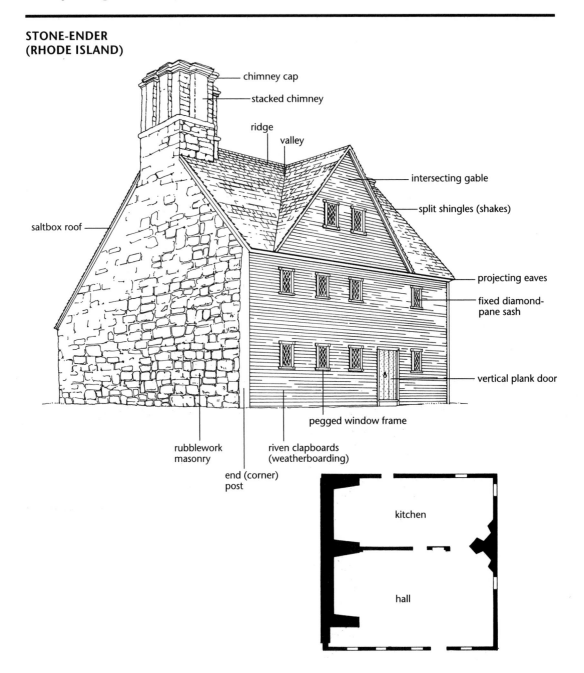

chimney cap

stacked chimney

ridge

valley

intersecting gable

split shingles (shakes)

saltbox roof

projecting eaves

fixed diamond-pane sash

vertical plank door

rubblework masonry

riven clapboards (weatherboarding)

pegged window frame

end (corner) post

kitchen

hall

Anatomy of a Post-and-Beam Frame

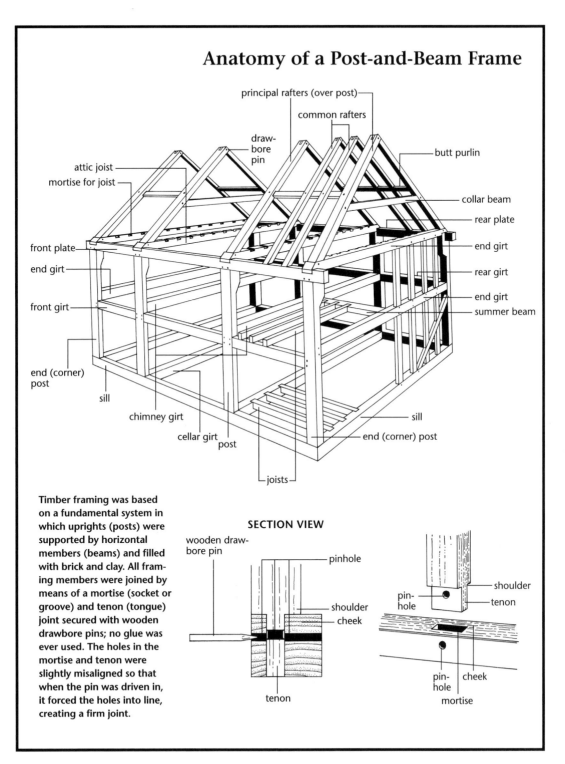

principal rafters (over post)

common rafters

draw-bore pin

attic joist

mortise for joist

butt purlin

collar beam

rear plate

front plate

end girt

end girt

rear girt

front girt

end girt

summer beam

end (corner) post

sill

chimney girt

cellar girt

post

sill

end (corner) post

joists

Timber framing was based on a fundamental system in which uprights (posts) were supported by horizontal members (beams) and filled with brick and clay. All framing members were joined by means of a mortise (socket or groove) and tenon (tongue) joint secured with wooden drawbore pins; no glue was ever used. The holes in the mortise and tenon were slightly misaligned so that when the pin was driven in, it forced the holes into line, creating a firm joint.

SECTION VIEW

wooden draw-bore pin

pinhole

shoulder

cheek

tenon

shoulder

pin-hole

tenon

pin-hole

cheek

mortise

Early English Colonial

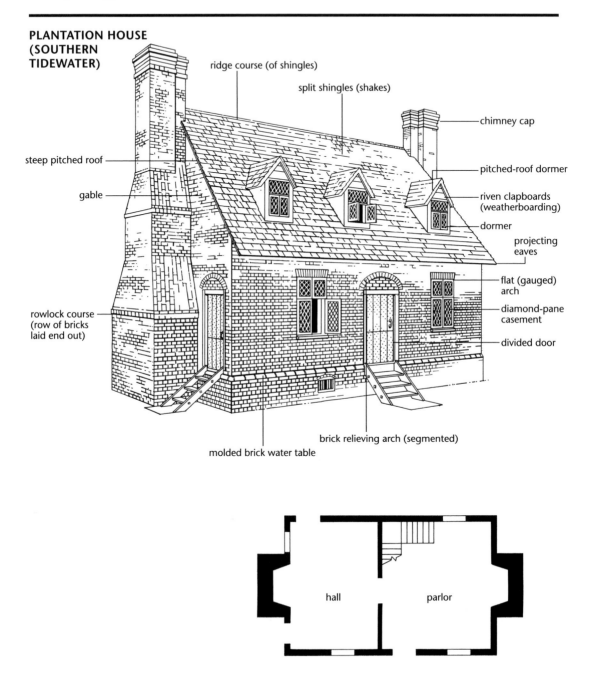

PLANTATION HOUSE (SOUTHERN TIDEWATER)

ridge course (of shingles)

split shingles (shakes)

chimney cap

steep pitched roof

pitched-roof dormer

gable

riven clapboards (weatherboarding)

dormer

projecting eaves

flat (gauged) arch

diamond-pane casement

rowlock course (row of bricks laid end out)

divided door

brick relieving arch (segmented)

molded brick water table

hall

parlor

Anatomy of Brick Bonds

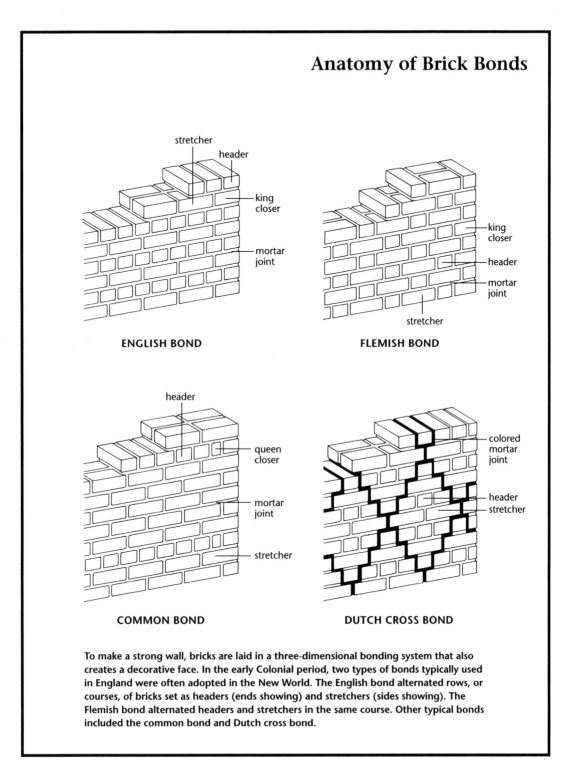

ENGLISH BOND

stretcher
header
king closer
mortar joint

FLEMISH BOND

king closer
header
mortar joint
stretcher

COMMON BOND

header
queen closer
mortar joint
stretcher

DUTCH CROSS BOND

colored mortar joint
header
stretcher

To make a strong wall, bricks are laid in a three-dimensional bonding system that also creates a decorative face. In the early Colonial period, two types of bonds typically used in England were often adopted in the New World. The English bond alternated rows, or courses, of bricks set as headers (ends showing) and stretchers (sides showing). The Flemish bond alternated headers and stretchers in the same course. Other typical bonds included the common bond and Dutch cross bond.

Early English Colonial

**PLANTATION HOUSES
(MID-ATLANTIC AND SOUTH)**

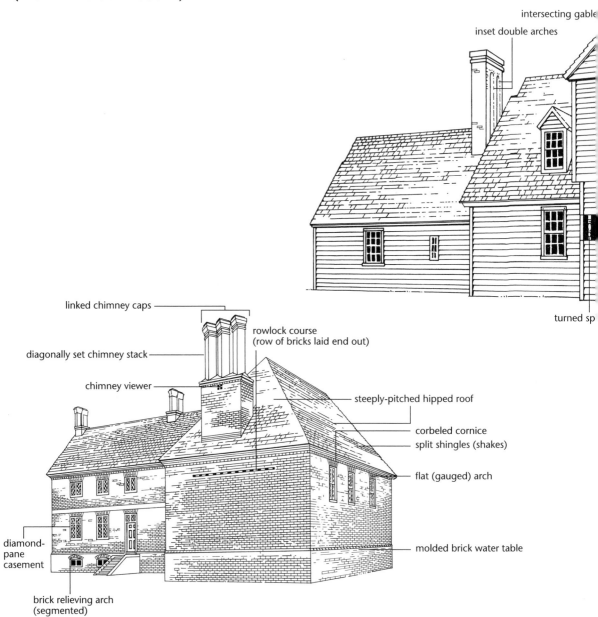

intersecting gable

inset double arches

turned sp

linked chimney caps

rowlock course
(row of bricks laid end out)

diagonally set chimney stack

chimney viewer

steeply-pitched hipped roof

corbeled cornice

split shingles (shakes)

flat (gauged) arch

diamond-
pane
casement

molded brick water table

brick relieving arch
(segmented)

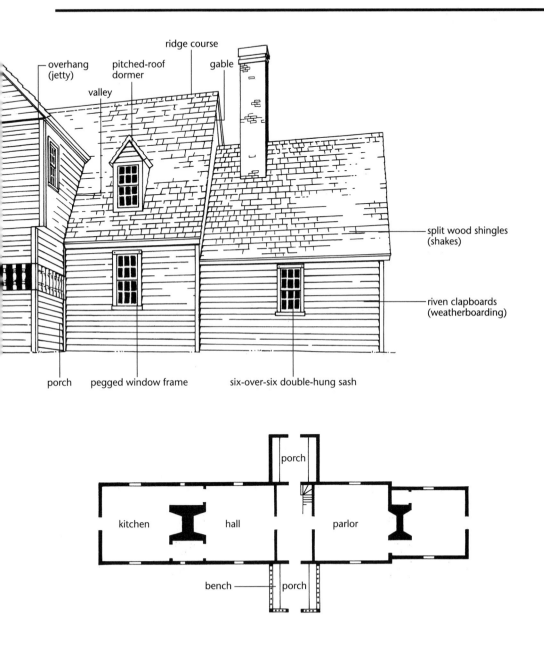

ridge course

overhang (jetty)

pitched-roof dormer

gable

valley

split wood shingles (shakes)

riven clapboards (weatherboarding)

porch

pegged window frame

six-over-six double-hung sash

porch

kitchen

hall

parlor

bench

porch

Early English Colonial

HALL (FIREROOM)

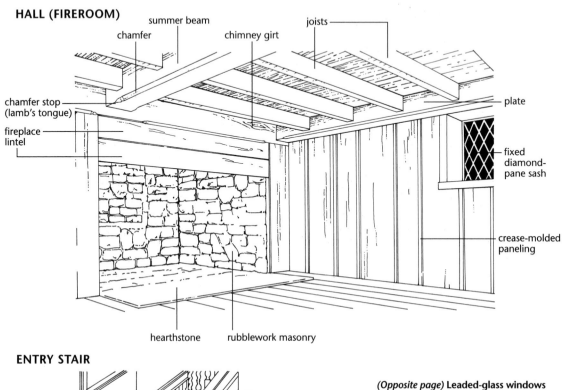

summer beam

chamfer

chimney girt

joists

chamfer stop
(lamb's tongue)

plate

fireplace
lintel

fixed
diamond-
pane sash

crease-molded
paneling

hearthstone   rubblework masonry

ENTRY STAIR

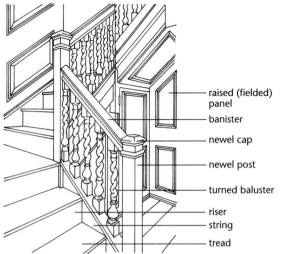

raised (fielded)
panel

banister

newel cap

newel post

turned baluster

riser

string

tread

(*Opposite page*) Leaded-glass windows persisted well into the second quarter of the 1700s and were typically either fixed or hinged casements (double-hung sashes were rare). English casements were set on the outside of the window opening and opened outward; they were never used with shutters. During the 1600s most glass used in the colonies was imported from England. Bubbled glass was considered inferior; clear, high-quality "crown" glass could cost fifteen times as much and was thus reserved for rooms in the front of the finest houses.

DOORS (INTERIOR)

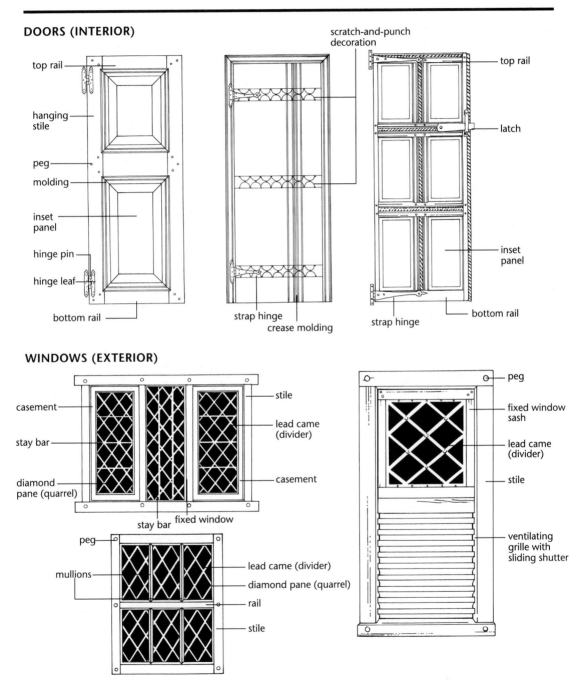

scratch-and-punch decoration

top rail

hanging stile

peg

molding

inset panel

hinge pin

hinge leaf

bottom rail

strap hinge

crease molding

top rail

latch

inset panel

bottom rail

strap hinge

WINDOWS (EXTERIOR)

casement

stay bar

diamond pane (quarrel)

stile

lead came (divider)

casement

stay bar   fixed window

peg

mullions

lead came (divider)

diamond pane (quarrel)

rail

stile

peg

fixed window sash

lead came (divider)

stile

ventilating grille with sliding shutter

Anatomy of a Purlin Roof Frame

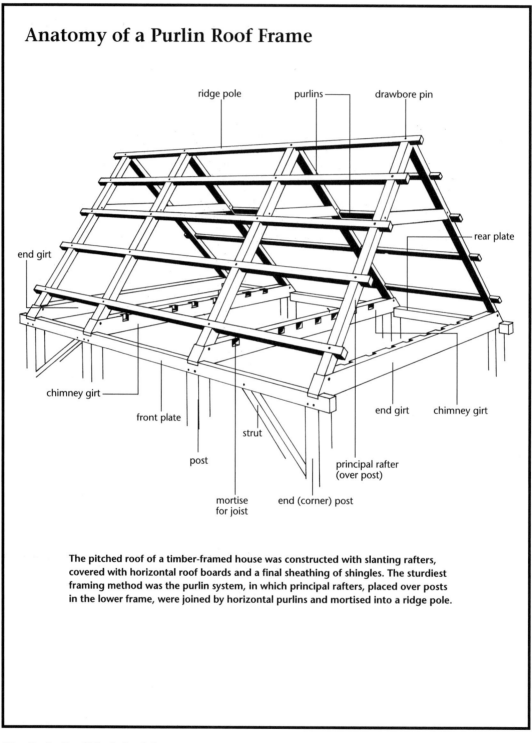

ridge pole

purlins

drawbore pin

rear plate

end girt

chimney girt

front plate

strut

post

mortise for joist

end (corner) post

principal rafter (over post)

end girt

chimney girt

The pitched roof of a timber-framed house was constructed with slanting rafters, covered with horizontal roof boards and a final sheathing of shingles. The sturdiest framing method was the purlin system, in which principal rafters, placed over posts in the lower frame, were joined by horizontal purlins and mortised into a ridge pole.

BARN

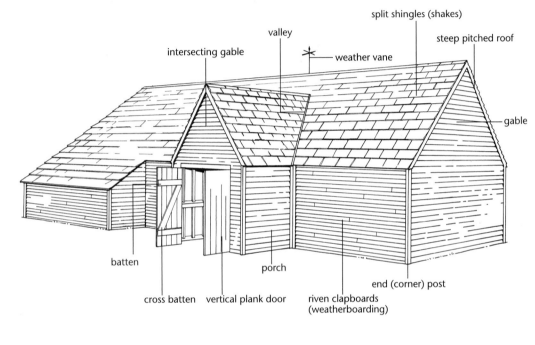

intersecting gable

valley

split shingles (shakes)

steep pitched roof

weather vane

gable

batten

cross batten

vertical plank door

porch

end (corner) post

riven clapboards
(weatherboarding)

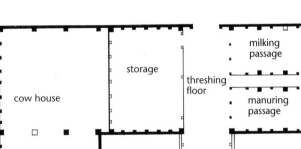

cow house

storage

threshing
floor

milking
passage

manuring
passage

porch

Chapter Four
The Georgian Era

The term "Georgian" generally refers to a period of architectural development in America from about 1700 to the Revolution (during the reigns of kings George I, II, and III). Rooted in the Classical design principles of ancient Rome, this English style came to America by way of British pattern books and an ever-swelling wave of masons, carpenters, and joiners who emigrated from England.

With its rigid symmetry, balanced proportion, and Classical detailing, the Georgian mode represented a final break from medieval architecture. Formal and dignified, it transcended geographical boundaries and was enthusiastically adopted for the imposing seaport mansions of New England's wealthy mercantile class, southern manors and plantation houses, and vernacular backcountry farmhouses, whose door and window designs were often copied directly from the pages of a carpenter's handbook. Surface ornament, usually concentrated on the centrally placed entry, was especially lavish during the early, Baroque phase of the style. A more academic, restrained approach in the mid- to late 1700s adhered more closely to the strict design principles of the Italian architect Andrea Palladio (1508–80).

As the notions of privacy and leisure time developed during the 1700s, the symmetrical Georgian center-hall plan evolved with larger rooms as well as more rooms designed for specialized uses, such as the dining room and library. The increasing availability of white lime plaster resulted in more sculptural interior ornament, often producing elaborate precast cornices and ceiling medallions.

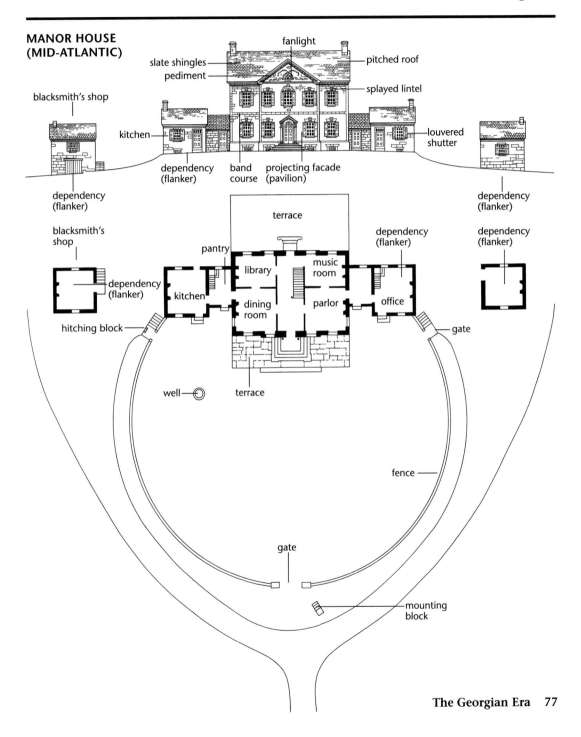

MANOR HOUSE (MID-ATLANTIC)

fanlight

slate shingles

pediment

pitched roof

splayed lintel

blacksmith's shop

kitchen

louvered shutter

dependency (flanker)

band course

projecting facade (pavilion)

dependency (flanker)

dependency (flanker)

blacksmith's shop

dependency (flanker)

dependency (flanker)

dependency (flanker)

terrace

pantry

library

music room

dependency (flanker)

kitchen

dining room

parlor

office

hitching block

gate

well

terrace

fence

gate

mounting block

Georgian

**PLANTATION HOUSE
(MID-ATLANTIC AND SOUTH)**

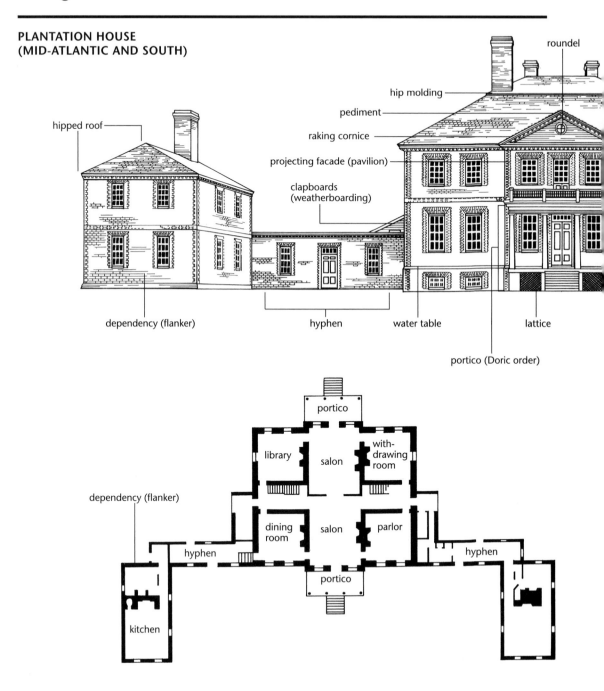

roundel

hip molding

pediment

raking cornice

projecting facade (pavilion)

clapboards
(weatherboarding)

hipped roof

dependency (flanker)

hyphen

water table

lattice

portico (Doric order)

portico

library

salon

with-drawing
room

dependency (flanker)

dining
room

salon

parlor

hyphen

hyphen

portico

kitchen

brick chimney

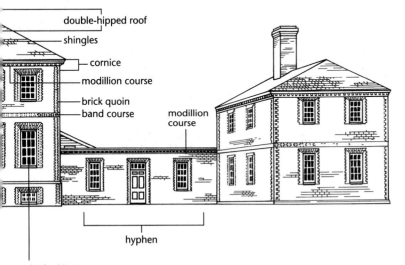

double-hipped roof

shingles

cornice

modillion course

brick quoin
band course

modillion
course

-over-six double-hung sash

hyphen

DOUBLE-HUNG SASH DETAIL

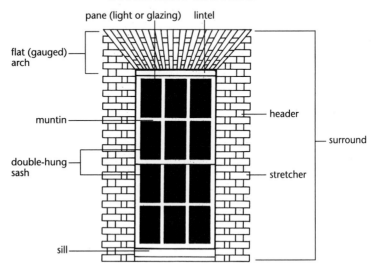

pane (light or glazing)   lintel

flat (gauged)
arch

muntin

double-hung
sash

sill

header

surround

stretcher

Pattern Book Designs

The most widely used 18th-century architectural books in both England and America were by the prolific English author Batty Langley (1696–1751), who wrote more than twenty practical handbooks designed for the average carpenter. These plates are from *The Builder's Jewel*, published in eleven editions from 1741 to 1787.

Georgian

END HOUSE (CHARLESTON)

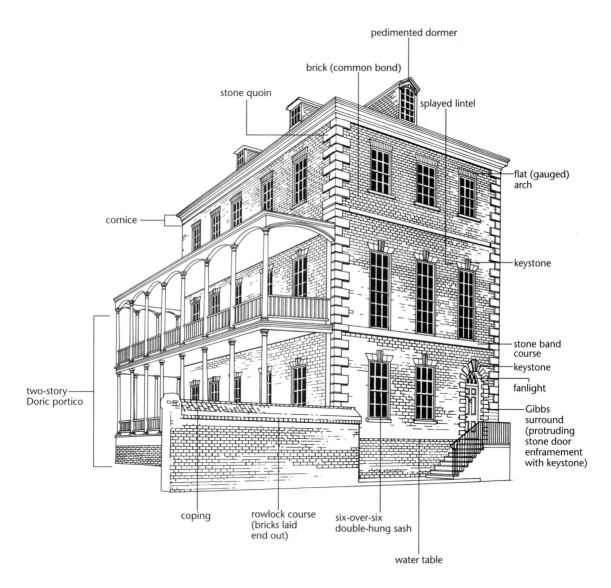

pedimented dormer

brick (common bond)

stone quoin

splayed lintel

flat (gauged) arch

cornice

keystone

stone band course

keystone

fanlight

Gibbs surround (protruding stone door enframement with keystone)

two-story Doric portico

coping

rowlock course (bricks laid end out)

six-over-six double-hung sash

water table

Georgian

MANOR HOUSE
(NEW ENGLAND)

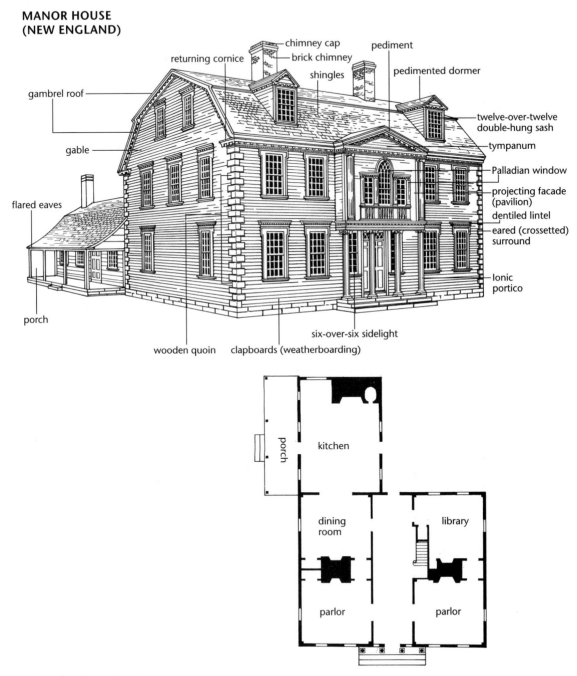

returning cornice

chimney cap

brick chimney

shingles

pediment

pedimented dormer

gambrel roof

gable

flared eaves

porch

wooden quoin

clapboards (weatherboarding)

six-over-six sidelight

twelve-over-twelve
double-hung sash

tympanum

Palladian window

projecting facade
(pavilion)

dentiled lintel

eared (crossetted)
surround

Ionic
portico

porch

kitchen

dining
room

library

parlor

parlor

Anatomy of a Gambrel Roof Frame

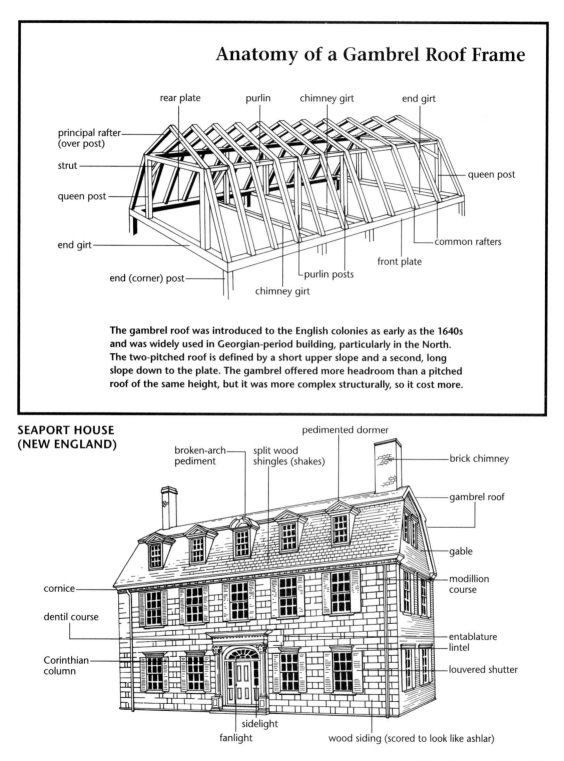

rear plate • purlin • chimney girt • end girt

principal rafter (over post)

strut

queen post

end girt

end (corner) post

chimney girt

purlin posts

front plate

common rafters

queen post

The gambrel roof was introduced to the English colonies as early as the 1640s and was widely used in Georgian-period building, particularly in the North. The two-pitched roof is defined by a short upper slope and a second, long slope down to the plate. The gambrel offered more headroom than a pitched roof of the same height, but it was more complex structurally, so it cost more.

SEAPORT HOUSE (NEW ENGLAND)

pedimented dormer

broken-arch pediment

split wood shingles (shakes)

brick chimney

gambrel roof

gable

modillion course

cornice

dentil course

Corinthian column

entablature
lintel

louvered shutter

sidelight

fanlight

wood siding (scored to look like ashlar)

Georgian

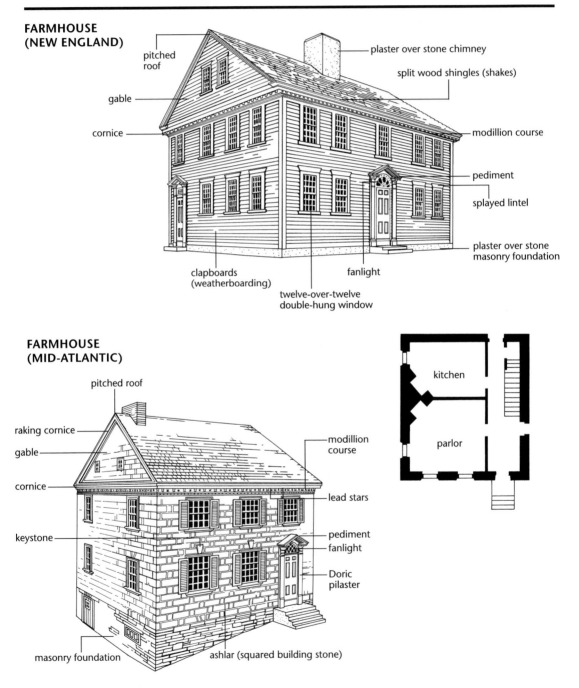

**FARMHOUSE
(NEW ENGLAND)**

pitched roof

gable

cornice

plaster over stone chimney

split wood shingles (shakes)

modillion course

pediment

splayed lintel

plaster over stone masonry foundation

clapboards (weatherboarding)

twelve-over-twelve double-hung window

fanlight

**FARMHOUSE
(MID-ATLANTIC)**

pitched roof

raking cornice

gable

cornice

keystone

modillion course

lead stars

pediment

fanlight

Doric pilaster

masonry foundation

ashlar (squared building stone)

kitchen

parlor

FIREPLACE WALLS

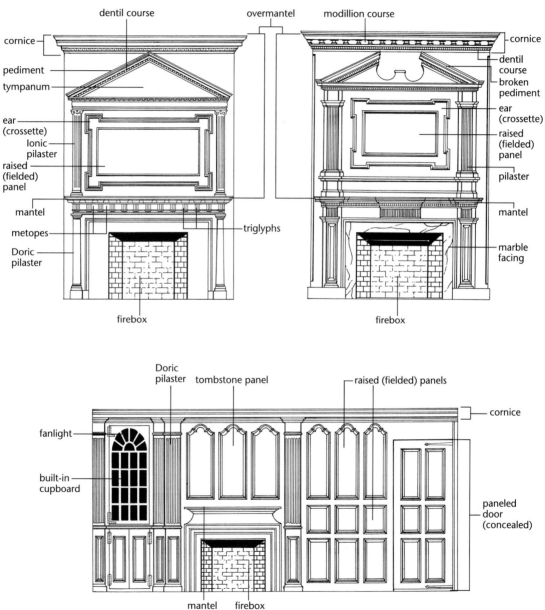

dentil course
overmantel
modillion course
cornice
pediment
tympanum
cornice
dentil course
broken pediment
ear (crossette)
Ionic pilaster
raised (fielded) panel
ear (crossette)
raised (fielded) panel
pilaster
mantel
metopes
triglyphs
mantel
marble facing
Doric pilaster
firebox
firebox

Doric pilaster
tombstone panel
raised (fielded) panels
cornice
fanlight
built-in cupboard
paneled door (concealed)
mantel
firebox

Anatomy of a Double-Hung Sash (Interior)

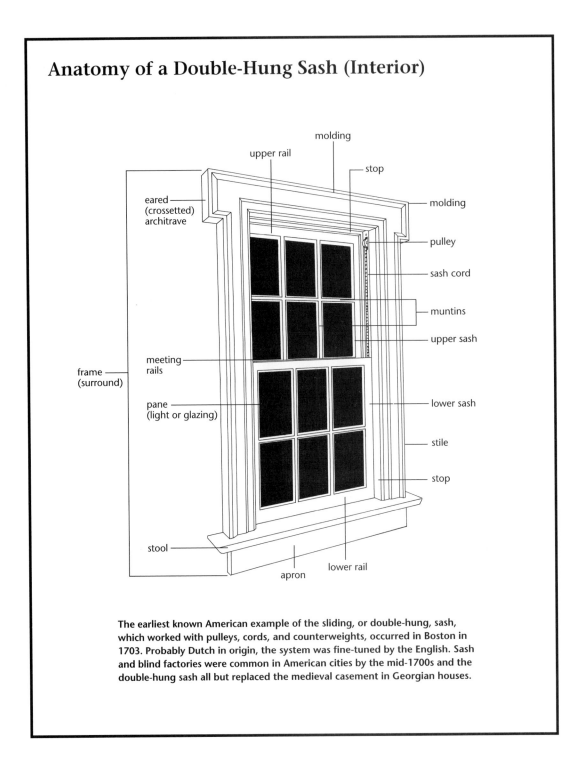

molding

upper rail

stop

eared (crossetted) architrave

molding

pulley

sash cord

muntins

upper sash

frame (surround)

meeting rails

lower sash

pane (light or glazing)

stile

stop

stool

apron

lower rail

The earliest known American example of the sliding, or double-hung, sash, which worked with pulleys, cords, and counterweights, occurred in Boston in 1703. Probably Dutch in origin, the system was fine-tuned by the English. Sash and blind factories were common in American cities by the mid-1700s and the double-hung sash all but replaced the medieval casement in Georgian houses.

WINDOWS (EXTERIOR)

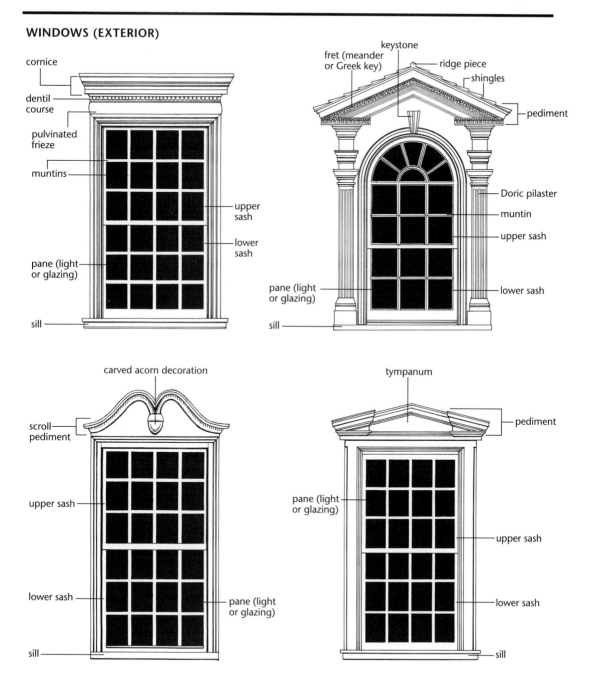

cornice

dentil course

pulvinated frieze

muntins

upper sash

lower sash

pane (light or glazing)

sill

keystone

fret (meander or Greek key)

ridge piece

shingles

pediment

Doric pilaster

muntin

upper sash

pane (light or glazing)

lower sash

sill

carved acorn decoration

scroll pediment

upper sash

lower sash

pane (light or glazing)

sill

tympanum

pediment

pane (light or glazing)

upper sash

lower sash

sill

Georgian

DOORS (EXTERIOR)

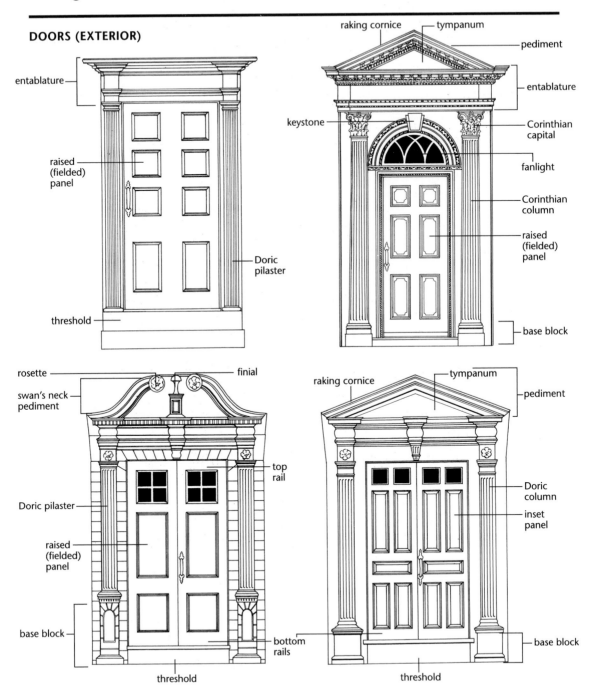

entablature

raised (fielded) panel

Doric pilaster

threshold

raking cornice — tympanum — pediment

entablature

keystone

Corinthian capital

fanlight

Corinthian column

raised (fielded) panel

base block

rosette — finial

swan's neck pediment

Doric pilaster

raised (fielded) panel

base block

top rail

bottom rails

threshold

raking cornice — tympanum — pediment

Doric column

inset panel

base block

threshold

GATES

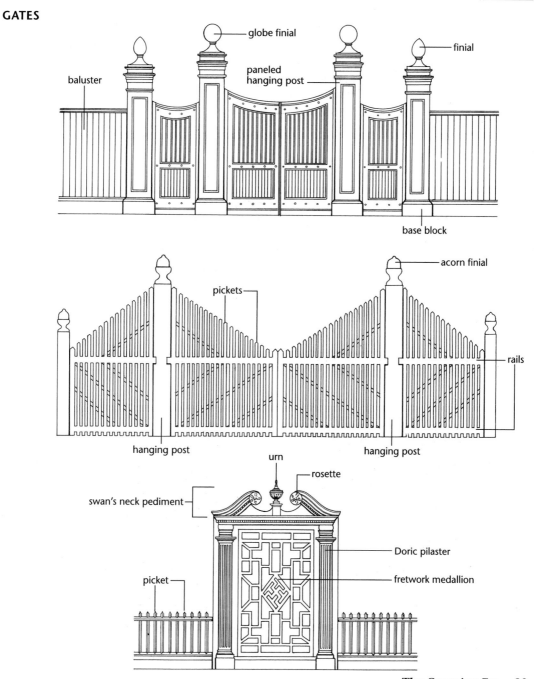

globe finial

finial

baluster

paneled
hanging post

base block

acorn finial

pickets

rails

hanging post

hanging post

urn

rosette

swan's neck pediment

Doric pilaster

fretwork medallion

picket

Chapter Five
Neoclassical Styles

The Neoclassical movement developed in Europe, especially in England and France, in the mid-18th century and began making its impact on American design after the Revolution. Like the Georgian mode, the Neoclassical was rooted in Classical orders (page 98) and concepts of proportion and decoration, but it differed in that it was based on a new perception of ancient Rome and Greece as separate and very distinct civilizations, each with its own merits. Whereas architects of the English Renaissance—the basis of the Georgian style—regarded ancient Rome as the leading authority on design matters, a new respect for ancient Greece now challenged this viewpoint.

Interest in the design principles of the two different cultures coincided with the emergence of archaeology as a serious science—major excavations began at Herculaneum in 1783 and at Pompeii in 1793. There was also a new class of superbly illustrated books that recorded individual monuments, including the buildings of the Acropolis, in unprecedented detail. Especially influential was the four-volume *Antiquities of Athens*, by James Stuart and Nicholas Revett, published in London between 1762 and 1816. As archeological studies progressed, a clearer understanding emerged of both the Roman interest in surface ornament and systems of proportion and the Greek passion for geometry and practical spatial function.

In America, Neoclassicism evolved into two distinct styles. The post-Colonial Federal style, based on Roman prototypes, lasted roughly from the 1780s to the 1820s, and the Greek Revival, based on Greek prototypes, extended from about 1820 through the 1840s.

Federal

URBAN HOUSE
(MID-ATLANTIC)

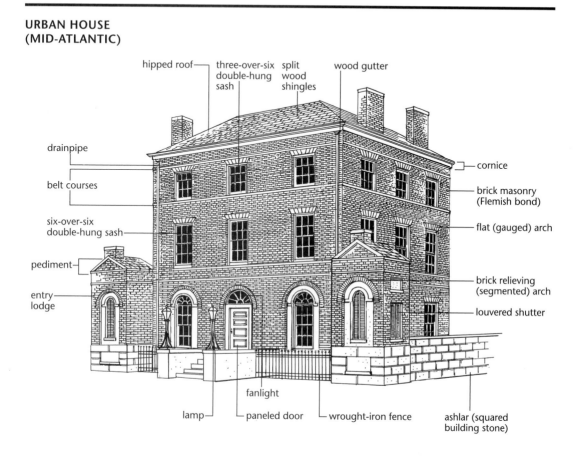

hipped roof

three-over-six double-hung sash

split wood shingles

wood gutter

drainpipe

belt courses

six-over-six double-hung sash

pediment

entry lodge

cornice

brick masonry (Flemish bond)

flat (gauged) arch

brick relieving (segmented) arch

louvered shutter

lamp

fanlight

paneled door

wrought-iron fence

ashlar (squared building stone)

Thoroughly British, Federal architecture began as the signature style of America's wealthy mercantile class, primarily members of the Federalist aristocracy whose international business trade kept them closely linked to England despite independence. Chaste, conservative, and gracefully elegant, the style first appeared primarily in important coastal cities, but eventually was adapted everywhere in simpler, vernacular forms.

Brick was the material of choice for simplified Federal-style facades, marked by refined decorations and elongated proportions. The interiors showed a new interest in how rooms related to one another in terms of volume and shape; round and oval spaces appeared for the first time, and ellipses and curves were constantly set off against rectilinear surfaces. A symmetrical facade often belied a varied plan, with rooms placed according to need rather than the dictates of a formal design. Based on the English Adamesque style, interior decoration featured elegant carved swags and garlands and other Classical details.

Federal

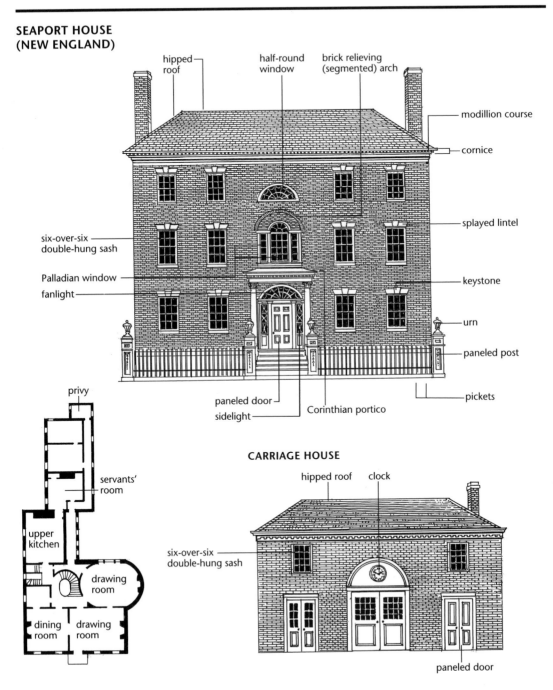

hipped roof

half-round window

brick relieving (segmented) arch

modillion course

cornice

six-over-six double-hung sash

splayed lintel

Palladian window

fanlight

keystone

urn

paneled post

pickets

paneled door

sidelight

Corinthian portico

privy

servants' room

upper kitchen

drawing room

dining room

drawing room

CARRIAGE HOUSE

hipped roof

clock

six-over-six double-hung sash

paneled door

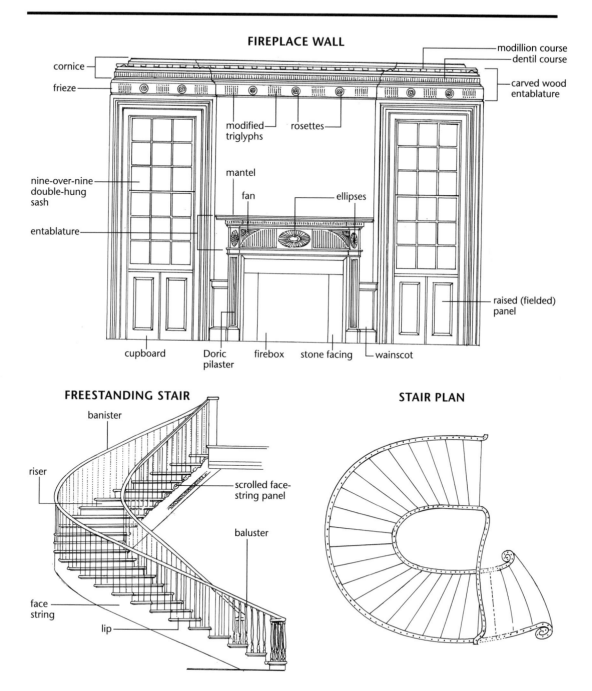

FIREPLACE WALL

cornice

frieze

modillion course

dentil course

carved wood entablature

modified triglyphs

rosettes

mantel

fan

ellipses

nine-over-nine double-hung sash

entablature

raised (fielded) panel

cupboard

Doric pilaster

firebox

stone facing

wainscot

FREESTANDING STAIR

banister

riser

scrolled face-string panel

baluster

face string

lip

STAIR PLAN

Federal

**ROW HOUSE
(NEW ENGLAND)**

CORNICE DETAIL

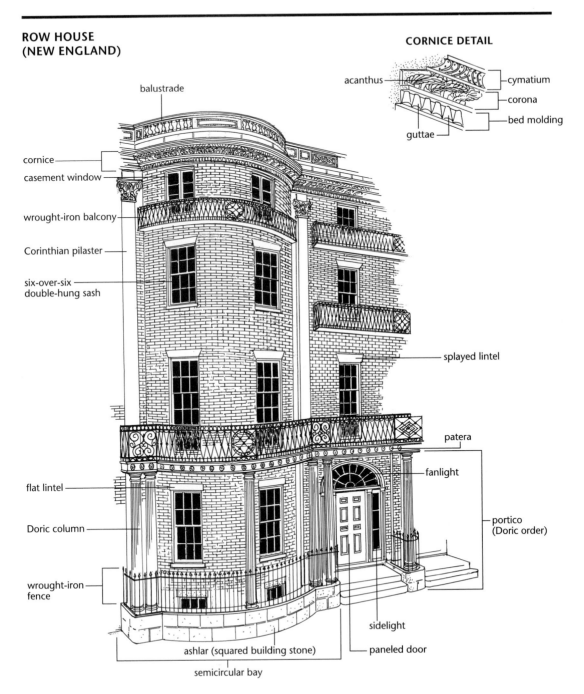

balustrade

cornice

casement window

wrought-iron balcony

Corinthian pilaster

six-over-six
double-hung sash

flat lintel

Doric column

wrought-iron
fence

acanthus — cymatium

corona

bed molding

guttae

splayed lintel

patera

fanlight

portico
(Doric order)

sidelight

paneled door

ashlar (squared building stone)

semicircular bay

URBAN HOUSE (CHARLESTON)

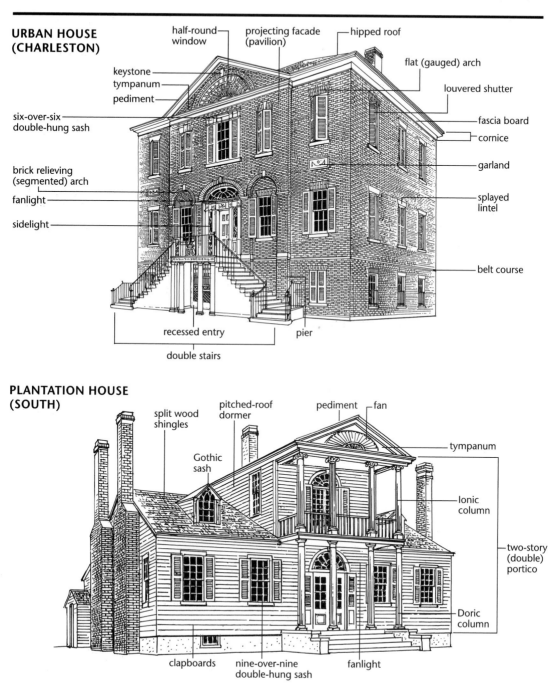

half-round window

projecting facade (pavilion)

hipped roof

keystone

tympanum

pediment

flat (gauged) arch

louvered shutter

six-over-six double-hung sash

fascia board

cornice

brick relieving (segmented) arch

garland

fanlight

splayed lintel

sidelight

belt course

recessed entry

pier

double stairs

PLANTATION HOUSE (SOUTH)

split wood shingles

pitched-roof dormer

pediment

fan

tympanum

Gothic sash

Ionic column

two-story (double) portico

Doric column

clapboards

nine-over-nine double-hung sash

fanlight

Federal

**SEAPORT HOUSE
(NEW ENGLAND)**

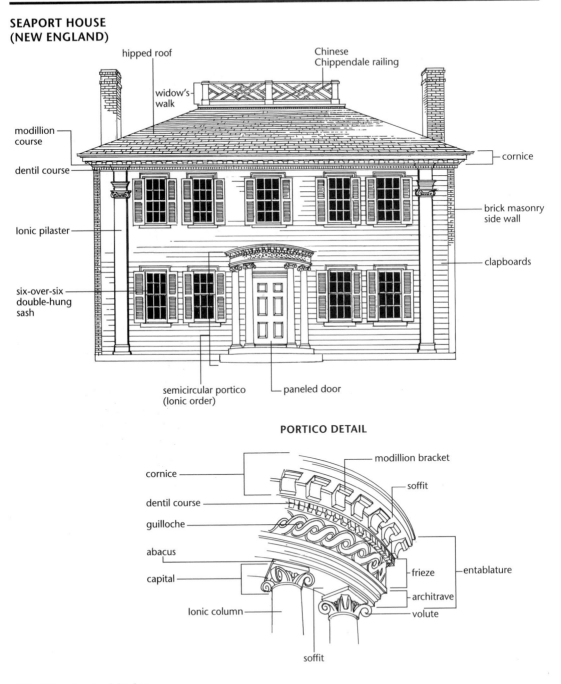

hipped roof

Chinese
Chippendale railing

widow's
walk

modillion
course

dentil course

Ionic pilaster

six-over-six
double-hung
sash

cornice

brick masonry
side wall

clapboards

semicircular portico
(Ionic order)

paneled door

PORTICO DETAIL

cornice

dentil course

guilloche

abacus

capital

Ionic column

modillion bracket

soffit

frieze

architrave

volute

entablature

soffit

**FARM HOUSE
(MID-ATLANTIC)**

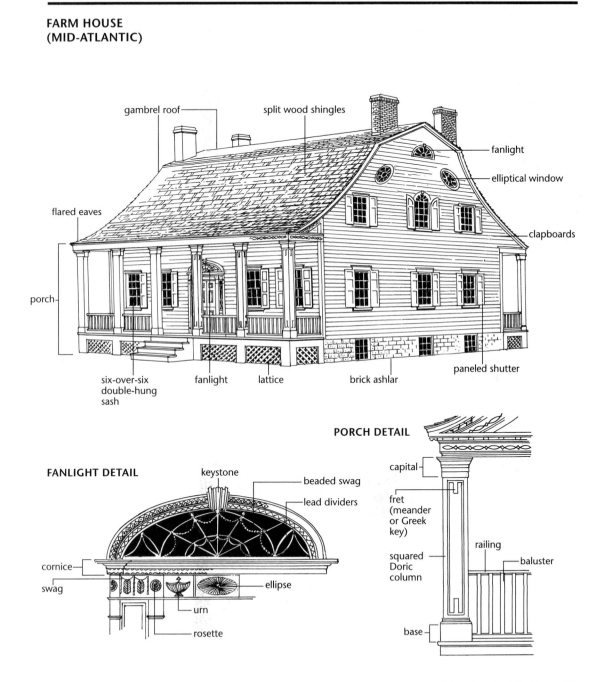

gambrel roof

split wood shingles

fanlight

elliptical window

flared eaves

clapboards

porch

paneled shutter

six-over-six
double-hung
sash

fanlight

lattice

brick ashlar

FANLIGHT DETAIL

keystone

beaded swag

lead dividers

cornice

swag

ellipse

urn

rosette

PORCH DETAIL

capital

fret
(meander
or Greek
key)

squared
Doric
column

railing

baluster

base

The Basic Orders

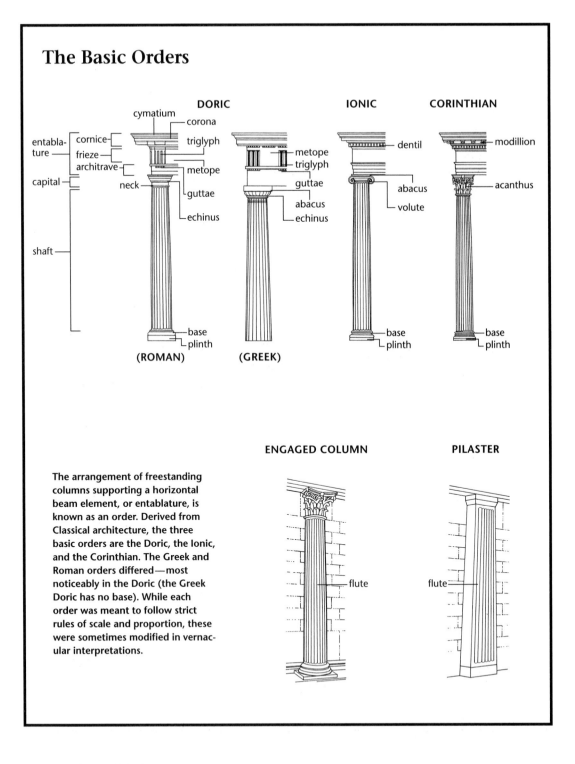

DORIC **IONIC** **CORINTHIAN**

cymatium
corona
entabla-
ture
cornice
frieze
architrave
capital
triglyph
metope
neck
guttae
echinus
shaft

metope
triglyph
guttae
abacus
echinus

dentil
abacus
volute

modillion
acanthus

base
plinth

base
plinth

base
plinth

base
plinth

(ROMAN) **(GREEK)**

ENGAGED COLUMN **PILASTER**

The arrangement of freestanding columns supporting a horizontal beam element, or entablature, is known as an order. Derived from Classical architecture, the three basic orders are the Doric, the Ionic, and the Corinthian. The Greek and Roman orders differed—most noticeably in the Doric (the Greek Doric has no base). While each order was meant to follow strict rules of scale and proportion, these were sometimes modified in vernacular interpretations.

flute

flute

DOORS (EXTERIOR)

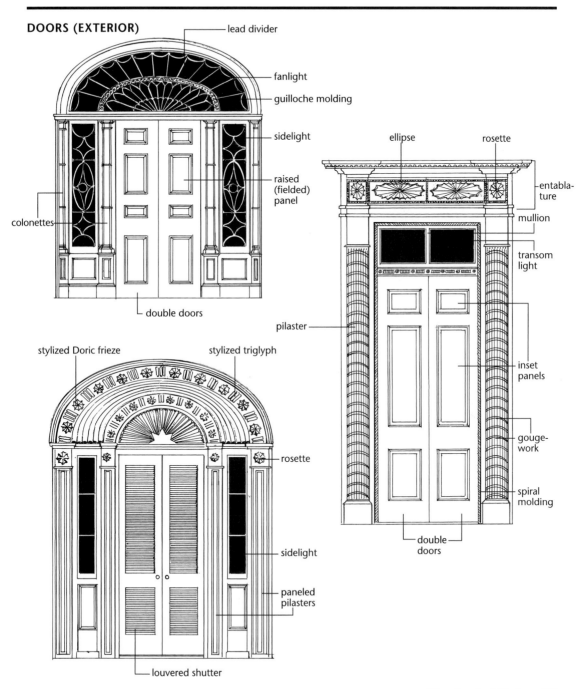

lead divider

fanlight

guilloche molding

sidelight

raised (fielded) panel

colonettes

double doors

ellipse

rosette

entablature

mullion

transom light

pilaster

inset panels

gougework

spiral molding

double doors

stylized Doric frieze

stylized triglyph

rosette

sidelight

paneled pilasters

louvered shutter

Greek Revival

Whereas the Federal style derived from the Palladian ideal of ancient Roman design, the Greek Revival adhered strictly to the Greek orders and systems of proportions and ornament. Modeled on English precedents, the Greek Revival was imported from abroad to America and spread rapidly along the coast and into the frontier. Linked by an educated elite to the ideals of ancient Greek democracy, it became associated with the young American democratic government and was considered a natural choice for civic monuments.

As a stylistic influence, the Greek Revival filtered down to even the most modest of rural farmhouses. Grander houses generally featured a columned portico supporting a triangular pediment—as on a Greek temple. Country builders accomplished the same effect simply by turning the gable end of a house to the street, boxing in the gable with a triangular raking cornice, adding pilasters to the corners, and painting the building a pristine white.

URBAN HOUSE

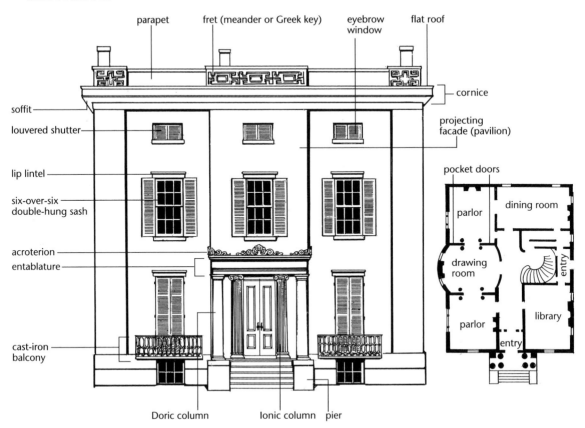

parapet · fret (meander or Greek key) · eyebrow window · flat roof · cornice · soffit · louvered shutter · projecting facade (pavilion) · lip lintel · pocket doors · six-over-six double-hung sash · parlor · dining room · acroterion · entablature · drawing room · entry · cast-iron balcony · parlor · library · entry · Doric column · Ionic column · pier

**ESTATE HOUSE
(NEW ENGLAND)**

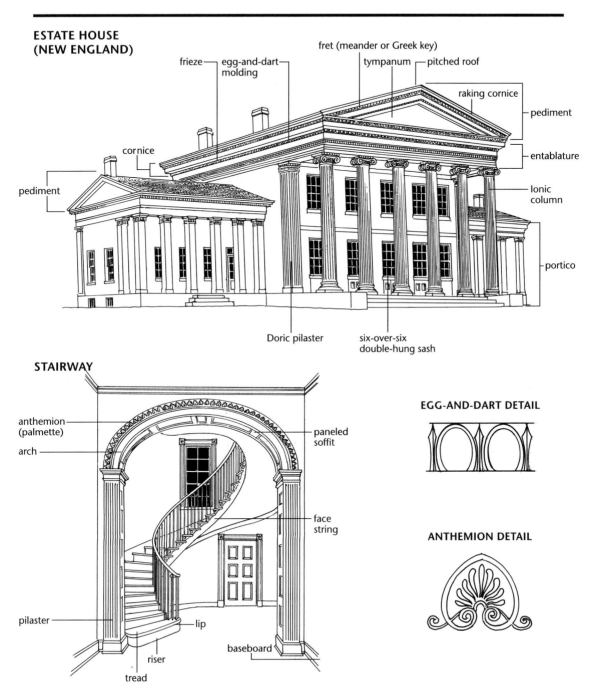

frieze

egg-and-dart molding

fret (meander or Greek key)

tympanum

pitched roof

raking cornice

pediment

cornice

entablature

Ionic column

pediment

portico

Doric pilaster

six-over-six double-hung sash

STAIRWAY

anthemion (palmette)

arch

paneled soffit

face string

pilaster

lip

baseboard

riser

tread

EGG-AND-DART DETAIL

ANTHEMION DETAIL

Greek Revival

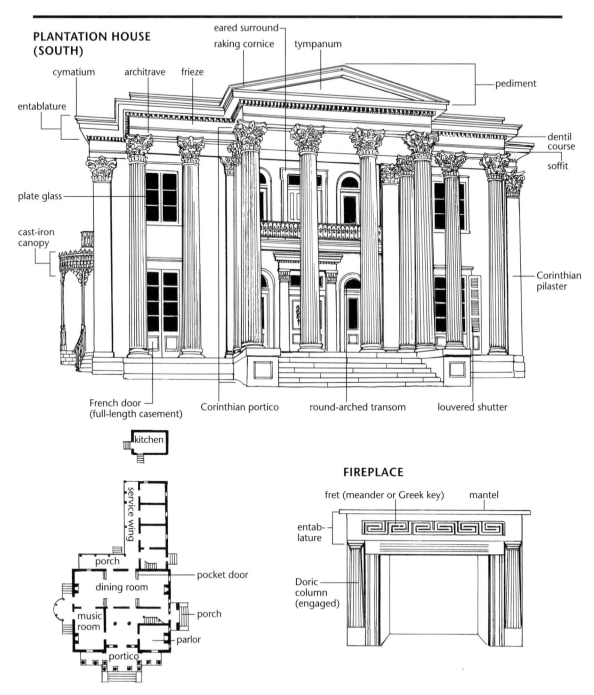

PLANTATION HOUSE (SOUTH)

eared surround

raking cornice

tympanum

pediment

cymatium

architrave

frieze

entablature

dentil course

soffit

plate glass

cast-iron canopy

Corinthian pilaster

French door (full-length casement)

Corinthian portico

round-arched transom

louvered shutter

kitchen

service wing

porch

pocket door

dining room

porch

music room

parlor

portico

FIREPLACE

fret (meander or Greek key)

mantel

entablature

Doric column (engaged)

PLANTATION HOUSE (SOUTH)

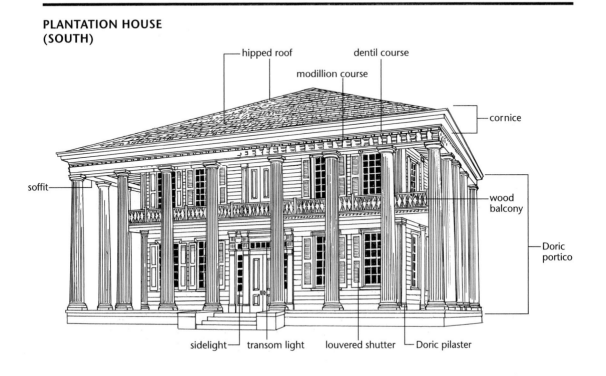

hipped roof

modillion course

dentil course

cornice

soffit

wood balcony

Doric portico

sidelight — transom light — louvered shutter — Doric pilaster

FIREPLACE

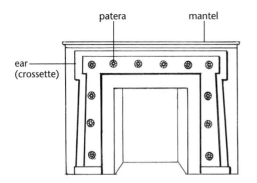

patera

mantel

ear (crossette)

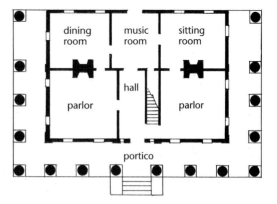

| dining room | music room | sitting room |
| parlor | hall | parlor |

portico

Greek Revival

ROW HOUSE
(NEW ORLEANS)

SECOND FLOOR

FIRST FLOOR

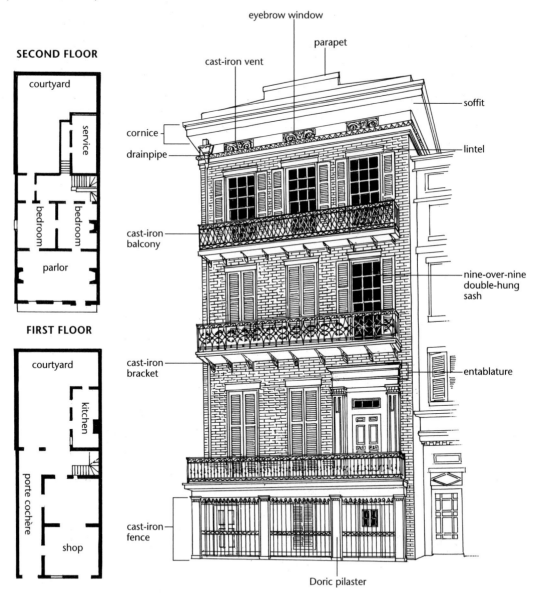

eyebrow window

parapet

cast-iron vent

cornice

drainpipe

soffit

lintel

cast-iron balcony

nine-over-nine double-hung sash

cast-iron bracket

entablature

cast-iron fence

Doric pilaster

courtyard

service

bedroom

bedroom

parlor

courtyard

kitchen

porte cochère

shop

DOORS (EXTERIOR)

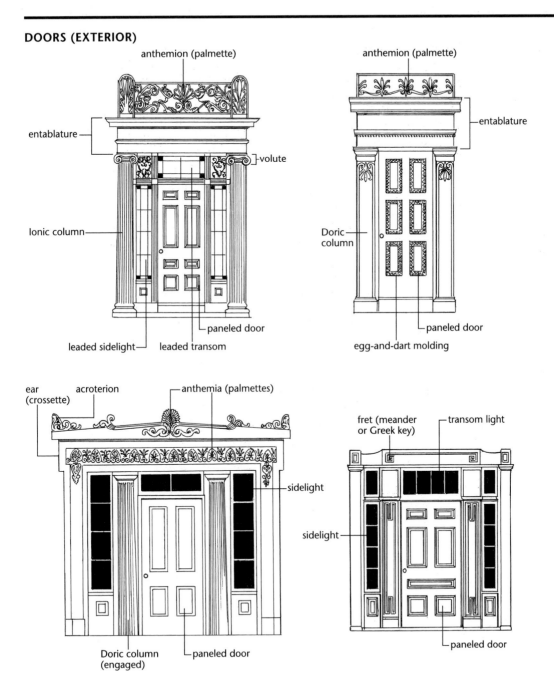

anthemion (palmette)

entablature

volute

Ionic column

leaded sidelight — leaded transom — paneled door

anthemion (palmette)

entablature

Doric column

paneled door

egg-and-dart molding

ear (crossette)   acroterion   anthemia (palmettes)

sidelight

Doric column (engaged) — paneled door

fret (meander or Greek key)   transom light

sidelight

paneled door

Greek Revival

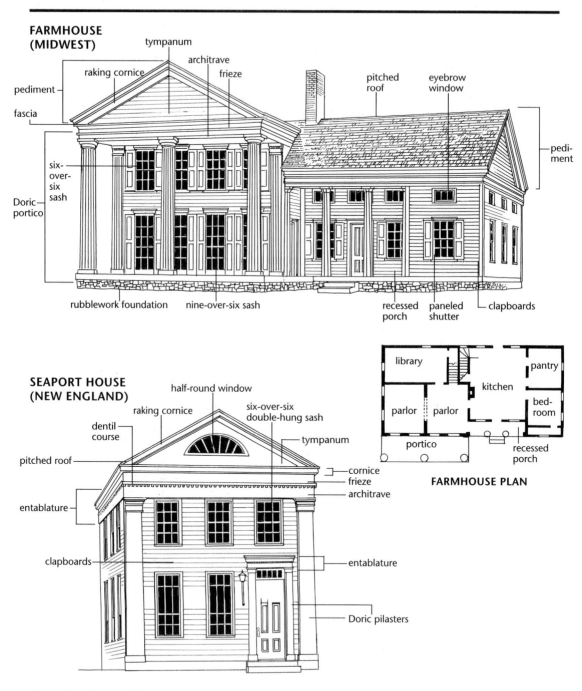

FARMHOUSE (MIDWEST)

pediment

fascia

raking cornice

tympanum

architrave

frieze

Doric portico

six-over-six sash

pitched roof

eyebrow window

pedi-ment

rubblework foundation

nine-over-six sash

recessed porch

paneled shutter

clapboards

SEAPORT HOUSE (NEW ENGLAND)

dentil course

pitched roof

raking cornice

half-round window

six-over-six double-hung sash

tympanum

cornice

frieze

architrave

entablature

clapboards

entablature

Doric pilasters

library

pantry

kitchen

parlor

parlor

bed-room

portico

recessed porch

FARMHOUSE PLAN

VILLA
(NEW ENGLAND)

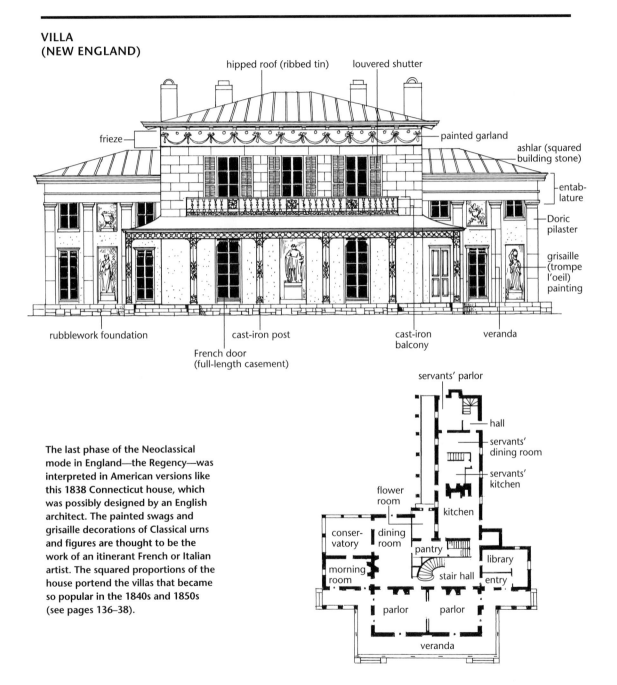

hipped roof (ribbed tin)   louvered shutter

frieze

painted garland

ashlar (squared building stone)

entab-lature

Doric pilaster

grisaille (trompe l'oeil) painting

rubblework foundation   cast-iron post

cast-iron balcony

veranda

French door (full-length casement)

servants' parlor

hall

servants' dining room

servants' kitchen

flower room

kitchen

conser-vatory

dining room

pantry

library

morning room

stair hall

entry

parlor   parlor

veranda

The last phase of the Neoclassical mode in England—the Regency—was interpreted in American versions like this 1838 Connecticut house, which was possibly designed by an English architect. The painted swags and grisaille decorations of Classical urns and figures are thought to be the work of an itinerant French or Italian artist. The squared proportions of the house portend the villas that became so popular in the 1840s and 1850s (see pages 136–38).

Chapter Six
Folk and Frontier Houses

Although architectural fashion has always been subject to the vagaries of contemporary taste, many regional building types in America were so well adapted to their specific locations that they endured even when the styles that formed them did not. Practical needs and available materials defined these so-called folk houses, whose distinctive forms—from the connected farms of northern Maine to the freestanding Conch houses of southern Florida—often reflected several different styles over the generations.

Most folk types outside of Colonial New England were the direct result of the great era of territorial expansion in the 19th century. With public land selling at $2.00 an acre, nearly one million settlers had spread into the vast area between the Appalachian Mountains and the Mississippi River by 1800. Texas was annexed in 1845, Florida gained statehood in the same year, and at the close of the Mexican War in 1848 the United States had possession of the territories of New Mexico and California.

Changing technology played a major role in shaping many new building types during this period. By the 1850s, cheap mass-produced nails became widely available, as did the circular saw, which was capable of milling vast quantities of lumber. Coinciding with the invention of the lightweight balloon frame (see page 127), these developments resulted in an unprecedented building boom of inexpensive frame houses across the country during the next decade.

Some vernacular traditions, such as the *Fachwerk* construction of German immigrants, reflected a specific ethnic heritage; others, such as sod and adobe houses, demonstrated the use of local building material. While often very different from one another, all types of folk houses shared one characteristic: common sense.

Cape Cod Cottage

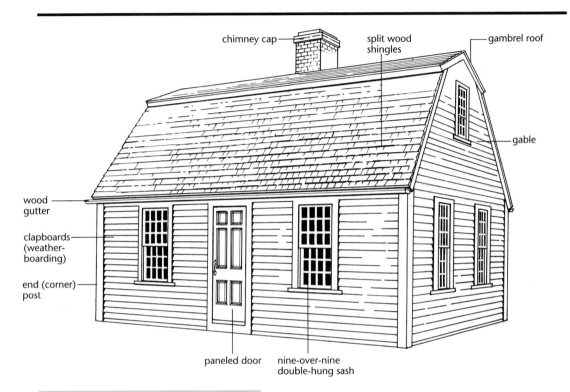

chimney cap

split wood shingles

gambrel roof

gable

wood gutter

clapboards (weather-boarding)

end (corner) post

paneled door

nine-over-nine double-hung sash

The Cape Cod cottage originated with English settlers in the mid-1600s; although it is associated with the early Colonial period, the type actually prevailed well into the 1800s. The basic form consisted of a one- or two-room house with a loft above and, often, a lean-to at the rear. Sometimes a third room was added at the end. A pitched, bowed, or gambrel roof sloped down just to the window tops.

Built low and broad to withstand prevailing winds, the shingled or clapboard Cape Cod cottage often sat directly on timber sills without a foundation. If the sandy soil underneath eroded or blew away, the house could be dragged or floated to a new location.

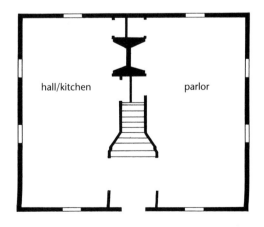

hall/kitchen

parlor

Connected Farm

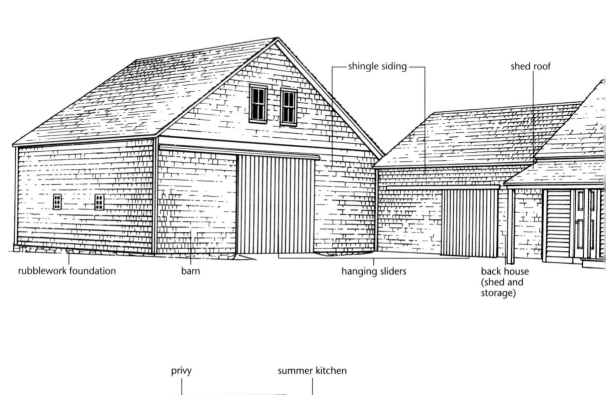

shingle siding

shed roof

rubblework foundation

barn

hanging sliders

back house
(shed and
storage)

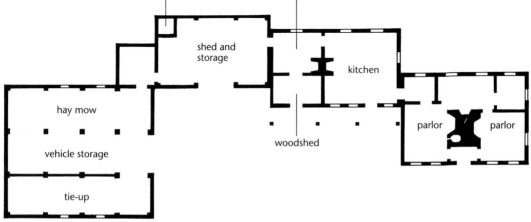

privy

summer kitchen

shed and
storage

kitchen

hay mow

vehicle storage

woodshed

parlor

parlor

tie-up

Connected Farm

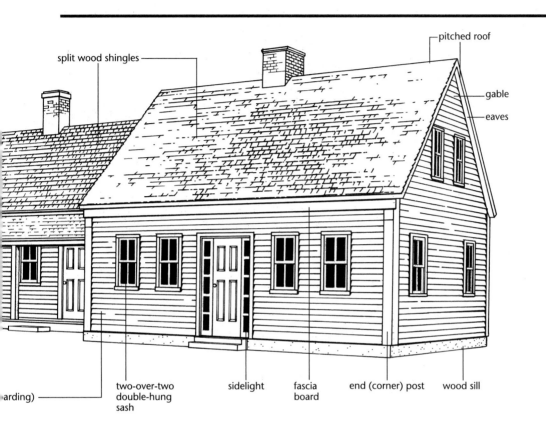

split wood shingles

pitched roof

gable

eaves

arding)

two-over-two
double-hung
sash

sidelight

fascia
board

end (corner) post

wood sill

The connected farm—a rambling complex of attached houses, barns, and animal sheds—is indigenous to northern New England. The supplementary buildings were usually added one by one over time, often as frugal Yankee farmers moved older, obsolete outbuildings from elsewhere on their property closer to the main house for reuse.

While the frigid winters of the region might explain this folk type, connected farms were not common until the mid-1800s and never appeared in other regions of the country that get just as cold as the Northeast. Rather, the connected farm probably developed in response to economic needs. As the 19th century progressed, the poor New England soil couldn't support the more progressive, large-scale farming adopted elsewhere. In an effort to compete, New Englanders combined smaller-scale family farms with cottage industries, such as needlecrafts and canning, and adopted a convenient arrangement of buildings to serve agriculture and home industry under the same roof.

Cracker House

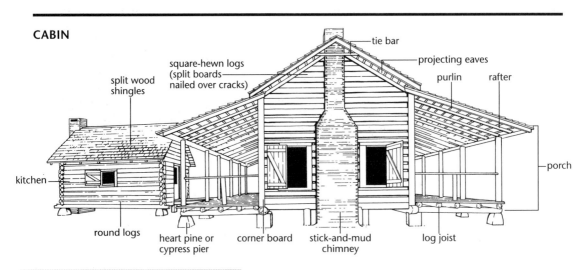

split wood shingles

square-hewn logs (split boards nailed over cracks)

tie bar

projecting eaves

purlin

rafter

porch

kitchen

round logs

heart pine or cypress pier

corner board

stick-and-mud chimney

log joist

The term "Cracker" is thought to have originated in southern Georgia, where cracked corn was a dietary staple, but it also refers to the whip-cracking cattle drivers who made their way across the Florida border in the 1800s. Many so-called Cracker houses, found primarily in central Florida and the panhandle, were log cabins of the standard single- or double-pen, saddlebag, or dogtrot types (see pages 119–21) adapted to a semi-tropical climate. A large, cool porch invariably surrounded the house, which was raised off the damp ground on rot-resistant piers of cypress, heart pine, or limestone. Chimneys were made of sticks where stones were scarce, and the kitchen was often in a separate building.

The more substantial "four-square" house, of balloon frame construction, featured ample front and back porches and a hipped roof covered in tin to deflect sun. A cupola provided natural air conditioning; as warm air rose out of louvered vents, cool air was drawn in through open windows and doors.

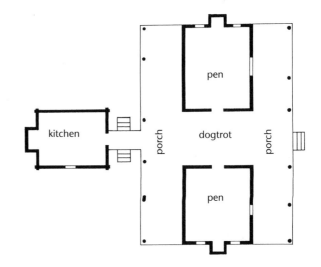

pen

kitchen

porch

dogtrot

porch

pen

FOUR-SQUARE HOUSE

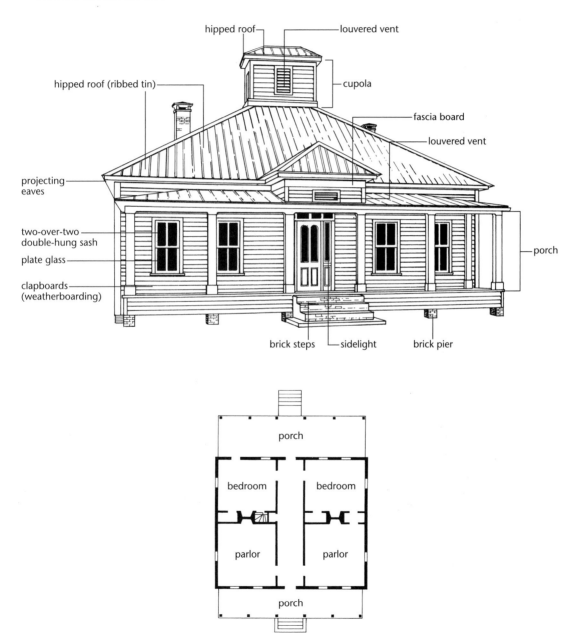

hipped roof

louvered vent

hipped roof (ribbed tin)

cupola

fascia board

louvered vent

projecting eaves

two-over-two double-hung sash

plate glass

clapboards (weatherboarding)

porch

brick steps

sidelight

brick pier

porch

bedroom

bedroom

parlor

parlor

porch

Creole House

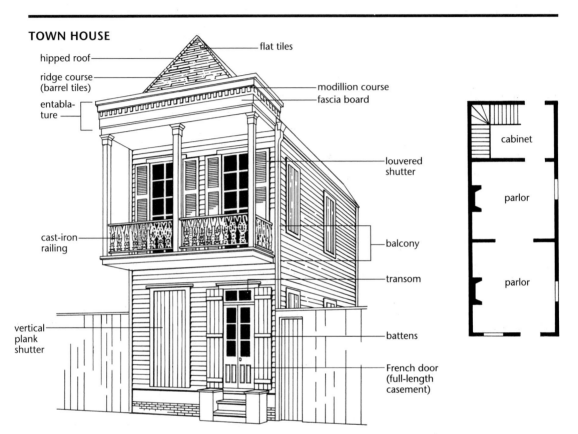

TOWN HOUSE

- hipped roof
- ridge course (barrel tiles)
- entabla-ture
- flat tiles
- modillion course
- fascia board
- louvered shutter
- cast-iron railing
- balcony
- transom
- vertical plank shutter
- battens
- French door (full-length casement)

cabinet

parlor

parlor

Once a common feature of the New Orleans streetscape during the 19th century, the Creole townhouse had a hipped or gabled roof and a one- or two-story gallery on both the front and the rear. The plan consisted of two large rooms; detached outbuildings served as the kitchen, washroom, and other work spaces. A typical construction technique consisted of vertical planks set directly onto the sill. These so-called flatboat boards were covered with horizontal weatherboarding, or clapboards.

The basic pavilion-roofed house of the French Colonial era (see page 52) evolved into a simple house that was common in Louisiana and on the Gulf Coast well into the 1800s. Called a Creole cottage (a Creole is a Louisiana native descended from French, Spanish, or West Indian settlers), or a *maison de maître*, its plan was a simple rectangle partitioned into two or four rooms (often all used for sleeping), usually with no interior halls. A rear stair in a cabinet (small room) sometimes led to rooms in a dormered attic. French doors opened onto a front gallery or directly onto the street. A secluded garden and a gallery, which both served as cool living spaces, were usually located behind the house.

Creole House

MAISON DE MAÎTRE

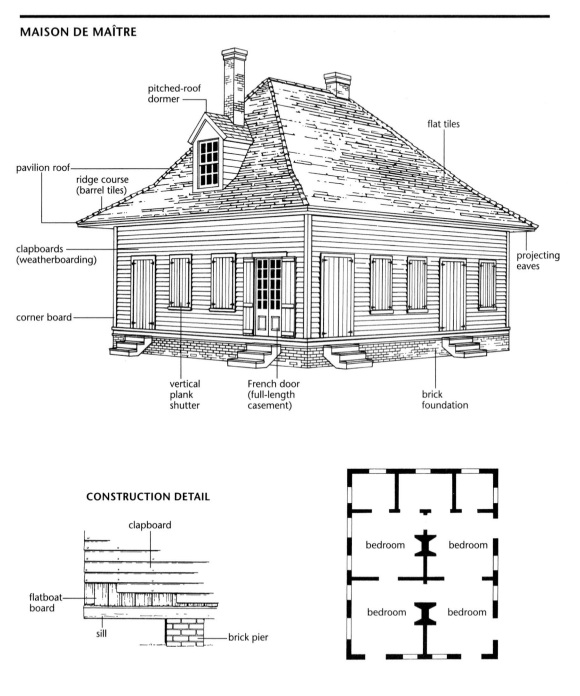

pitched-roof dormer

flat tiles

pavilion roof

ridge course (barrel tiles)

clapboards (weatherboarding)

corner board

vertical plank shutter

French door (full-length casement)

projecting eaves

brick foundation

CONSTRUCTION DETAIL

clapboard

flatboat board

sill

brick pier

bedroom

bedroom

bedroom

bedroom

Shotgun House

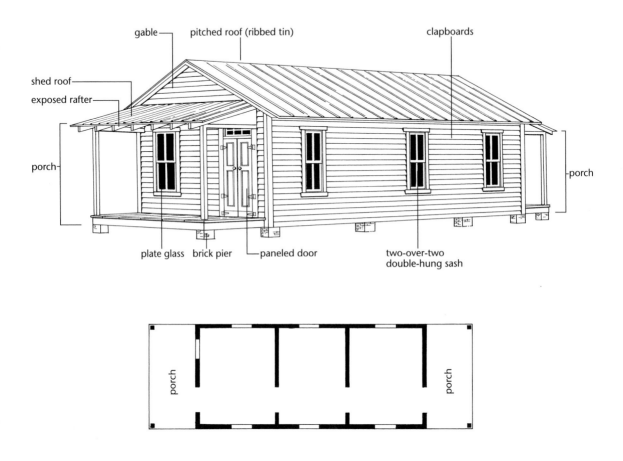

gable — pitched roof (ribbed tin) clapboards

shed roof

exposed rafter

porch porch

plate glass brick pier paneled door two-over-two double-hung sash

porch porch

One room wide, the shotgun house featured a gable-end entry and consisted of two or three all-purpose rooms placed back to back. It was said that if a gun were fired through the front door, the shot would pass through all the rooms in a straight line and go right out the back door. A second story was often raised over the rear room.

Associated primarily with New Orleans, the Gulf Coast, and the rural South, the shotgun was used for workers' and tenants' housing, and by the 1920s was found as far afield as California and Chicago. The long, narrow house type is believed to have first come to America during the 19th century by way of free blacks migrating from Haiti to Louisiana, where it developed as an amalgam of African, French, and Arawak building traditions.

Conch House

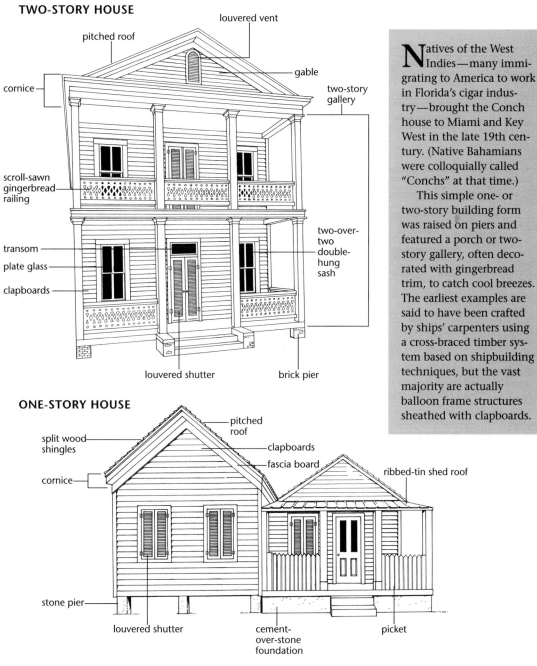

TWO-STORY HOUSE

louvered vent

pitched roof

gable

cornice

two-story gallery

scroll-sawn gingerbread railing

transom

plate glass

clapboards

two-over-two double-hung sash

louvered shutter

brick pier

ONE-STORY HOUSE

split wood shingles

pitched roof

clapboards

fascia board

cornice

ribbed-tin shed roof

stone pier

louvered shutter

cement-over-stone foundation

picket

Natives of the West Indies—many immigrating to America to work in Florida's cigar industry—brought the Conch house to Miami and Key West in the late 19th century. (Native Bahamians were colloquially called "Conchs" at that time.)

This simple one- or two-story building form was raised on piers and featured a porch or two-story gallery, often decorated with gingerbread trim, to catch cool breezes. The earliest examples are said to have been crafted by ships' carpenters using a cross-braced timber system based on shipbuilding techniques, but the vast majority are actually balloon frame structures sheathed with clapboards.

Sod House

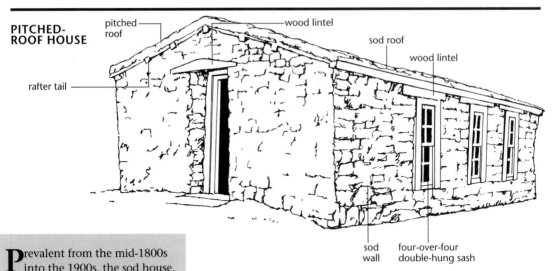

PITCHED-ROOF HOUSE

pitched roof

wood lintel

sod roof

wood lintel

rafter tail

sod wall

four-over-four double-hung sash

Prevalent from the mid-1800s into the 1900s, the sod house, or "soddie," was a product of the Plains, where lumber and other building materials were scarce. A specially designed breaking, or "grasshopper," plow allowed settlers to cut furrows without turning over and destroying the soil, producing foot-wide blocks of sod known as "Kansas brick" or, more optimistically, "Nebraska marble." Blocks were laid with staggered joints, as bricks would be, with every third course (row) set crosswise and the chinks filled in with fine dirt; the interior might be plastered with clay. A twelve- by fourteen-foot house took about an acre of sod and a week to build. Although dirty and leak-prone, the sod, preferably tough buffalo grass, kept the interior warm in winter and cool in summer, withstood wind, and was also good, according to one early settler, for "stopping arrows and slowing bullets."

BARREL-ROOF HOUSE

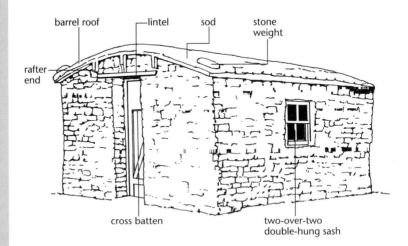

barrel roof

lintel

sod

stone weight

rafter end

cross batten

two-over-two double-hung sash

SINGLE-PEN CABIN

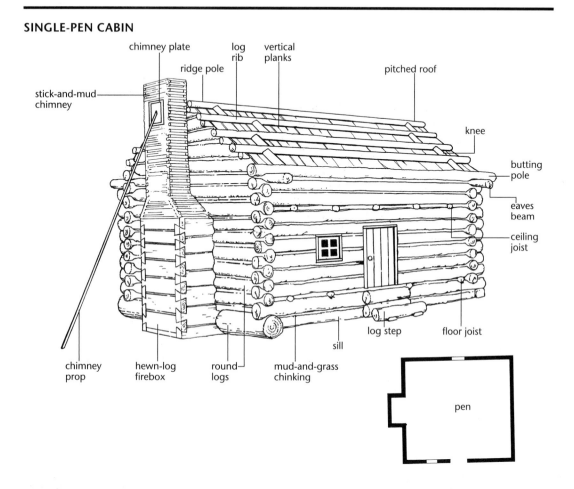

Labels (clockwise from top): chimney plate · log rib · vertical planks · pitched roof · ridge pole · knee · butting pole · eaves beam · ceiling joist · floor joist · log step · sill · mud-and-grass chinking · round logs · hewn-log firebox · chimney prop · stick-and-mud chimney · pen

Although the Swedes were the first settlers to build log structures in America, the major tradition of log building here originated independently in the late 1600s to the early 1700s with German-speaking settlers (see pages 40–42) in the mid-Atlantic region. From Pennsylvania and Virginia, the tradition of log building began spreading south and west with migrating Germans and Scots-Irish in the 1730s and reached its height during the period of frontier expansion from the mid-18th to mid-19th centuries.

The basic log house form was the one-room, or single-pen, plan. The central-chimney "saddlebag" plan evolved when the single-pen house was enlarged by setting the gable end of a second log building against the chimney of the existing structure. An easier way to add on to a log house was to place a second cabin next to the first, gable to gable, and simply roof over the intervening space, producing the "dogtrot" (two pens and a passage) house. Pine and spruce were the preferred woods.

Log Building

SADDLEBAG CABIN

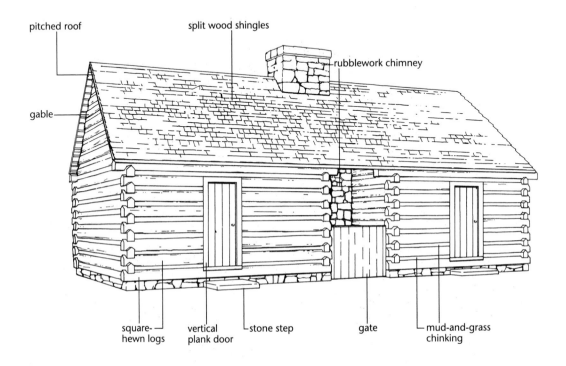

pitched roof

split wood shingles

rubblework chimney

gable

square-hewn logs

vertical plank door

stone step

gate

mud-and-grass chinking

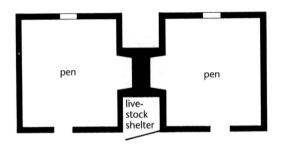

pen

pen

live-stock shelter

DOGTROT CABIN

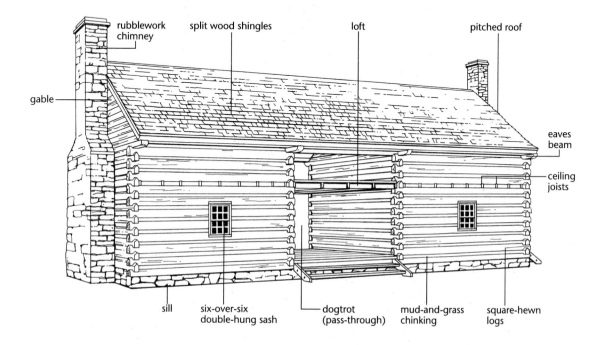

rubblework chimney

split wood shingles

loft

pitched roof

gable

eaves beam

ceiling joists

sill

six-over-six double-hung sash

dogtrot (pass-through)

mud-and-grass chinking

square-hewn logs

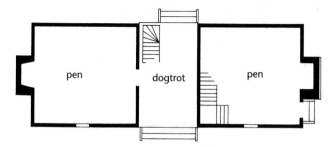

pen

dogtrot

pen

Log Building

NORDIC LOG HOUSE

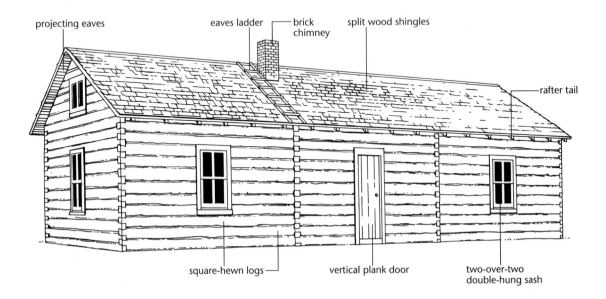

projecting eaves · eaves ladder · brick chimney · split wood shingles · rafter tail · square-hewn logs · vertical plank door · two-over-two double-hung sash

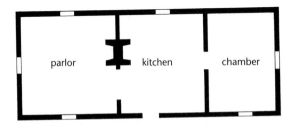

parlor · kitchen · chamber

The square-hewn log house built by Nordic settlers, primarily in the upper Midwest, was characterized by a two-room plan, often with a third room added to make an I- or T-shaped layout. The door opened directly into the kitchen, an all-purpose room used for sleeping and daily work activities. The parlor was reserved for visitors.

Anatomy of Log Notching

SADDLE NOTCHES

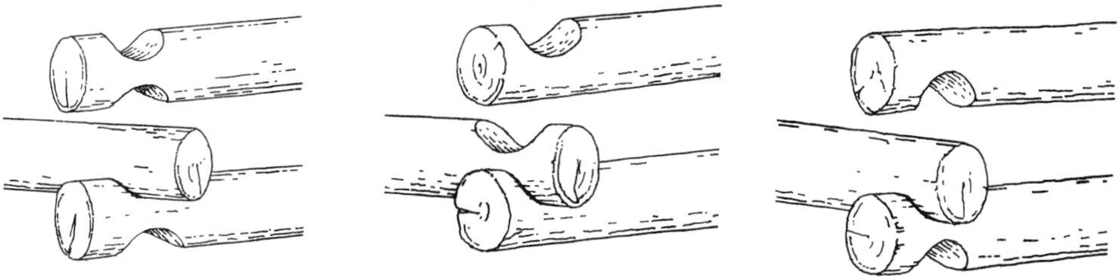

V-NOTCH

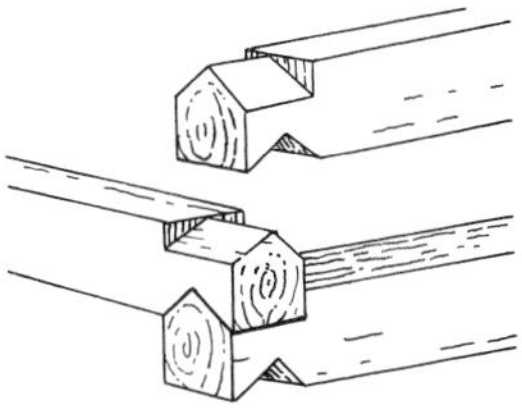

SQUARE NOTCH

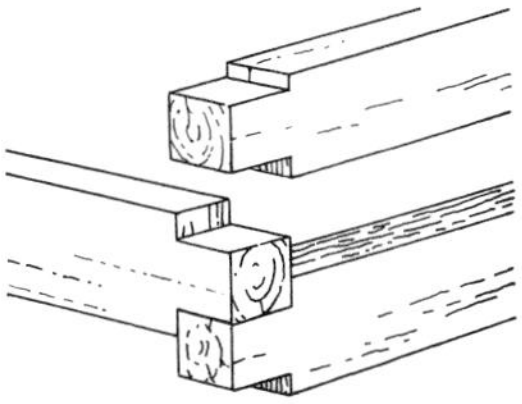

DOVETAIL NOTCH

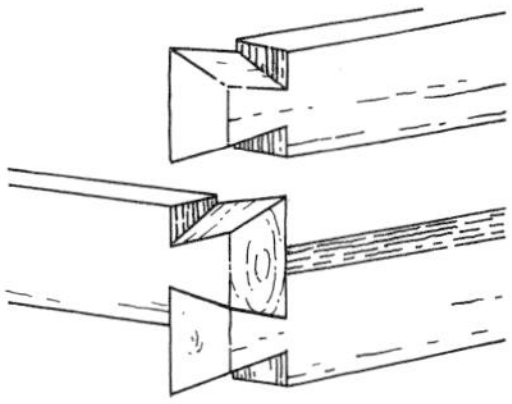

STOVEWOOD CONSTRUCTION

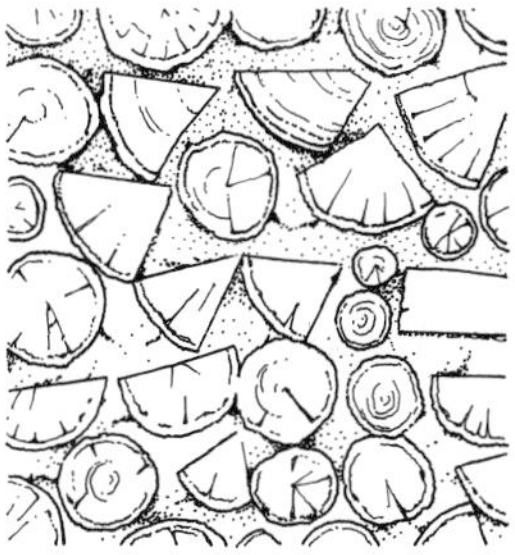

Several different systems of corner notching were used in log construction. The saddle notch was employed universally for round logs, while various lapped (overlaid) and dovetail joints functioned best with squared logs. All logs were locked into place by their own weight. Joints were typically chinked with mud plaster or covered with narrow split boards. Stovewood log construction, found primarily in Wisconsin, involved embedding 8- to 10-inch-long log chunks, ends out, in limestone cement.

Fachwerk Building

FARMHOUSE (WISCONSIN)

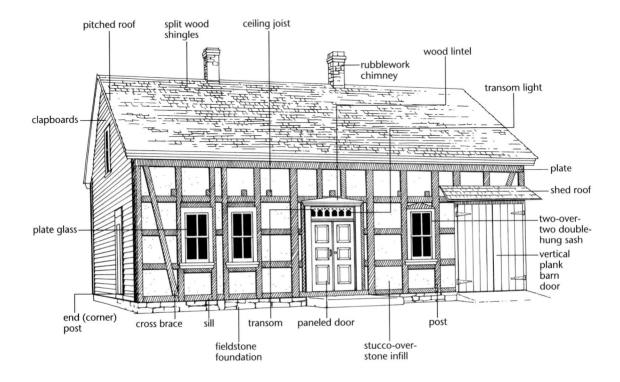

A distinctive addition to the 19th-century frontier landscape of Wisconsin and Texas, where Germanic settlers homesteaded, was the small farmhouse built of *Fachwerk*, or half-timbering. *Fachwerk* consisted of a braced timber frame, usually of white oak or cedar, set on a squared timber sill over a fieldstone foundation. The open framework was filled with an insulation of mud and straw, sandstone, or nogging (kiln-fired brick). A coat of adobe or lime plaster was often applied over the walls, but the *Fachwerk* might also be left exposed.

Fachwerk Building

FARMHOUSE (TEXAS)

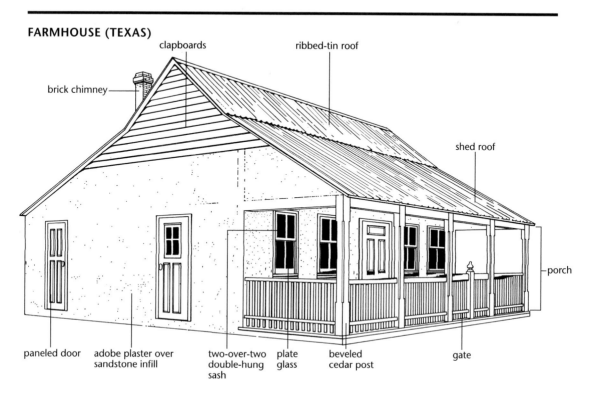

brick chimney

clapboards

ribbed-tin roof

shed roof

porch

paneled door

adobe plaster over sandstone infill

two-over-two double-hung sash

plate glass

beveled cedar post

gate

FRAMING DETAIL (HEWN CEDAR)

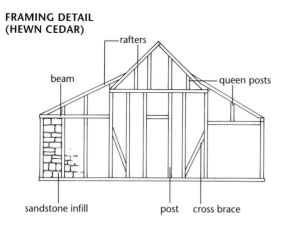

rafters

beam

queen posts

sandstone infill

post

cross brace

kitchen

bedroom

parlor

porch

Box-and-Strip Building

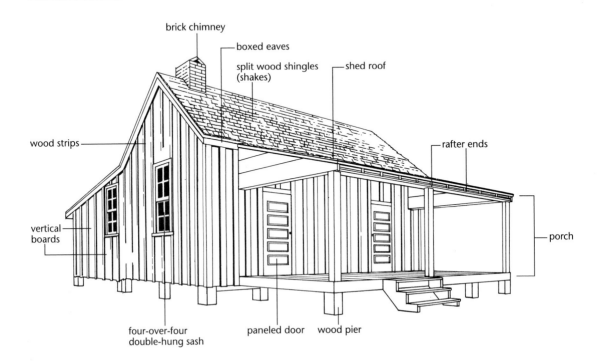

brick chimney

boxed eaves

split wood shingles
(shakes)

shed roof

wood strips

rafter ends

vertical
boards

porch

four-over-four
double-hung sash

paneled door

wood pier

The simple box-and-strip construction technique appeared in the
Plains and in Texas in the late 1800s
after milled lumber became available
but was still expensive in some hard-
to-reach areas. Requiring a minimum
of wood, the building method involved
nailing vertical boards to a bottom sill
and top plate, then merely covering up
the cracks with thin wood strips. The
look was similar to board-and-batten
siding, but the strips were wider and
rougher, and there was no balloon
frame for support underneath.

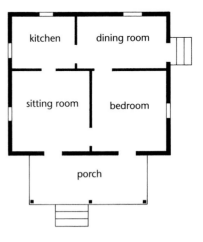

kitchen   dining room

sitting room   bedroom

porch

Anatomy of a Balloon Frame

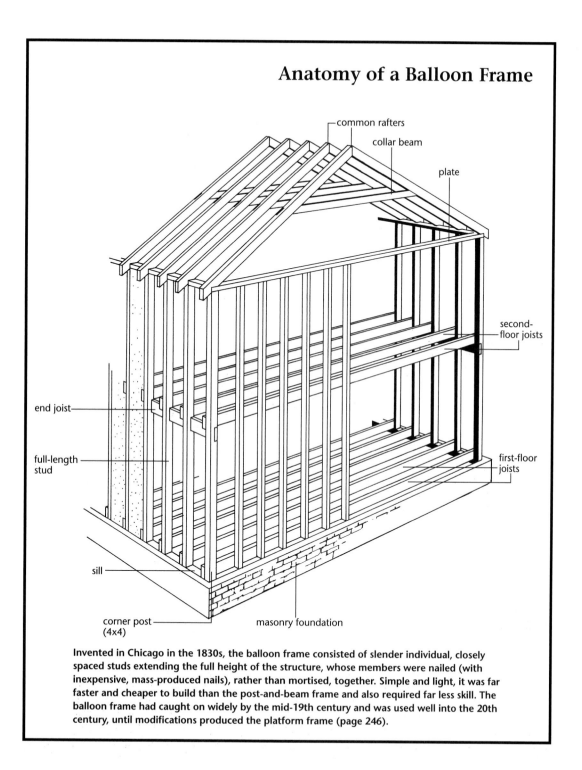

common rafters

collar beam

plate

second-floor joists

end joist

full-length stud

first-floor joists

sill

corner post (4x4)

masonry foundation

Invented in Chicago in the 1830s, the balloon frame consisted of slender individual, closely spaced studs extending the full height of the structure, whose members were nailed (with inexpensive, mass-produced nails), rather than mortised, together. Simple and light, it was far faster and cheaper to build than the post-and-beam frame and also required far less skill. The balloon frame had caught on widely by the mid-19th century and was used well into the 20th century, until modifications produced the platform frame (page 246).

Spanish Territorial Architecture

CASA DEL POBLADOR (TOWN HOUSE)

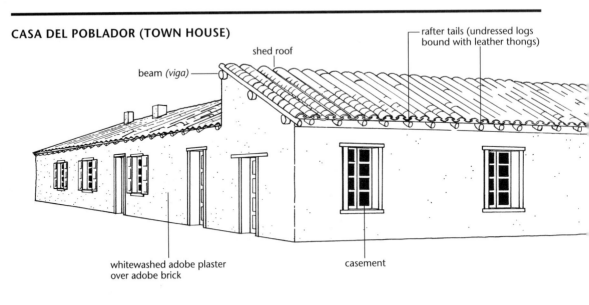

rafter tails (undressed logs bound with leather thongs)

shed roof

beam *(viga)*

whitewashed adobe plaster over adobe brick

casement

MISSION TILE DETAIL

After the Spanish Colonial period ended in 1821, a second generation of Spanish folk architecture developed in the Southwest and California territories, holding strong well into the 1900s. Beginning in the 1820s, wagon trains bearing Anglo settlers and goods from the East arrived along the Santa Fe Trail; later, with the railroads in the 1880s, factory-made window sashes, doors, gingerbread trim, and tin and shingle roofing materials traveled west. Adobe was still the basic building material, but wood clapboards appeared as commercial sawmills became common in the mid-1800s. Anglo and Spanish traditions melded; houses grew a story and gained porches and hipped and peaked roofs, producing a style sometimes known as "Monterey." Local craftsmen carved their own versions of factory-milled ornaments, yielding distinctive gates, window grilles, doors, and porch brackets.

Spanish Territorial Architecture

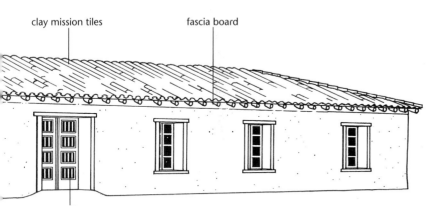

clay mission tiles

fascia board

grille

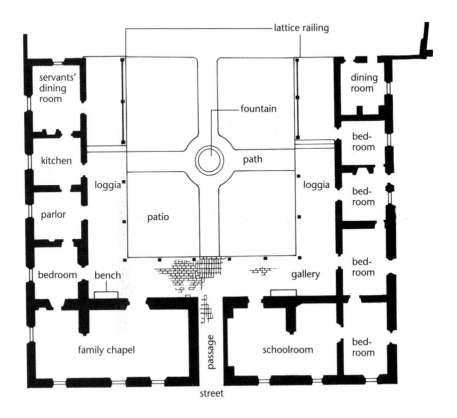

lattice railing

servants' dining room

dining room

fountain

kitchen

bed-room

path

loggia

loggia

bed-room

parlor

patio

bedroom

bench

bed-room

gallery

family chapel

passage

schoolroom

bed-room

street

Spanish Territorial Architecture

RANCHO

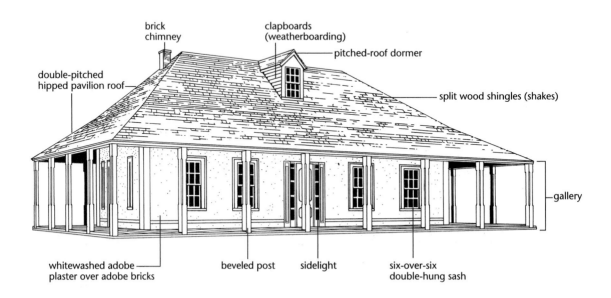

brick chimney

clapboards (weatherboarding)

pitched-roof dormer

double-pitched hipped pavilion roof

split wood shingles (shakes)

gallery

whitewashed adobe plaster over adobe bricks

beveled post

sidelight

six-over-six double-hung sash

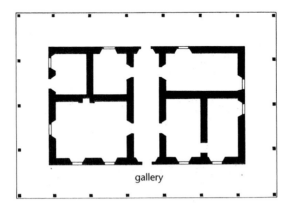

gallery

MONTEREY-STYLE HOUSE

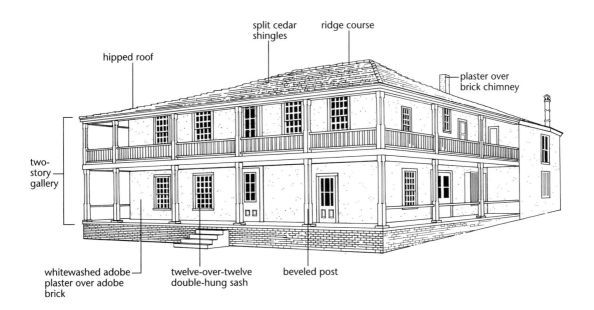

split cedar shingles

ridge course

hipped roof

plaster over brick chimney

two-story gallery

whitewashed adobe plaster over adobe brick

twelve-over-twelve double-hung sash

beveled post

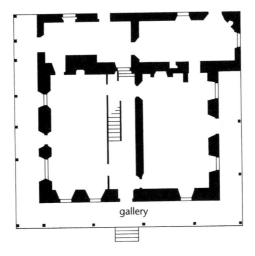

gallery

Spanish Territorial Architecture

BARN

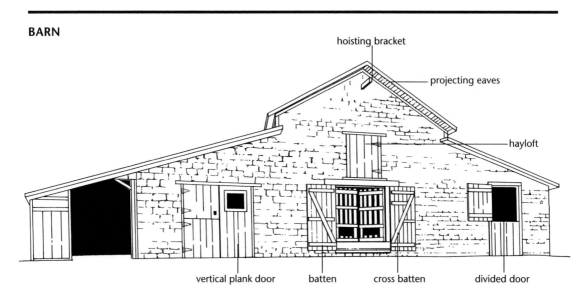

hoisting bracket

projecting eaves

hayloft

vertical plank door   batten   cross batten   divided door

ADOBE BRICK DETAIL

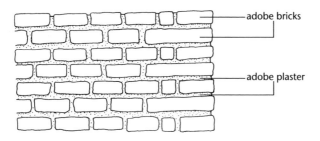

adobe bricks

adobe plaster

WINDOW GRILLES

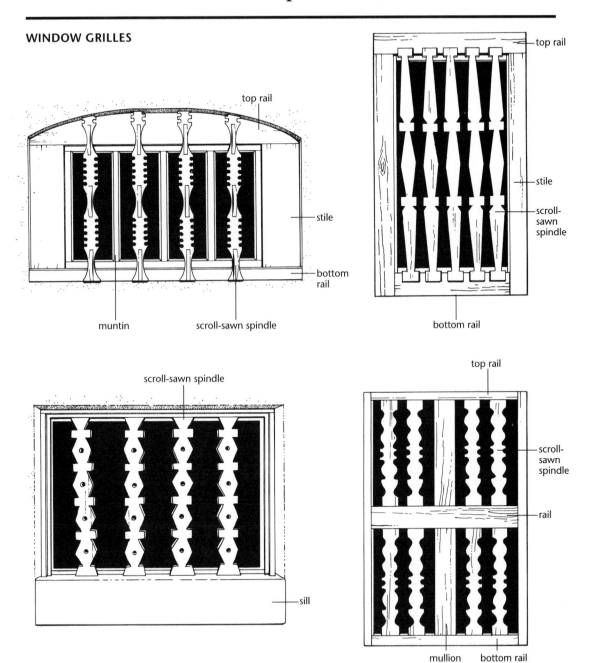

top rail

stile

bottom rail

muntin

scroll-sawn spindle

top rail

stile

scroll-sawn spindle

bottom rail

scroll-sawn spindle

sill

top rail

scroll-sawn spindle

rail

mullion

bottom rail

Chapter Seven
The Victorian Era

The Victorian era, which stretched from the 1830s to the turn of the century, was an age of great romanticism. Whereas the Renaissance-inspired interest in Classicism of the past century stressed intellect and reason, the Romantic movement appealed directly to the imagination, evoking mystery, passion, and nostalgia. Moody revivals of medieval European architecture came into fashion, and the ordered, sensible architecture of the Classical past fell out. Texture, color, and asymmetry replaced geometry and balance, and a broad range of lively, unconventional, and complex styles emerged.

The early Victorian styles, including the Gothic Revival and Italianate, were a direct reflection of the Picturesque, an aesthetic point of view celebrating the variety, texture, and irregularity inherent in nature. This resulted in a new and very strong interest in how a building related to its natural setting. Loggias, verandas, towers, and sleeping porches proliferated to take advantage of uplifting views and healthful fresh air, while asymmetrical floor plans designed to complement the natural site yielded wonderfully odd-shaped rooms.

As the century progressed, American architects continued to interpret and embellish European influences in their own ways, both looking to the inspiration of the past in the Queen Anne style and emulating current Parisian fashion with the Second Empire style. A fascination with decorative effect and material yielded the Stick and Shingle styles. And in an era of true eclecticism that fully embraced the eccentric, there was room not only for oddities such as the Octagon house, but also for the Adirondack style, the only Victorian building mode with entirely indigenous roots.

ROW HOUSE

The Gothic Revival was the first of the Victorian-era styles to challenge the symmetry and ordered reason of Classicism. Brooding and romantic, it was a Picturesque mode, with vaulted ceilings, battlements, lancet-arch windows, and tracery all suggesting the mysterious architectural vocabulary of a distant past.

Popular in the 1830s and 1840s, the Gothic Revival was well suited to the dark brownstone increasingly used for the urban row house, but it was most commonly applied to the large country "villa" and to the small cottage, the first house type in America designed specifically for the middle class. The villa and cottage were introduced by the architect Alexander Jackson Davis (1803–92) in his 1837 volume *Rural Residences* and widely promoted by the influential landscape designer, Andrew Jackson Downing (1815–52), who also published several books. Widely used by the 1840s, the high-speed mechanical scroll saw, or jigsaw, allowed for the creation of exuberant gingerbread trim in wood, often found in what is called the Carpenter Gothic style.

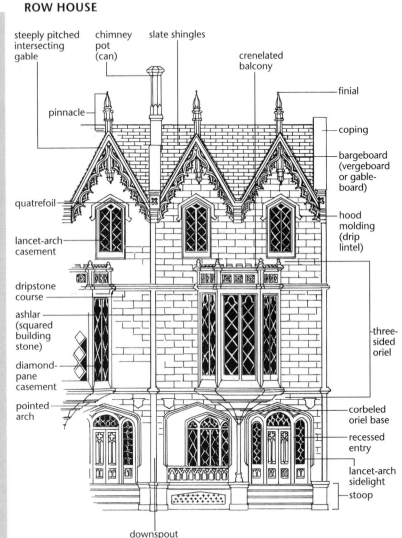

steeply pitched intersecting gable

chimney pot (can)

slate shingles

crenelated balcony

finial

coping

pinnacle

bargeboard (vergeboard or gable-board)

quatrefoil

hood molding (drip lintel)

lancet-arch casement

dripstone course

three-sided oriel

ashlar (squared building stone)

diamond-pane casement

pointed arch

corbeled oriel base

recessed entry

lancet-arch sidelight

stoop

downspout

Gothic Revival

VILLA (MASONRY)

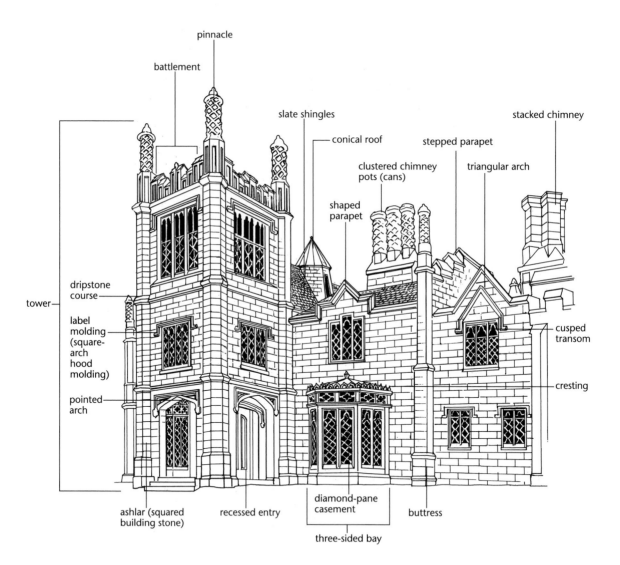

pinnacle

battlement

slate shingles

conical roof

stacked chimney

stepped parapet

clustered chimney pots (cans)

triangular arch

shaped parapet

tower

dripstone course

label molding (square-arch hood molding)

pointed arch

cusped transom

cresting

ashlar (squared building stone)

recessed entry

diamond-pane casement

buttress

three-sided bay

Gothic Revival

BOSS DETAIL

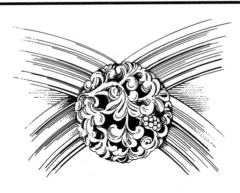

RECEPTION HALL

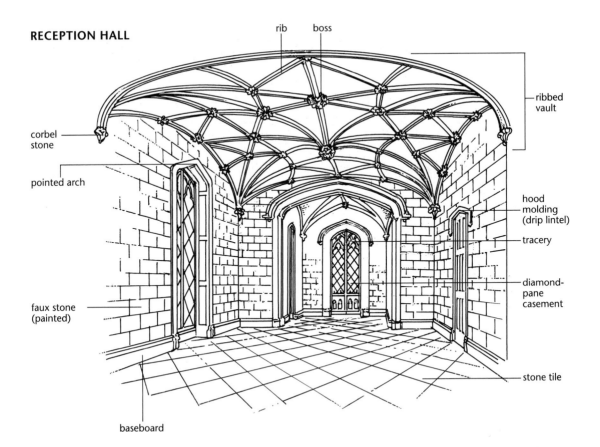

rib

boss

ribbed vault

corbel stone

pointed arch

hood molding (drip lintel)

tracery

faux stone (painted)

diamond-pane casement

stone tile

baseboard

Gothic Revival

VILLA (CARPENTER GOTHIC)

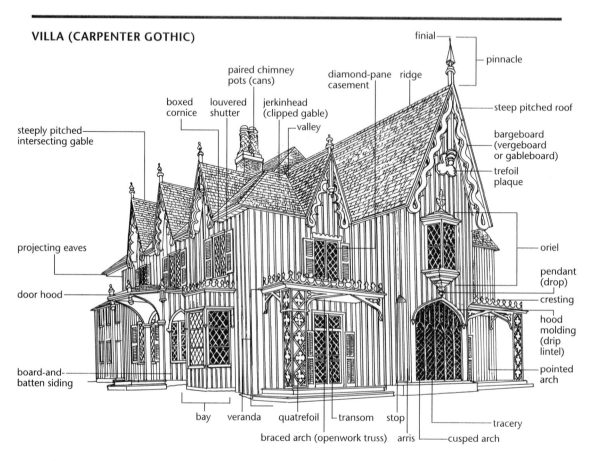

- finial
- pinnacle
- paired chimney pots (cans)
- diamond-pane casement
- ridge
- steep pitched roof
- boxed cornice
- louvered shutter
- jerkinhead (clipped gable)
- valley
- bargeboard (vergeboard or gableboard)
- trefoil plaque
- steeply pitched intersecting gable
- projecting eaves
- oriel
- pendant (drop)
- door hood
- cresting
- hood molding (drip lintel)
- board-and-batten siding
- pointed arch
- bay
- veranda
- quatrefoil
- transom
- stop
- tracery
- braced arch (openwork truss)
- arris
- cusped arch

BOARD-AND-BATTEN DETAIL

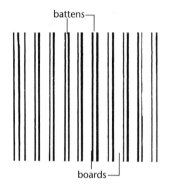

- battens
- boards

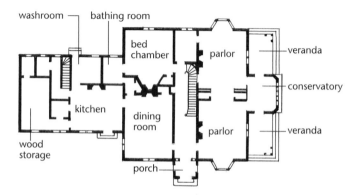

- washroom
- bathing room
- bed chamber
- parlor
- veranda
- kitchen
- conservatory
- dining room
- parlor
- veranda
- wood storage
- porch

COTTAGE

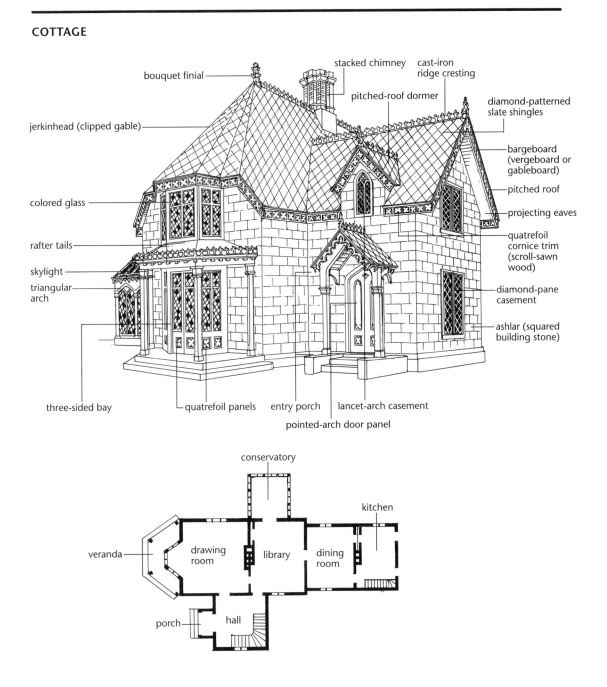

bouquet finial

stacked chimney

cast-iron ridge cresting

pitched-roof dormer

diamond-patterned slate shingles

jerkinhead (clipped gable)

bargeboard (vergeboard or gableboard)

pitched roof

colored glass

projecting eaves

quatrefoil cornice trim (scroll-sawn wood)

rafter tails

diamond-pane casement

skylight

triangular arch

ashlar (squared building stone)

three-sided bay

quatrefoil panels

entry porch

lancet-arch casement

pointed-arch door panel

conservatory

kitchen

veranda

drawing room

library

dining room

porch

hall

Pattern Book Fences

The Model Architect (1852–53) by the popular 19th-century Philadelphia architect Samuel Sloan was an extremely successful Victorian-era pattern book, containing designs for many finishing details such as these fences. The top fence, claimed the author, was a fine specimen of rustic pattern, suitable for any ornamental villa. The center design ($1.50 per foot), made of cast iron, was best for a large building, while the last was intended as a "neat" pattern for a cottage or farmhouse.

TERRA-COTTA CHIMNEY POTS (CANS)

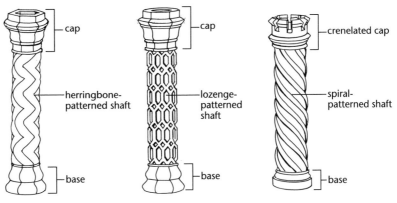

cap

cap

crenelated cap

herringbone-patterned shaft

lozenge-patterned shaft

spiral-patterned shaft

base

base

base

WINDOWS (EXTERIOR)

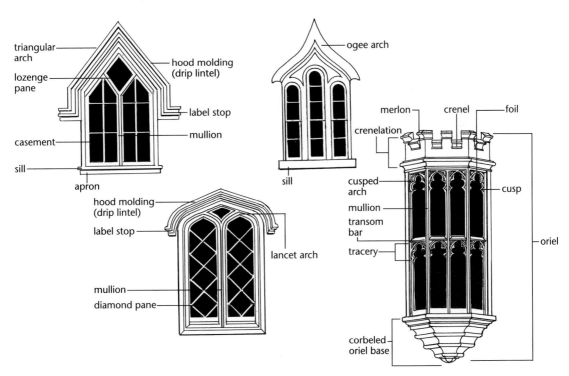

triangular arch

hood molding (drip lintel)

lozenge pane

label stop

mullion

casement

sill

apron

ogee arch

merlon

crenel

foil

crenelation

sill

cusped arch

cusp

hood molding (drip lintel)

mullion

label stop

transom bar

lancet arch

tracery

oriel

mullion

diamond pane

corbeled oriel base

Gothic Revival

COTTAGE (RUSTIC)

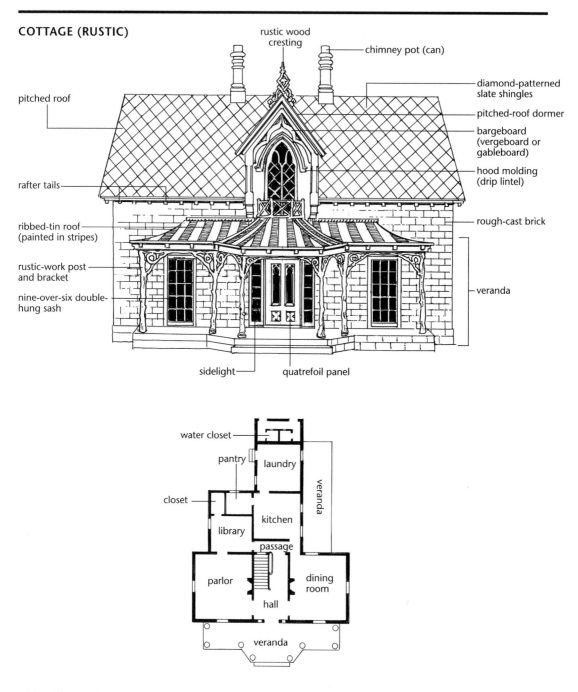

rustic wood cresting

chimney pot (can)

diamond-patterned slate shingles

pitched roof

pitched-roof dormer

bargeboard (vergeboard or gableboard)

hood molding (drip lintel)

rafter tails

ribbed-tin roof (painted in stripes)

rough-cast brick

rustic-work post and bracket

nine-over-six double-hung sash

veranda

sidelight

quatrefoil panel

water closet

pantry

laundry

closet

veranda

library

kitchen

passage

parlor

dining room

hall

veranda

PANELED DOUBLE DOORS (EXTERIOR)

W̲ell represented on the pages of pattern books, the Italianate style emerged in the 1830s along with the Gothic Revival and eventually proved more popular, lasting into the 1870s. With their square towers, asymmetrical plans, broad roofs, and generous verandas, the rambling Italianate houses that began to appear in both the suburbs and the countryside were rather free and highly romanticized interpretations of the villas of Tuscany, Umbria, and Lombardy. During the mid-1800s, the Italianate style was enthusiastically adapted for urban row house architecture and reached its zenith in the brownstone-fronted rows of New York, characterized by ornate door and window designs, weighty bracketed cornices, and high stoops with robust cast-iron stair rails.

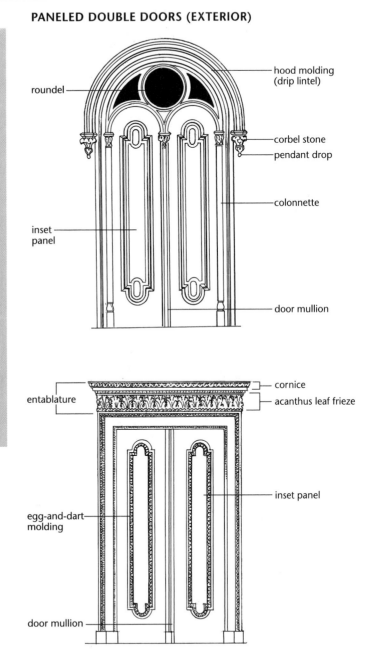

roundel

hood molding (drip lintel)

corbel stone

pendant drop

colonnette

inset panel

door mullion

entablature

cornice

acanthus leaf frieze

inset panel

egg-and-dart molding

door mullion

Italianate

VILLA

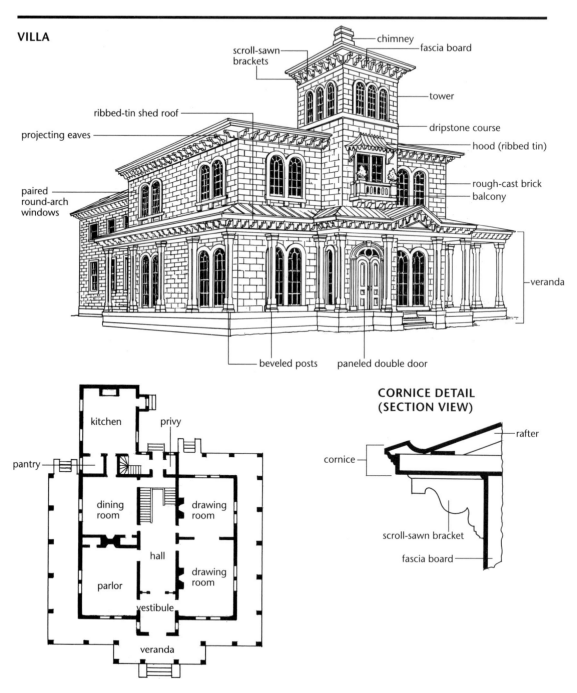

chimney

fascia board

scroll-sawn brackets

tower

ribbed-tin shed roof

dripstone course

projecting eaves

hood (ribbed tin)

rough-cast brick

balcony

paired round-arch windows

veranda

beveled posts

paneled double door

CORNICE DETAIL (SECTION VIEW)

kitchen

privy

rafter

pantry

cornice

dining room

drawing room

hall

scroll-sawn bracket

parlor

drawing room

fascia board

vestibule

veranda

Italianate

ROW HOUSE

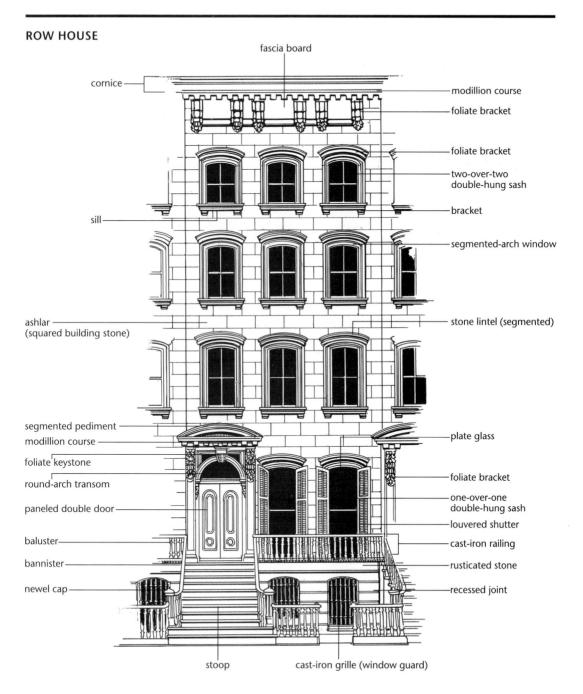

- fascia board
- cornice
- modillion course
- foliate bracket
- foliate bracket
- two-over-two double-hung sash
- sill
- bracket
- segmented-arch window
- ashlar (squared building stone)
- stone lintel (segmented)
- segmented pediment
- modillion course
- plate glass
- foliate keystone
- round-arch transom
- foliate bracket
- paneled double door
- one-over-one double-hung sash
- louvered shutter
- baluster
- cast-iron railing
- bannister
- rusticated stone
- newel cap
- recessed joint
- stoop
- cast-iron grille (window guard)

Octagon

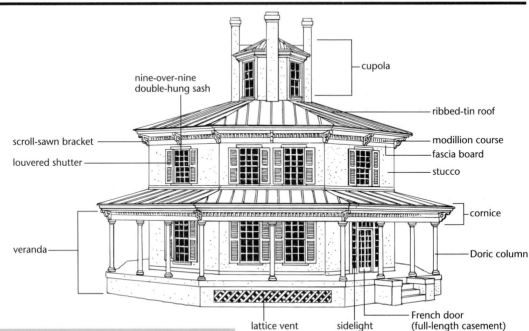

- cupola
- ribbed-tin roof
- modillion course
- fascia board
- stucco
- cornice
- Doric column
- nine-over-nine double-hung sash
- scroll-sawn bracket
- louvered shutter
- veranda
- lattice vent
- sidelight
- French door (full-length casement)

In 1848, Orson Fowler (1809–87)—an extraordinary self-styled Renaissance man who made a living as a phrenologist, sex educator, and marriage counselor—published a wildly successful architectural handbook. Meant to bring "comfortable dwellings within the reach of the poorer classes," *A Home for All* introduced plans for the eight-sided house. Dismissing the square plan as woefully outdated, Fowler felt the Octagon plan made better use of a square or rectangular space because a wall of the same perimeter could enclose some 20 percent more floor area. Promoting comfort and convenience, he also advocated the use of central heating, dumbwaiters, speaking tubes, and indoor water closets. The fad for Octagon building faded with the financial panic of 1857, but by then thousands of Octagon homes, as well as Octagon barns, pig sties, and even a few seance chambers, had already been built.

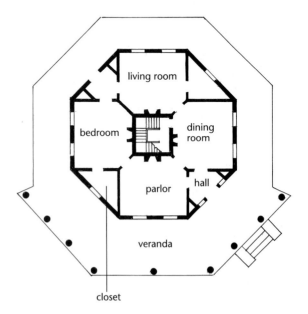

- living room
- bedroom
- dining room
- parlor
- hall
- veranda
- closet

BARN

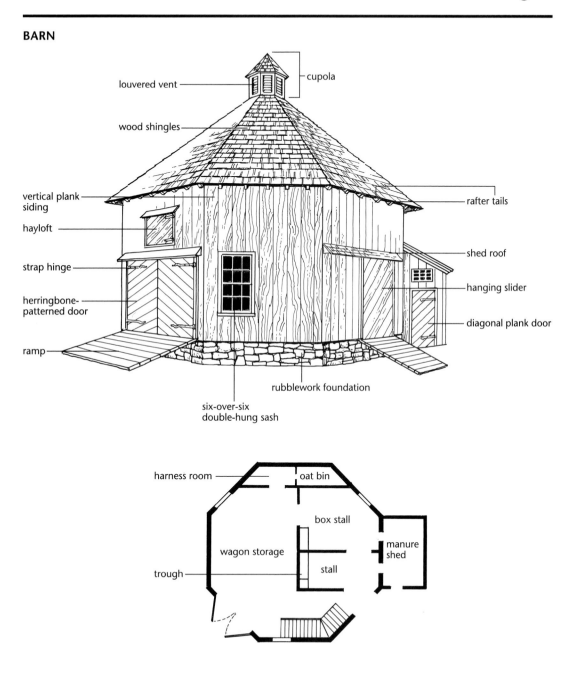

louvered vent — cupola

wood shingles

vertical plank siding — rafter tails

hayloft

strap hinge — shed roof

herringbone-patterned door — hanging slider

ramp — diagonal plank door

rubblework foundation

six-over-six double-hung sash

harness room — oat bin

box stall

wagon storage — manure shed

stall

trough

Second Empire

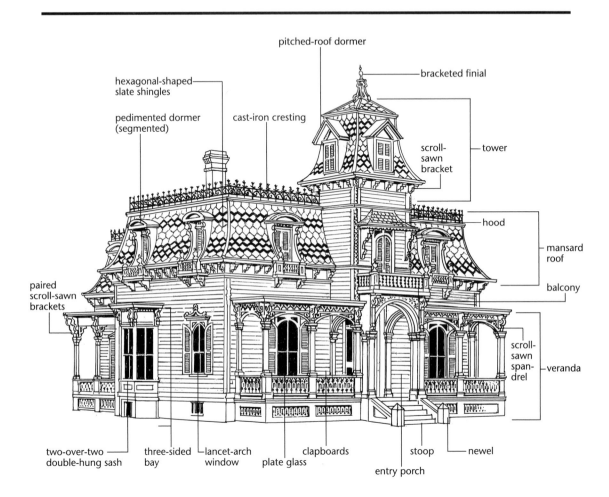

pitched-roof dormer

bracketed finial

hexagonal-shaped slate shingles

pedimented dormer (segmented)

cast-iron cresting

scroll-sawn bracket

tower

hood

mansard roof

balcony

paired scroll-sawn brackets

scroll-sawn spandrel

veranda

two-over-two double-hung sash

three-sided bay

lancet-arch window

plate glass

clapboards

stoop

newel

entry porch

The Second Empire style took its inspiration directly from the skyline of Paris, which had been dramatically overhauled under the reign of Napoleon III during France's Second Empire period (1852–70). Two well-attended Paris exhibitions in 1855 and 1867 attracted enormous attention to the grandiose style, which found its first expression in public and civic buildings in America in the 1850s. It was particularly favored during the boom period following the Civil War under the administration of Ulysses S. Grant (1869–77). The signature mansard roof—which made good used of attic space—prominent cornices, ornate cresting, projecting pavilion fronts, and round dormers were adopted for splendid private homes and row houses across the country. The style began to fade by 1880.

Second Empire

CAST-IRON CRESTING

SLATE SHINGLES

STABLE

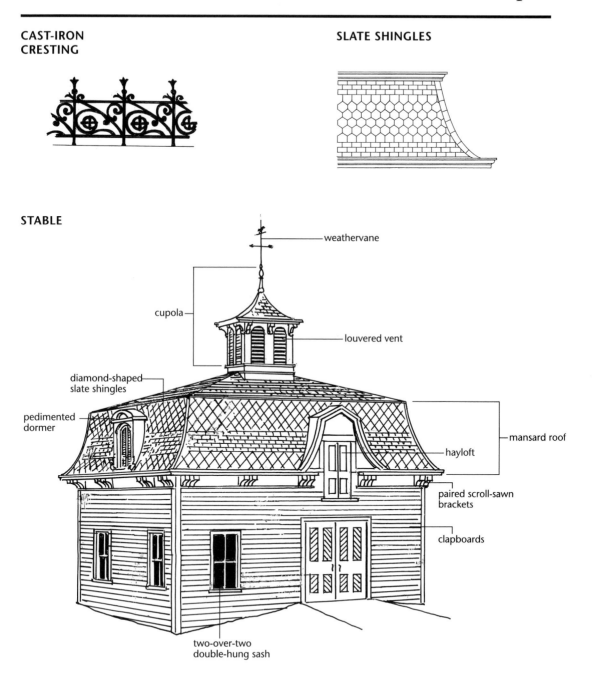

weathervane

cupola

louvered vent

diamond-shaped slate shingles

pedimented dormer

mansard roof

hayloft

paired scroll-sawn brackets

clapboards

two-over-two double-hung sash

Stick Style

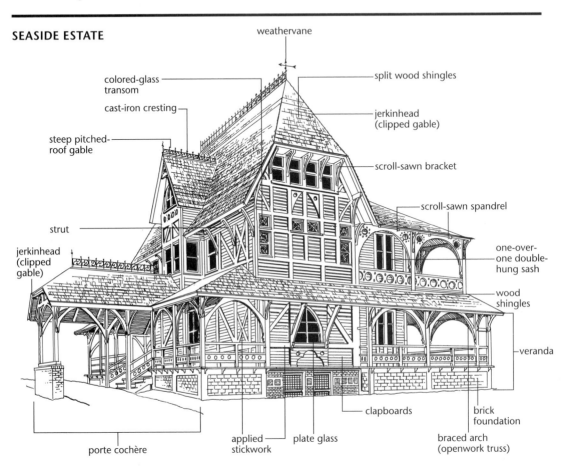

weathervane

colored-glass transom

cast-iron cresting

steep pitched-roof gable

strut

jerkinhead (clipped gable)

porte cochère

applied stickwork

plate glass

clapboards

split wood shingles

jerkinhead (clipped gable)

scroll-sawn bracket

scroll-sawn spandrel

one-over-one double-hung sash

wood shingles

veranda

brick foundation

braced arch (openwork truss)

The highly picturesque Stick style, which is thought to have developed as a resort architecture, was richly expressed in several houses designed by Richard Morris Hunt (1827–95) in Newport, Rhode Island. Hunt was one of many American architects influenced by a mid–19th-century European revival of late-medieval rustic country architecture, most notably the gingerbread-ornamented chalets of the Alps and the half-timbered cottages of Normandy and Tudor England. The revival spread to America largely by way of several widely circulated German architectural journals.

The charm of the Stick style was impossible to resist, with its bright, contrasting paint colors, ornamental brackets and bargeboards, lacy openwork balconies, overhanging eaves, colored shingles, and the purely decorative criss-cross timbers, or stickwork, for which the style was later named (in the mid-1900s). By the 1860s, marvelously elaborate Stick style confections were appearing across the country, and the style remained popular in resorts, suburbs, and small towns well into the 1870s.

COTTAGE

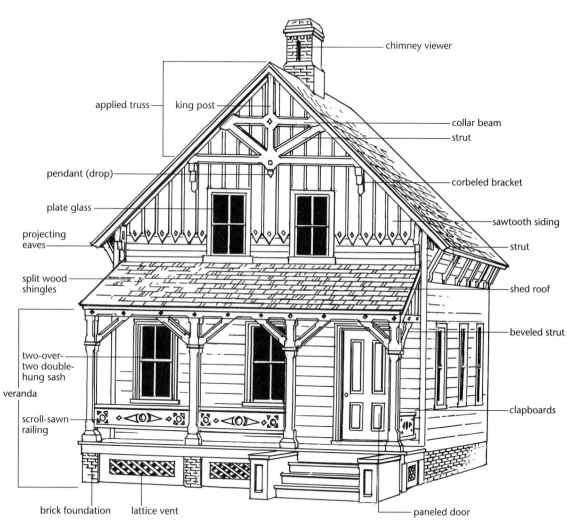

chimney viewer

applied truss — king post —

collar beam
strut

pendant (drop) —

corbeled bracket

plate glass —

sawtooth siding

projecting
eaves

strut

split wood
shingles

shed roof

beveled strut

two-over-
two double-
hung sash

veranda

clapboards

scroll-sawn
railing

brick foundation   lattice vent

paneled door

Stick Style

PARLOR

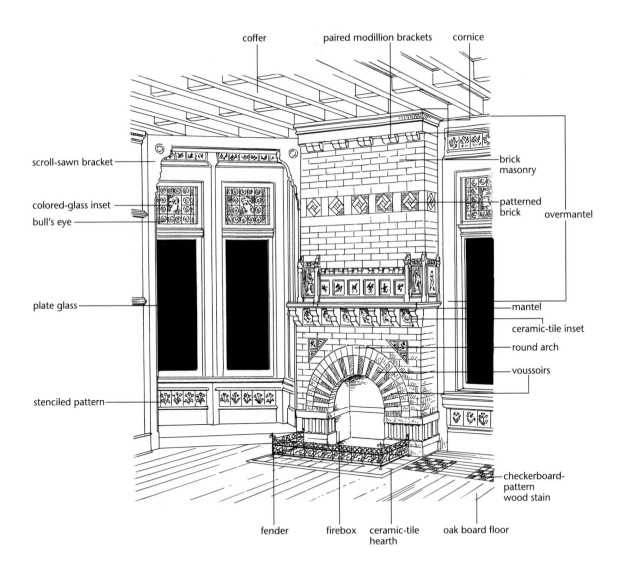

coffer

paired modillion brackets

cornice

scroll-sawn bracket

colored-glass inset

bull's eye

plate glass

stenciled pattern

brick masonry

patterned brick

overmantel

mantel

ceramic-tile inset

round arch

voussoirs

fender

firebox

ceramic-tile hearth

oak board floor

checkerboard-pattern wood stain

SEASIDE COTTAGE

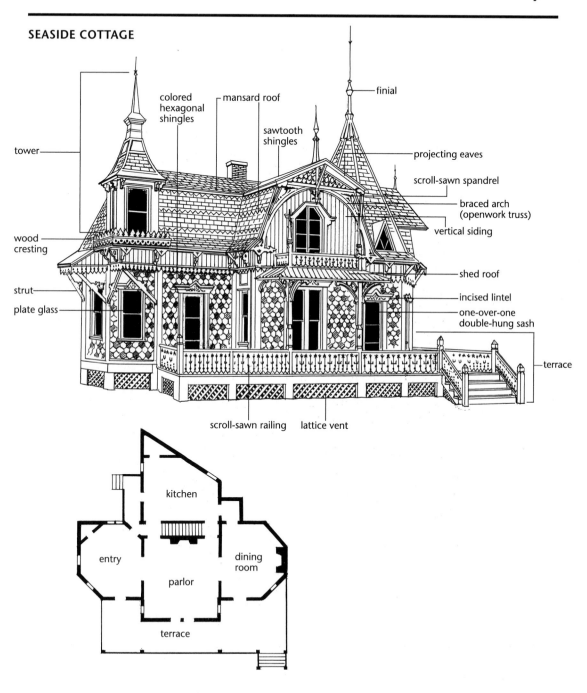

tower

wood cresting

strut

plate glass

colored hexagonal shingles

mansard roof

sawtooth shingles

finial

projecting eaves

scroll-sawn spandrel

braced arch (openwork truss)

vertical siding

shed roof

incised lintel

one-over-one double-hung sash

terrace

scroll-sawn railing

lattice vent

kitchen

entry

dining room

parlor

terrace

Queen Anne

ROW HOUSE

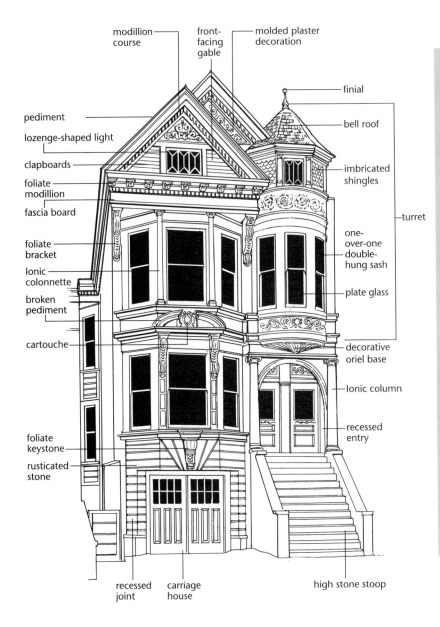

modillion course — front-facing gable — molded plaster decoration

finial

pediment

bell roof

lozenge-shaped light

clapboards

imbricated shingles

foliate modillion

fascia board

turret

foliate bracket

one-over-one double-hung sash

Ionic colonnette

broken pediment

plate glass

cartouche

decorative oriel base

Ionic column

foliate keystone

recessed entry

rusticated stone

recessed joint

carriage house

high stone stoop

Among the attractions generating considerable interest at the 1876 Centennial Exhibition in Philadelphia were several English buildings designed in the Queen Anne style, which would be widely influential in America from the 1870s until the turn of the century. The style was identified with the Scottish-born architect Richard Norman Shaw (1831–1912) and his followers, whose domestic work in England was a tremendously free and eclectic hybrid of forms drawn from a range of sources, including Classical, Tudor, and Flemish architecture.

Queen Anne style dismissed the impractical Gothic by emphasizing human scale and domestic comfort. Its facades showed a great variety, featuring projecting oriels, bay win-

Queen Anne

ROW HOUSE

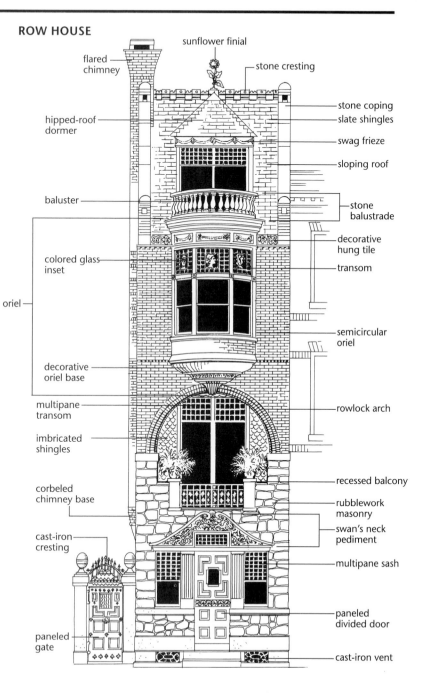

sunflower finial

flared chimney

stone cresting

stone coping

slate shingles

hipped-roof dormer

swag frieze

sloping roof

baluster

stone balustrade

decorative hung tile

colored glass inset

transom

oriel

semicircular oriel

decorative oriel base

multipane transom

rowlock arch

imbricated shingles

corbeled chimney base

recessed balcony

rubblework masonry

swan's neck pediment

cast-iron cresting

multipane sash

paneled gate

paneled divided door

cast-iron vent

dows, and odd roof-lines. It was also rich in texture, with cut and molded brick, terra-cotta, and ornamental plaster. The open, asymmetrical plan centered around a "great hall" with an enormous fire-place and homey built-in inglenooks.

In America, the style found an exuberant expression in wood, and frequently incorporated Classical columns and decorative motifs borrowed from our own Colonial architecture. The Queen Anne style was favored for everything from row houses to sprawling seaside retreats, whose designs frequently came from pattern books. All were resplendent in patterned shingles, spindles, brackets, and curlicue cutouts; many boasted ample verandas, turrets, and sleeping porches.

Queen Anne

ROW HOUSE

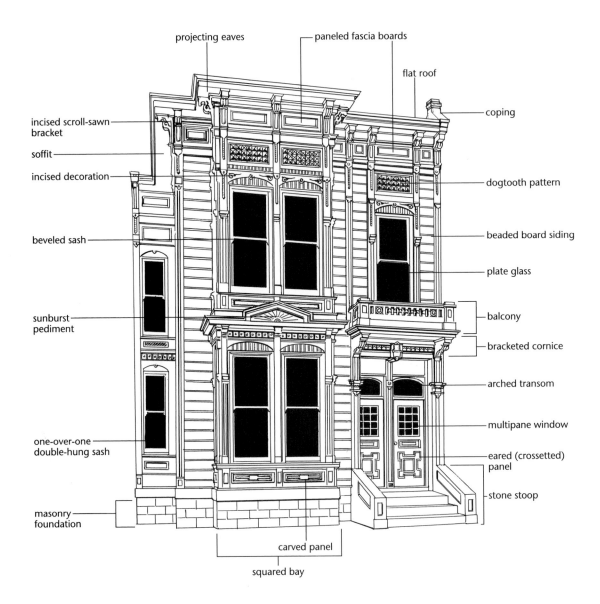

projecting eaves

paneled fascia boards

flat roof

incised scroll-sawn bracket

coping

soffit

incised decoration

dogtooth pattern

beveled sash

beaded board siding

plate glass

sunburst pediment

balcony

bracketed cornice

arched transom

multipane window

one-over-one double-hung sash

eared (crossetted) panel

stone stoop

masonry foundation

carved panel

squared bay

DRAWING ROOM

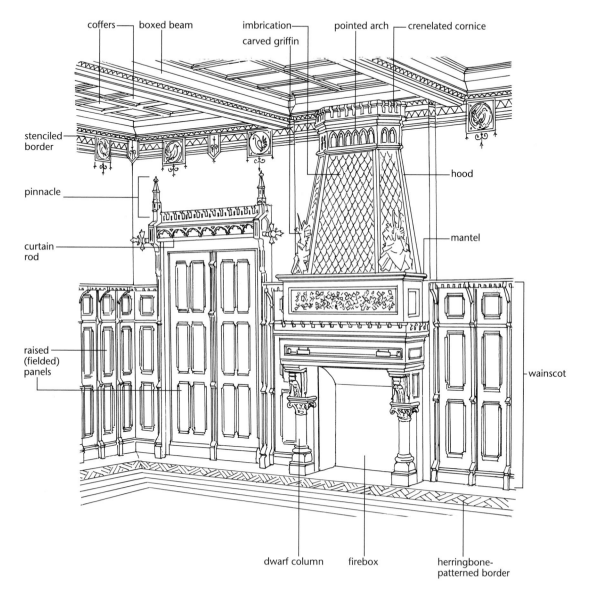

coffers   boxed beam   imbrication   pointed arch   crenelated cornice

carved griffin

stenciled border

pinnacle

curtain rod

raised (fielded) panels

hood

mantel

wainscot

dwarf column   firebox   herringbone-patterned border

Queen Anne

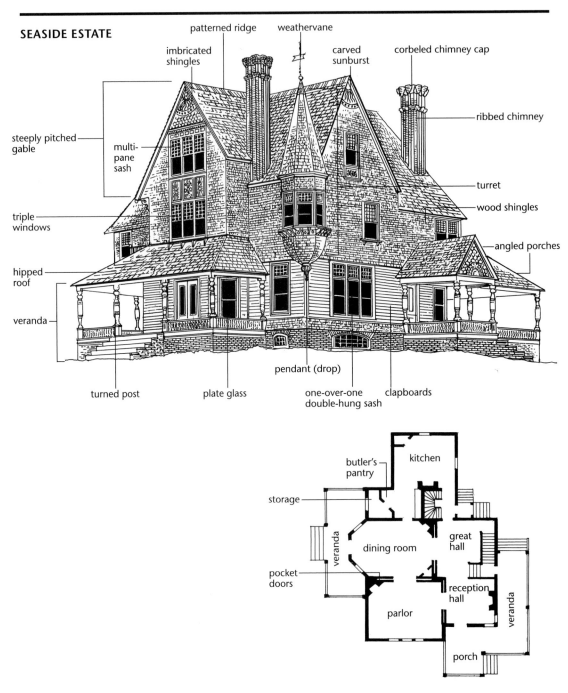

steeply pitched gable

multi-pane sash

triple windows

hipped roof

veranda

imbricated shingles

patterned ridge

weathervane

carved sunburst

corbeled chimney cap

ribbed chimney

turret

wood shingles

angled porches

turned post

plate glass

pendant (drop)

one-over-one double-hung sash

clapboards

butler's pantry

kitchen

storage

veranda

dining room

great hall

pocket doors

reception hall

parlor

veranda

porch

SEASIDE COTTAGE

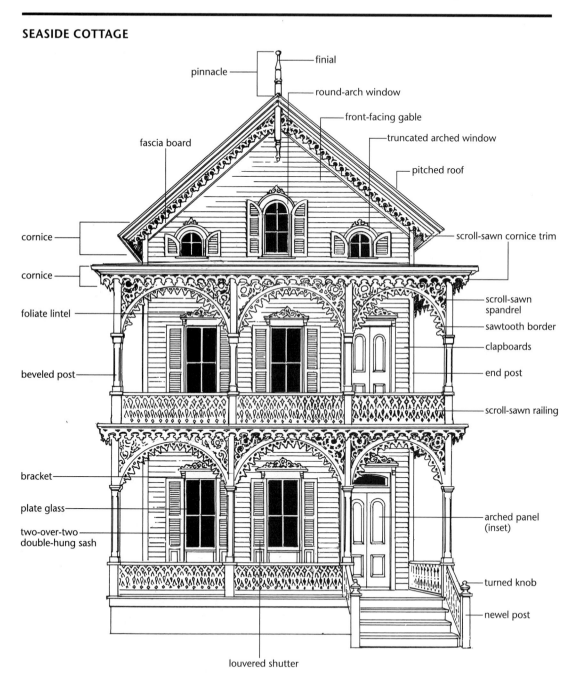

pinnacle — finial

round-arch window

front-facing gable

truncated arched window

fascia board

pitched roof

cornice

scroll-sawn cornice trim

cornice

scroll-sawn spandrel

foliate lintel

sawtooth border

clapboards

beveled post

end post

scroll-sawn railing

bracket

plate glass

two-over-two double-hung sash

arched panel (inset)

turned knob

newel post

louvered shutter

Queen Anne

STAIRS

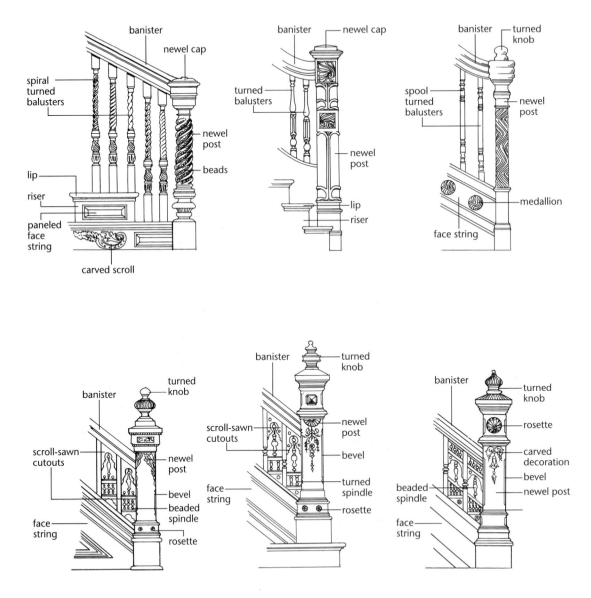

banister

newel cap

spiral turned balusters

newel post

lip

riser

beads

paneled face string

carved scroll

banister

newel cap

turned balusters

newel post

lip

riser

banister

turned knob

spool turned balusters

newel post

medallion

face string

banister

turned knob

scroll-sawn cutouts

newel post

bevel

beaded spindle

face string

rosette

banister

turned knob

scroll-sawn cutouts

newel post

bevel

turned spindle

face string

rosette

banister

turned knob

rosette

carved decoration

bevel

newel post

beaded spindle

face string

Queen Anne

INTERIOR FEATURES

DOUBLE DOORS

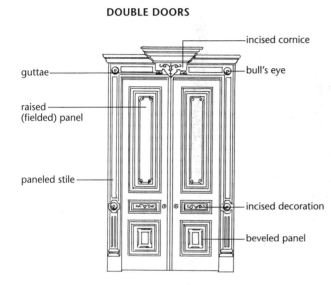

incised cornice

guttae

bull's eye

raised (fielded) panel

paneled stile

incised decoration

beveled panel

ONE-OVER-ONE DOUBLE-HUNG SASH

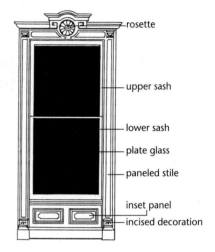

rosette

upper sash

lower sash

plate glass

paneled stile

inset panel

incised decoration

EXTERIOR FEATURES

THREE-SIDED BAY

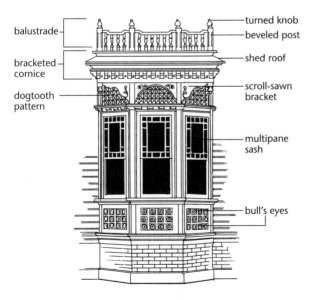

balustrade

bracketed cornice

dogtooth pattern

turned knob

beveled post

shed roof

scroll-sawn bracket

multipane sash

bull's eyes

SQUARED BAY

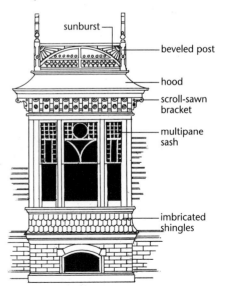

sunburst

beveled post

hood

scroll-sawn bracket

multipane sash

imbricated shingles

Queen Anne

BARGEBOARDS

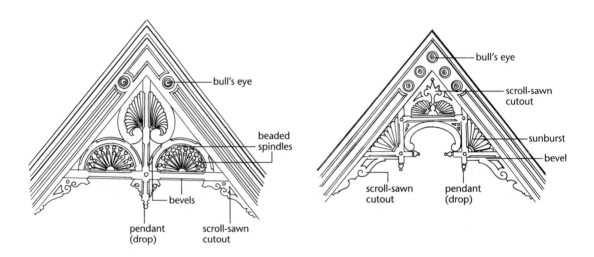

bull's eye

beaded spindles

bevels

pendant (drop)

scroll-sawn cutout

bull's eye

scroll-sawn cutout

sunburst

bevel

scroll-sawn cutout

pendant (drop)

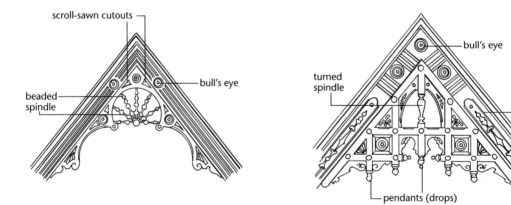

scroll-sawn cutouts

bull's eye

beaded spindle

bull's eye

turned spindle

bevel

pendants (drops)

Shingle Style

SEASIDE ESTATE

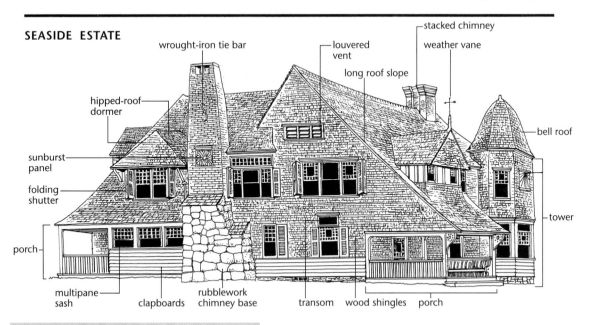

Labels (clockwise from top): stacked chimney, weather vane, louvered vent, long roof slope, wrought-iron tie bar, hipped-roof dormer, sunburst panel, folding shutter, porch, multipane sash, clapboards, rubblework chimney base, transom, wood shingles, porch, bell roof, tower

The Shingle style had its genesis in the Boston area in the early 1880s. Over the next two decades it spread across the country, although it was favored for the rambling seaside estates and resorts of the New England coast. Like the Queen Anne style, the Shingle style was influenced by the work of the architect Richard Norman Shaw. This is especially evident in the innovative free-flowing plan, with large rooms and porches loosely arranged around an open "great hall," dominated by a grand staircase. On the exterior—stripped of excess decoration—shingles form a continuous covering, stretched smooth over roof lines and around corners in a kind of contoured envelope.

Henry Hobson Richardson (1836–86) is credited with developing the style and used it for most of his country and suburban houses, as did many prominent architects. The firm of McKim, Mead and White is also closely associated with the Shingle style; the partners often incorporated Colonial Revival motifs.

Floor plan labels: dining room, parlor, shed, pantry, kitchen, great hall, porch, bath, porch

Shingle Style

COUNTRY HOUSE

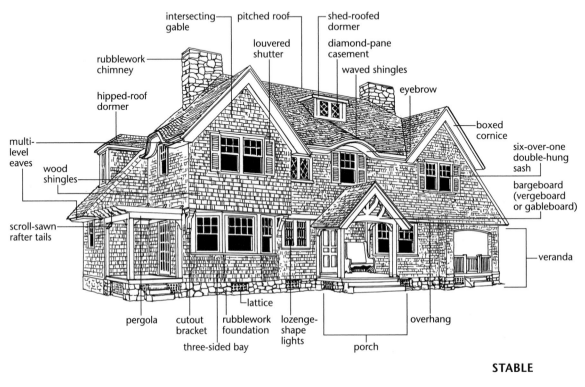

intersecting gable · pitched roof · shed-roofed dormer

louvered shutter · diamond-pane casement

rubblework chimney · waved shingles · eyebrow

hipped-roof dormer · boxed cornice

multi-level eaves · six-over-one double-hung sash

wood shingles · bargeboard (vergeboard or gableboard)

scroll-sawn rafter tails · veranda

pergola · cutout bracket · rubblework foundation · lozenge-shape lights · overhang

lattice · three-sided bay · porch

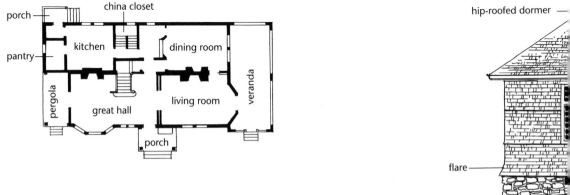

porch · china closet

pantry · kitchen · dining room

pergola · great hall · living room · veranda

porch

STABLE

hip-roofed dormer —

flare —

rubblework fo

GREAT HALL

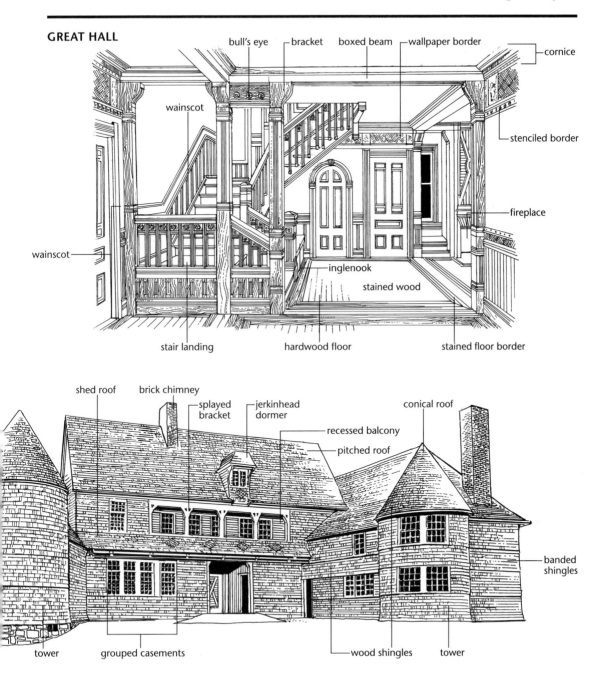

bull's eye — bracket — boxed beam — wallpaper border — cornice

wainscot

stenciled border

wainscot

fireplace

inglenook

stained wood

stair landing

hardwood floor

stained floor border

shed roof — brick chimney — splayed bracket — jerkinhead dormer — recessed balcony — conical roof — pitched roof

banded shingles

tower — grouped casements — wood shingles — tower

Romanesque Revival

The robust masonry forms and rich texture of this romantic style derive from the medieval Romanesque architecture of France and Spain. The characteristic features of the Romanesque Revival, including heavy rough-cut stone, round arches, squat dwarf columns, deeply recessed windows, and densely carved decoration with interlaced motifs, were imaginatively interpreted in massive freestanding houses and substantial row houses.

The architect Henry Hobson Richardson developed the style in the Boston area in the 1870s, and a monograph of his work published soon after his death in 1886 had a major influence throughout the country. Constructed of solid masonry, Romanesque Revival houses were expensive and, with the exception of row houses built on speculation, largely the purview of architects designing for affluent clients. The style was popular in urban and suburban areas. Interest in it faded in the 1890s.

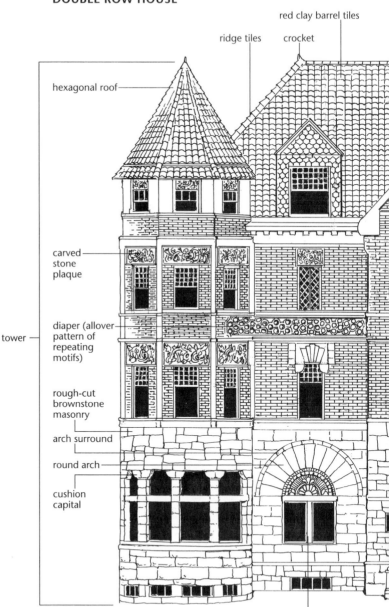

- red clay barrel tiles
- ridge tiles
- crocket
- hexagonal roof
- carved stone plaque
- tower
- diaper (allover pattern of repeating motifs)
- rough-cut brownstone masonry
- arch surround
- round arch
- cushion capital
- stone mullion

Romanesque Revival

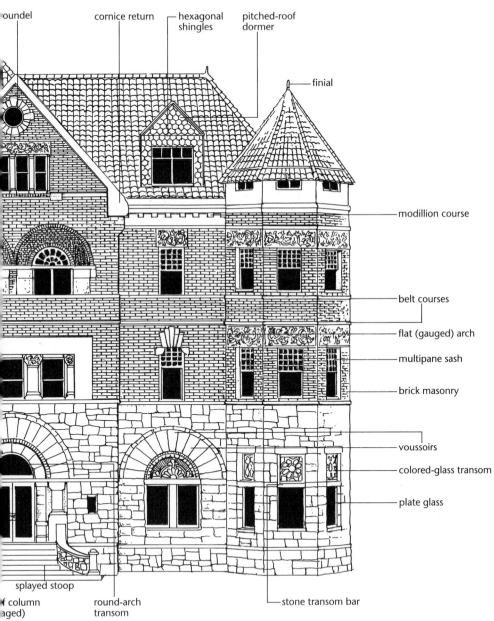

ecting gable

oundel

cornice return

hexagonal shingles

pitched-roof dormer

finial

modillion course

belt courses

flat (gauged) arch

multipane sash

brick masonry

voussoirs

colored-glass transom

plate glass

splayed stoop

f column aged)

round-arch transom

stone transom bar

Romanesque Revival

URBAN HOUSE

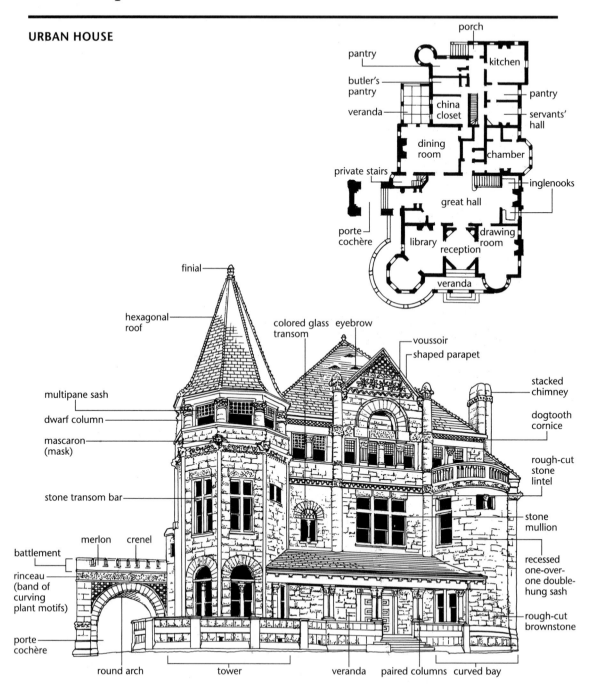

porch

pantry

kitchen

butler's pantry

pantry

veranda

china closet

servants' hall

dining room

chamber

private stairs

inglenooks

great hall

porte cochère

drawing room

library

reception

veranda

finial

hexagonal roof

colored glass transom

eyebrow

voussoir

shaped parapet

stacked chimney

multipane sash

dogtooth cornice

dwarf column

mascaron (mask)

rough-cut stone lintel

stone transom bar

stone mullion

merlon

crenel

battlement

recessed one-over-one double-hung sash

rinceau (band of curving plant motifs)

rough-cut brownstone

porte cochère

round arch

tower

veranda

paired columns

curved bay

STABLE

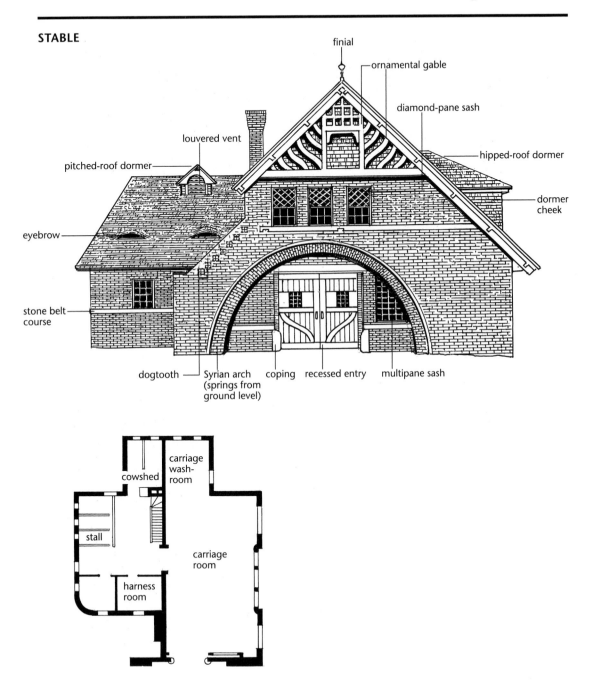

finial

ornamental gable

diamond-pane sash

louvered vent

hipped-roof dormer

pitched-roof dormer

dormer cheek

eyebrow

stone belt course

dogtooth — Syrian arch (springs from ground level) — coping — recessed entry — multipane sash

cowshed

carriage wash-room

stall

carriage room

harness room

Adirondack

While America's high-society industrialists and capitalists were lavishing millions on the palaces of Newport and other resorts, they also had a taste for "roughing it" in the wilderness. The result was the Great Camp of the Adirondack Mountains in northern New York State. Set up for extended summer stays, these sprawling complexes, and similar ones that appeared in other mountain regions of the country, included elaborate boathouses, guest quarters, kitchens, laundry and dining buildings, and hot running water. The look, however, was rustic, achieved with stone, logs, and twigs used in their natural state.

GREAT CAMP

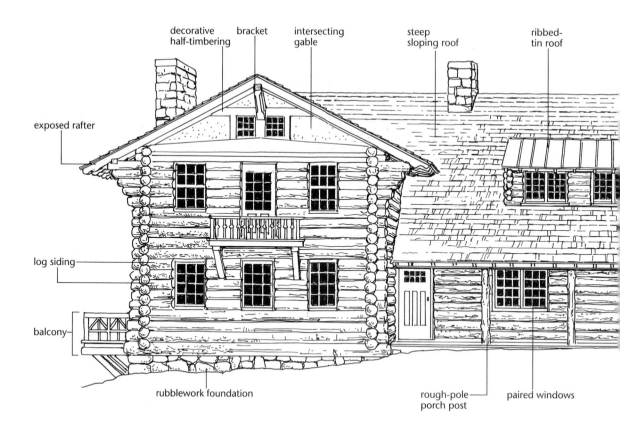

decorative half-timbering · bracket · intersecting gable · steep sloping roof · ribbed-tin roof

exposed rafter

log siding

balcony

rubblework foundation

rough-pole porch post

paired windows

Adirondack

While they were usually built by local woodsmen, the camps were invariably designed by society architects; several were also the work of William West Durant, a New York State speculator who was credited with originating the Great Camp. For families of more modest means, many of the popular periodicals and handbooks of the day offered plans for woodland cabins that could be built for a few hundred dollars. The heyday of this rustic style lasted from the 1870s to the onset of the Depression.

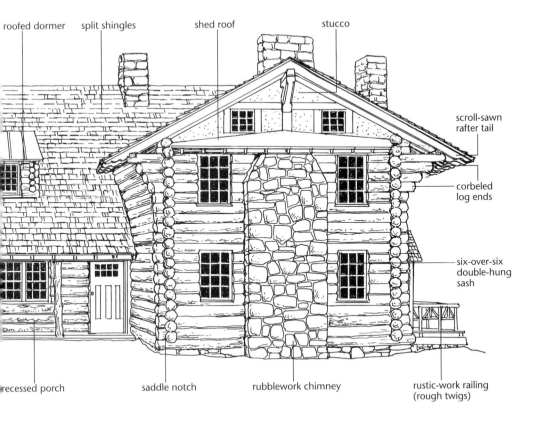

roofed dormer   split shingles   shed roof   stucco

scroll-sawn rafter tail

corbeled log ends

six-over-six double-hung sash

recessed porch   saddle notch   rubblework chimney   rustic-work railing (rough twigs)

A Rustic Dog Kennel

Dog Kennels
Jocks Lake Herkimer

Mc Dutton Barber Owner

The camp style of architecture was a wholehearted celebration of the joys of nature. As a result, the rustic approach to decoration and design influenced every structure in a camp complex—even dog kennels like this one, pictured in the 1889 edition of *Log Cabins and Cottages: How to Build and Furnish Them* by William S. Wicks. The inherent picturesque quality of log construction was a big draw. Log cabins and outbuildings were closely associated with the nation's frontier heroes of the 19th century, suggesting—according to one contemporary periodical—"a certain glamor of romance."

Adirondack

BOATHOUSE

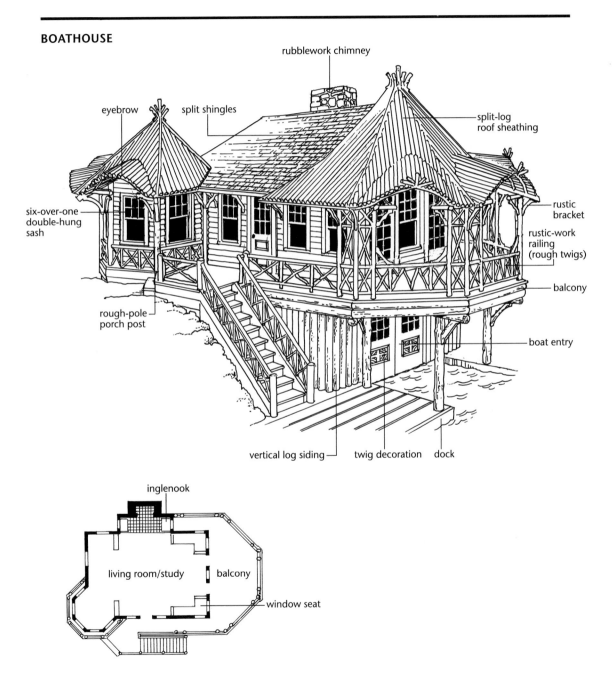

rubblework chimney

eyebrow

split shingles

split-log
roof sheathing

six-over-one
double-hung
sash

rustic
bracket

rustic-work
railing
(rough twigs)

balcony

rough-pole
porch post

boat entry

vertical log siding

twig decoration

dock

inglenook

living room/study

balcony

window seat

Adirondack

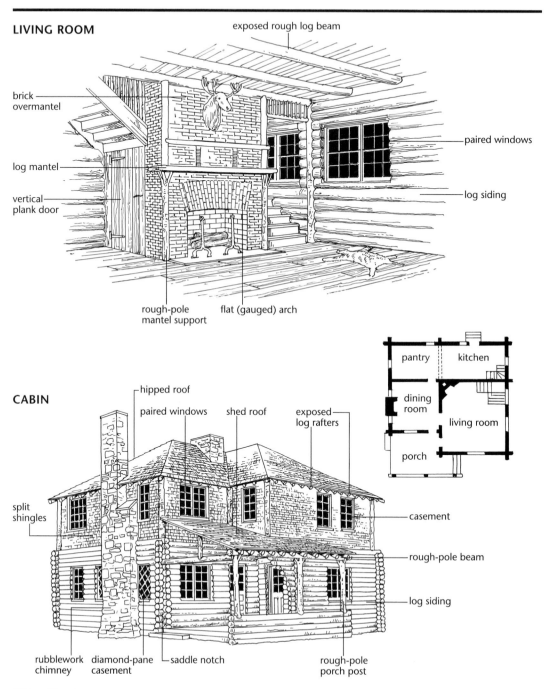

LIVING ROOM

exposed rough log beam

brick overmantel

log mantel

vertical plank door

paired windows

log siding

rough-pole mantel support

flat (gauged) arch

CABIN

hipped roof

paired windows

shed roof

exposed log rafters

split shingles

casement

rough-pole beam

log siding

rubblework chimney

diamond-pane casement

saddle notch

rough-pole porch post

pantry

kitchen

dining room

living room

porch

Victorian Fireplaces

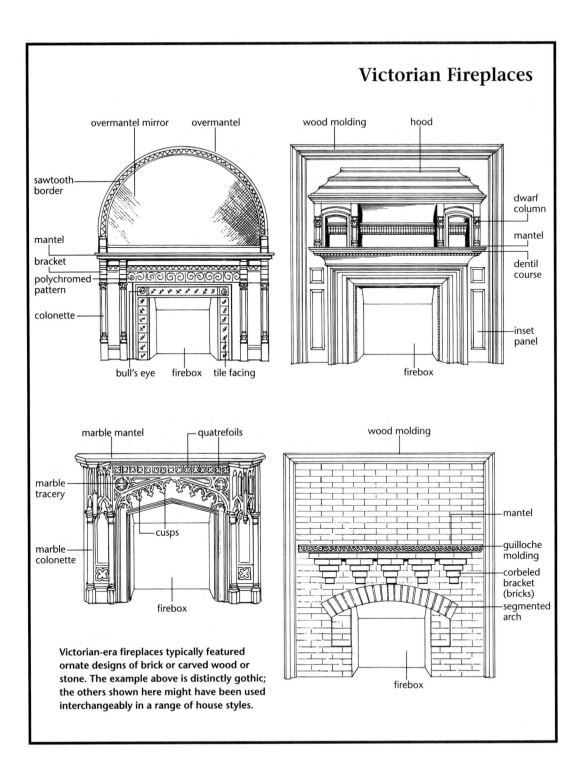

overmantel mirror overmantel

wood molding hood

sawtooth border

mantel

bracket

polychromed pattern

colonette

bull's eye firebox tile facing

dwarf column

mantel

dentil course

inset panel

firebox

marble mantel quatrefoils

wood molding

marble tracery

cusps

marble colonette

firebox

mantel

guilloche molding

corbeled bracket (bricks)

segmented arch

firebox

Victorian-era fireplaces typically featured ornate designs of brick or carved wood or stone. The example above is distinctly gothic; the others shown here might have been used interchangeably in a range of house styles.

Chapter Eight
Classicism and the Revivals

As the Victorian era waned, there emerged a new current in American architecture that consciously rejected the Picturesque. This "Academic Reaction," led by the influential New York firm of McKim, Mead and White, marked a return to formal, disciplined order and the kind of literal, archaeological adaptation of historical styles that had gone out with the Greek Revival. Rooted in a broader cultural movement then known as the American Renaissance, the renewed interest in historical European design (especially Classical and Renaissance forms), as well as a new interest in America's own Colonial past, could be seen in the overwhelming response to the Classically inspired design of the 1893 World's Columbian Exposition in Chicago. Equally influential were the principles of the Ecole des Beaux-Arts in Paris, which emphasized "correct" interpretations of historic architecture. While bookish and programmatic, the style known as Beaux Arts made up for its lack of spontaneity with an architecture outstanding for its balance and clarity, reasoned solutions to spatial and circulation problems, and true sense of grandeur, permanence, and "good taste."

With the 20th century came a related interest in a variety of period styles. Safe and conservative designs—based, for example, on the half-timbered manor houses of Tudor England and the country estates of Normandy and Spain—attracted the well-heeled clients who provided the bulk of business for the prestigious architectural firms of the day. While it took some time, the influence of these popular period revivals eventually spread to more modest suburban residences and was widespread by the 1940s, lasting into the present.

CHERUB (PUTTO)

CORBEL STONE

**GARGOYLE
(WATERSPOUT)**

Popularized in the 1880s by the fashionable society architect Richard Morris Hunt (1827–95), the Chateauesque was perhaps the most grandiose of the late Victorian styles, epitomizing all the excesses of the Gilded Age. The Chateauesque was loosely based on the 15th- and 16th-century French chateaux of the Loire Valley. The American versions, built primarily in New York and other eastern cities, were in fact modified stone castles, complete with steeply pitched hipped roofs, elaborate dormers and gable parapets, towers, spires, and all manner of florid Gothic detailing, from gargoyles to griffins. Not to be outdone, the interiors boasted enormous reception halls, picture galleries, and conservatories, along with the latest in technological innovations, including electric passenger elevators and central steam heating. The style was fashionable into the first decade of the 1900s.

Chateauesque

URBAN HOUSE

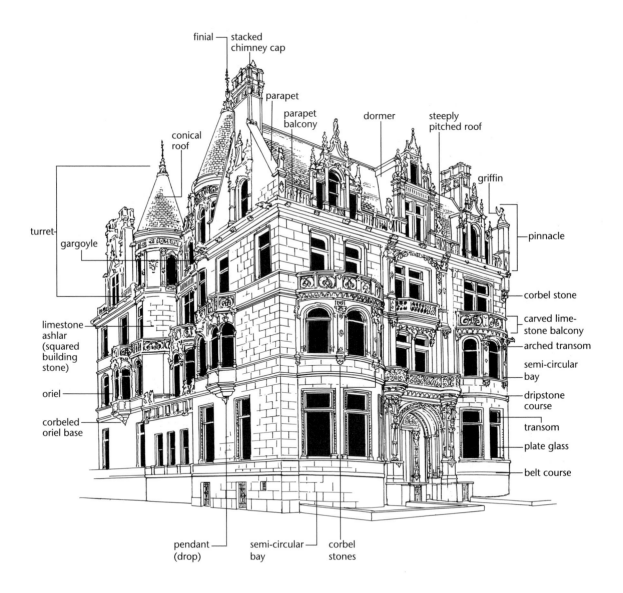

finial — stacked chimney cap

parapet

parapet balcony

dormer

steeply pitched roof

conical roof

griffin

turret

gargoyle

pinnacle

corbel stone

limestone ashlar (squared building stone)

carved limestone balcony

arched transom

semi-circular bay

oriel

dripstone course

corbeled oriel base

transom

plate glass

belt course

pendant (drop)

semi-circular bay

corbel stones

Italian Renaissance

URBAN HOUSE

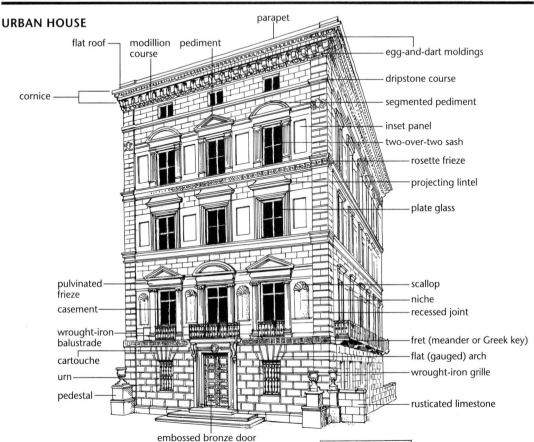

- parapet
- flat roof
- modillion course
- pediment
- cornice
- egg-and-dart moldings
- dripstone course
- segmented pediment
- inset panel
- two-over-two sash
- rosette frieze
- projecting lintel
- plate glass
- pulvinated frieze
- casement
- wrought-iron balustrade
- cartouche
- urn
- pedestal
- scallop
- niche
- recessed joint
- fret (meander or Greek key)
- flat (gauged) arch
- wrought-iron grille
- rusticated limestone
- embossed bronze door

The Italian Renaissance revival, directly inspired by the great Renaissance houses of Italy, was one of the most popular of the Beaux Arts design modes, lasting from the late 1800s until the 1920s. While the Victorian Italianate (pages 143–45) was essentially a loose interpretation of Italian architecture, drawn primarily from pattern books, the Italian Renaissance revival took a much more academic approach, with design features often copied directly from actual Renaissance landmarks. Roman, Florentine, and Venetian prototypes—ducal palazzi or country villas—were translated into American "palaces," primarily in cities such as New York and fashionable resorts like Newport, Rhode Island.

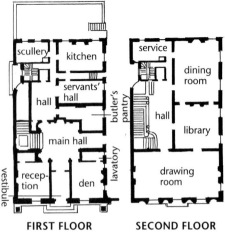

FIRST FLOOR

- scullery
- kitchen
- hall
- servants' hall
- butler's pantry
- main hall
- lavatory
- reception
- den
- vestibule

SECOND FLOOR

- service
- dining room
- hall
- library
- drawing room

Italian Renaissance

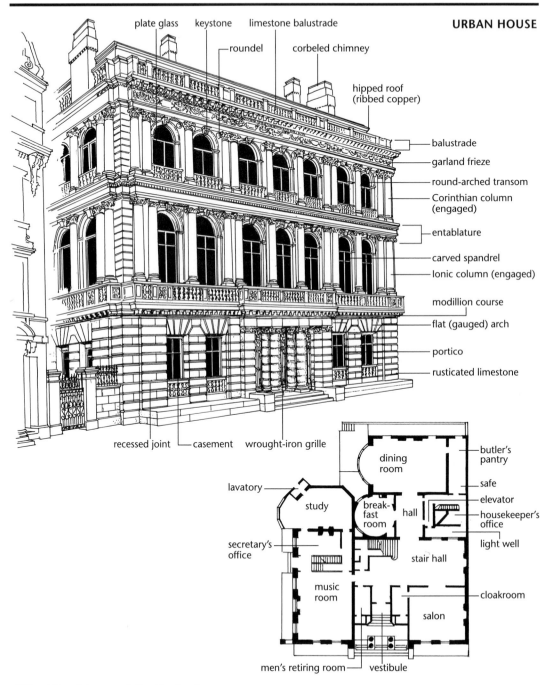

URBAN HOUSE

plate glass
keystone
limestone balustrade
roundel
corbeled chimney
hipped roof
(ribbed copper)

balustrade
garland frieze
round-arched transom
Corinthian column
(engaged)
entablature
carved spandrel
Ionic column (engaged)
modillion course
flat (gauged) arch
portico
rusticated limestone

recessed joint
casement
wrought-iron grille

dining
room

butler's
pantry

lavatory

safe
elevator
housekeeper's
office

study

break-
fast
room

hall

secretary's
office

light well

stair hall

music
room

cloakroom

salon

men's retiring room
vestibule

Italian Renaissance

ROW HOUSE

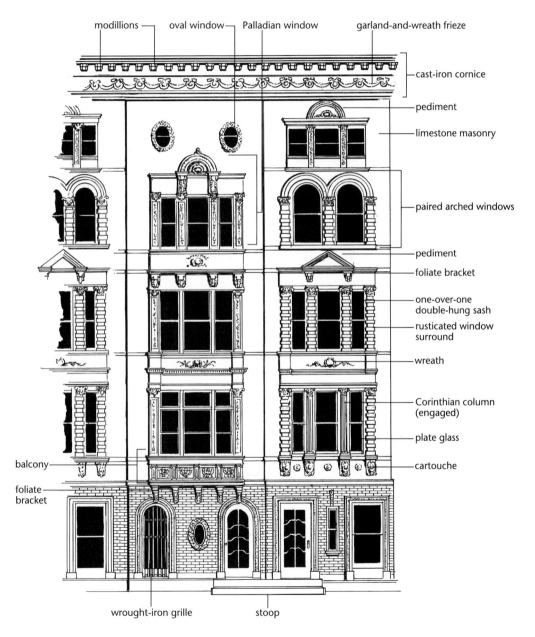

modillions — oval window — Palladian window — garland-and-wreath frieze

cast-iron cornice

pediment

limestone masonry

paired arched windows

pediment

foliate bracket

one-over-one double-hung sash

rusticated window surround

wreath

Corinthian column (engaged)

plate glass

cartouche

balcony

foliate bracket

wrought-iron grille — stoop

Italian Renaissance

SUBURBAN HOUSE

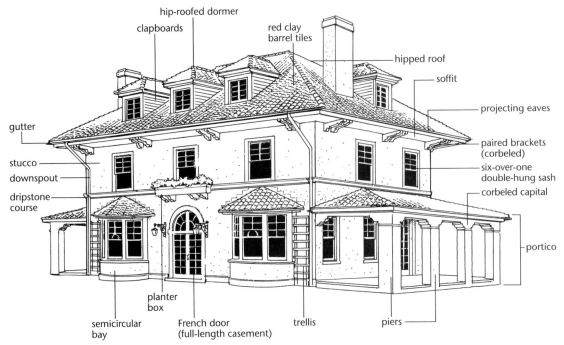

hip-roofed dormer

clapboards

red clay
barrel tiles

hipped roof

soffit

projecting eaves

gutter

paired brackets
(corbeled)

stucco

six-over-one
double-hung sash

downspout

corbeled capital

dripstone
course

portico

planter
box

semicircular
bay

French door
(full-length casement)

trellis

piers

GARAGE
(AUTO BARN)

keystone

wood shingles

arched multipane doors

pediment

hipped roof

fascia board

pediment

entablature

squared columns

rubblework masonry

Beaux Arts

ROW HOUSE

Broadly speaking, the term "Beaux Arts" refers to the American Renaissance period from about 1885 to the 1920s and encompasses the Italian Renaissance and Neoclassical revivals. It is also used specifically to describe buildings derivative of contemporary work in France, based on Baroque architecture. In America, the Beaux Arts style was interpreted in imposing row and freestanding town houses as well as grandiose country estates. Characteristically, these impressive residences featured facades of pristine white limestone or elegant buff-colored or yellow brick in a narrow gauge, often accented with enormous cartouches dripping with sculptural ornament.

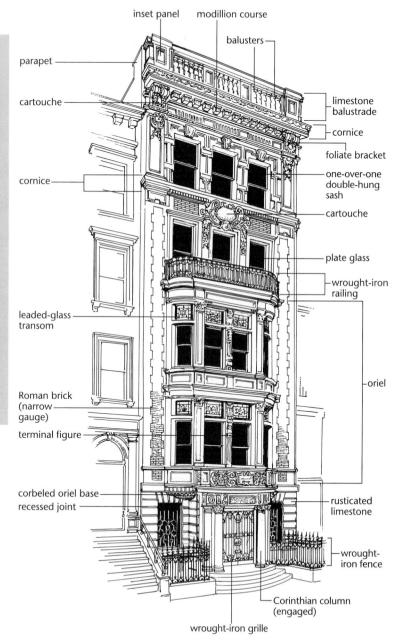

inset panel — modillion course — balusters — parapet — cartouche — limestone balustrade — cornice — foliate bracket — cornice — one-over-one double-hung sash — cartouche — plate glass — leaded-glass transom — wrought-iron railing — oriel — Roman brick (narrow gauge) — terminal figure — corbeled oriel base — recessed joint — rusticated limestone — wrought-iron fence — Corinthian column (engaged) — wrought-iron grille

Beaux Arts

ENTRANCE HALL AND GRAND STAIRCASE

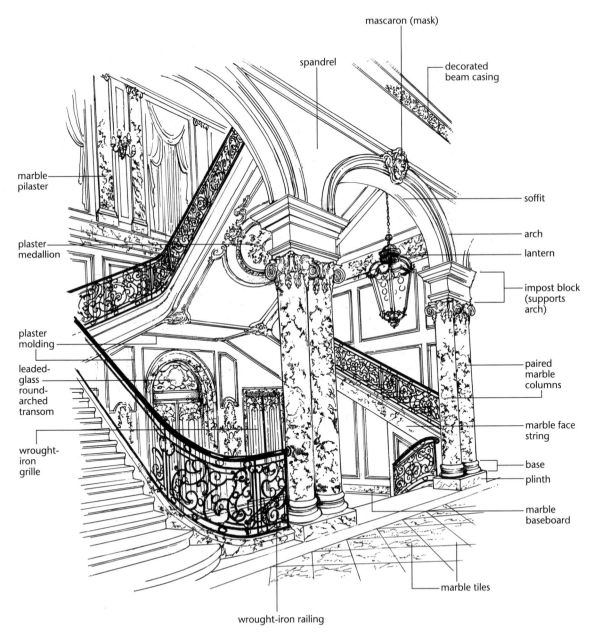

mascaron (mask)

spandrel

decorated
beam casing

marble
pilaster

soffit

plaster
medallion

arch

lantern

impost block
(supports
arch)

plaster
molding

leaded-
glass
round-
arched
transom

paired
marble
columns

marble face
string

wrought-
iron
grille

base

plinth

marble
baseboard

marble tiles

wrought-iron railing

URBAN HOUSE

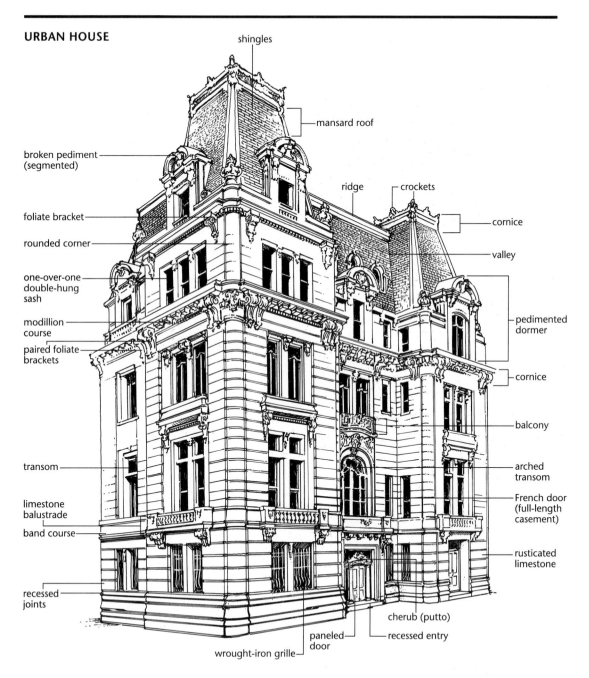

shingles

mansard roof

broken pediment (segmented)

ridge

crockets

cornice

foliate bracket

rounded corner

valley

one-over-one double-hung sash

modillion course

paired foliate brackets

pedimented dormer

cornice

balcony

transom

arched transom

limestone balustrade

French door (full-length casement)

band course

rusticated limestone

recessed joints

cherub (putto)

paneled door

recessed entry

wrought-iron grille

Neoclassical

ESTATE HOUSE

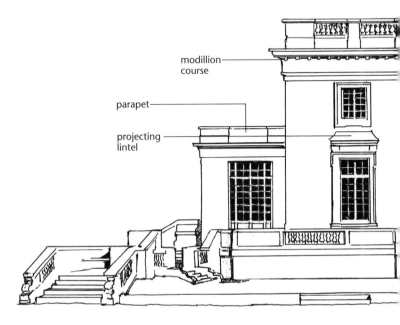

modillion course

parapet

projecting lintel

The Neoclassical revival was based on the Neoclassical architecture of 18th-century France and England. In America, fashion favored the French Neoclassical, which provided a striking alternative to the ostentatious sculptural ornament associated with the Beaux Arts style. By contrast, the flat-roofed Neoclassical house was subdued and dignified, although equally monumental in scale. Facades were markedly symmetrical, gaining interest from a deliberate play of clear glass against solid expanses of stone, and punctuated by rhythmic rows of columns, windows, and French doors. A grand two-story portico often emphasized the centrality of the design.

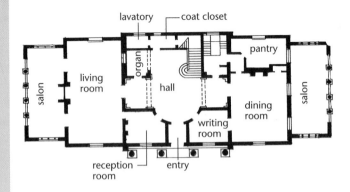

lavatory   coat closet

pantry

salon

living room

organ

hall

salon

dining room

writing room

reception room   entry

Neoclassical

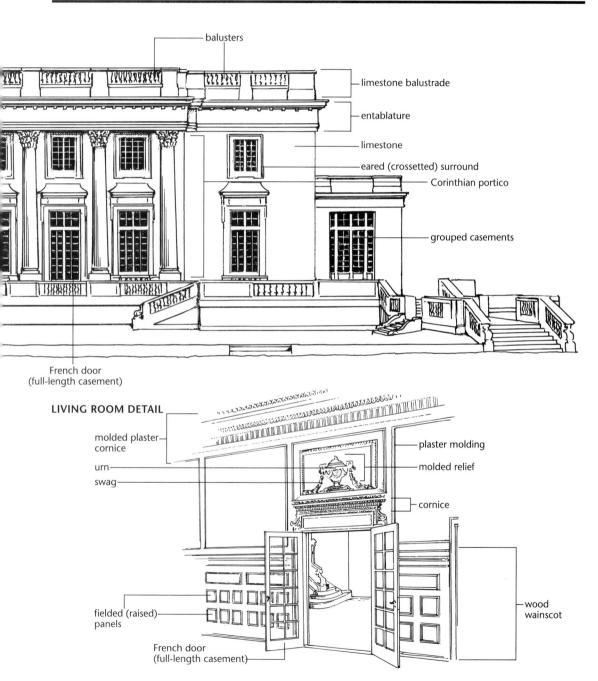

balusters

limestone balustrade

entablature

limestone

eared (crossetted) surround

Corinthian portico

grouped casements

French door
(full-length casement)

LIVING ROOM DETAIL

molded plaster cornice

urn

swag

plaster molding

molded relief

cornice

fielded (raised) panels

French door
(full-length casement)

wood wainscot

Classicism and the Revivals 187

Colonial Revival

ROW HOUSE

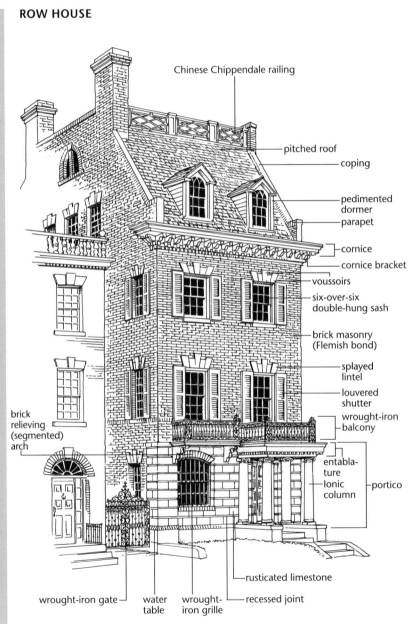

Chinese Chippendale railing

pitched roof

coping

pedimented dormer

parapet

cornice

cornice bracket

voussoirs

six-over-six double-hung sash

brick masonry (Flemish bond)

splayed lintel

louvered shutter

wrought-iron balcony

entablature

Ionic column

portico

rusticated limestone

recessed joint

brick relieving (segmented) arch

wrought-iron gate

water table

wrought-iron grille

Following on the heels of America's Centennial celebrations, the Colonial Revival emerged in the early 1880s. The style, which borrowed heavily from early American architecture—particularly Georgian and Federal buildings—was largely an outgrowth of a new pride in America's past and a rapidly growing interest in historic preservation. Among the leaders of the movement were the partners at McKim, Mead and White, who had made a tour of New England's historic towns in 1878.

In this early phase, the Colonial Revival style remained the exclusive domain of fashionable architectural firms and was favored for the large residences of wealthy clients. Designs incorporated characteristic features of Colonial buildings, including Palladian windows, gambrel roofs, pedimented porticos, columns, Classical detailing such as swags and urns, and crisp white trim. The new buildings, however, were much larger than their historic counterparts, with the details also enlarged and plans laid out on a grandiose scale.

Colonial Revival

FREESTANDING STAIRCASE

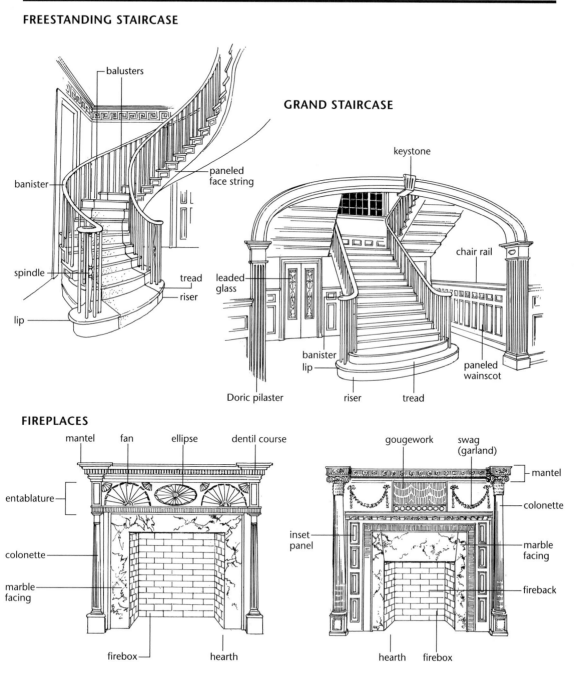

balusters

paneled face string

banister

spindle

tread

riser

lip

GRAND STAIRCASE

keystone

chair rail

leaded glass

banister

lip

paneled wainscot

Doric pilaster

riser

tread

FIREPLACES

mantel   fan   ellipse   dentil course

entablature

colonette

marble facing

firebox   hearth

gougework   swag (garland)

mantel

colonette

inset panel

marble facing

fireback

hearth   firebox

Colonial Revival

ESTATE HOUSES

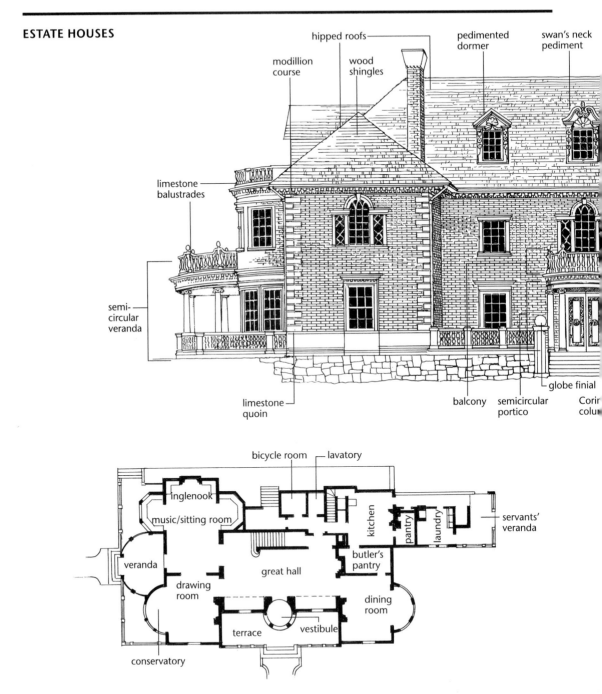

modillion course

hipped roofs

wood shingles

pedimented dormer

swan's neck pediment

limestone balustrades

semi-circular veranda

limestone quoin

balcony

semicircular portico

globe finial

Corir colu

bicycle room

lavatory

inglenook

music/sitting room

kitchen

pantry

laundry

servants' veranda

veranda

butler's pantry

great hall

drawing room

dining room

terrace

vestibule

conservatory

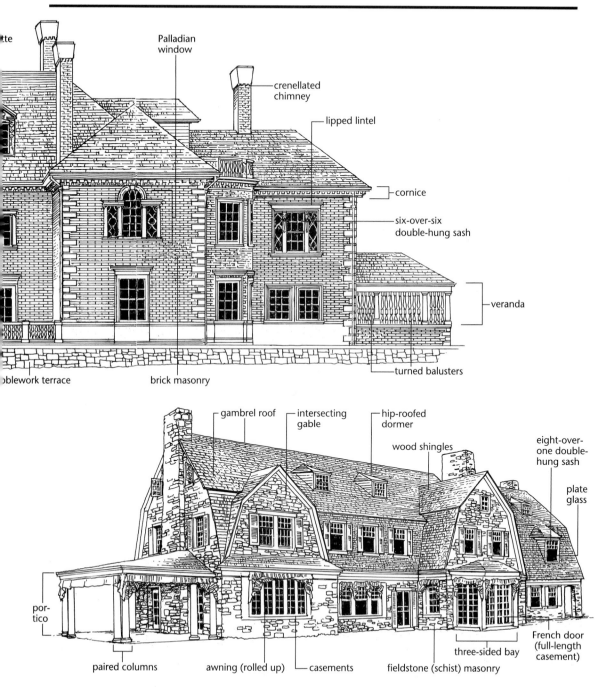

tte

Palladian
window

crenellated
chimney

lipped lintel

cornice

six-over-six
double-hung sash

veranda

blework terrace

brick masonry

turned balusters

gambrel roof

intersecting
gable

hip-roofed
dormer

wood shingles

eight-over-
one double-
hung sash

plate
glass

por-
tico

paired columns

awning (rolled up)

casements

fieldstone (schist) masonry

three-sided bay

French door
(full-length
casement)

Classicism and the Revivals 191

Colonial Revival

ESTATE HOUSES

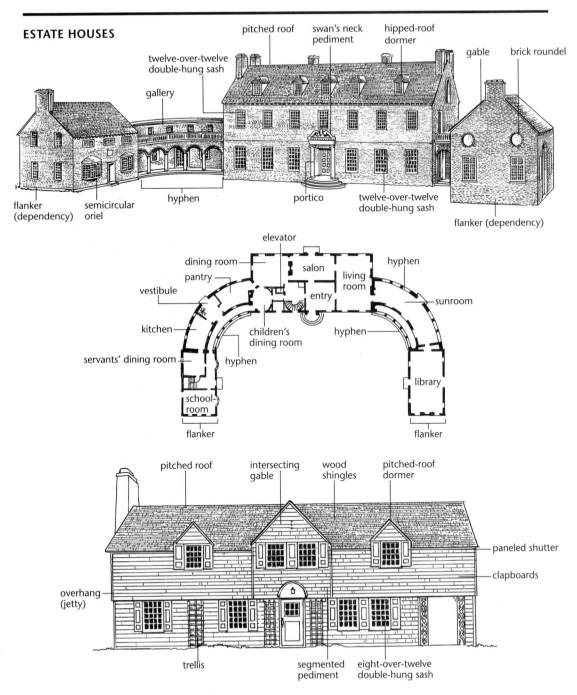

pitched roof

swan's neck pediment

hipped-roof dormer

gable

brick roundel

twelve-over-twelve double-hung sash

gallery

flanker (dependency)

semicircular oriel

hyphen

portico

twelve-over-twelve double-hung sash

flanker (dependency)

elevator

dining room

pantry

vestibule

kitchen

servants' dining room

salon

entry

living room

hyphen

sunroom

children's dining room

hyphen

hyphen

school-room

flanker

library

flanker

pitched roof

intersecting gable

wood shingles

pitched-roof dormer

paneled shutter

clapboards

overhang (jetty)

trellis

segmented pediment

eight-over-twelve double-hung sash

French Revival

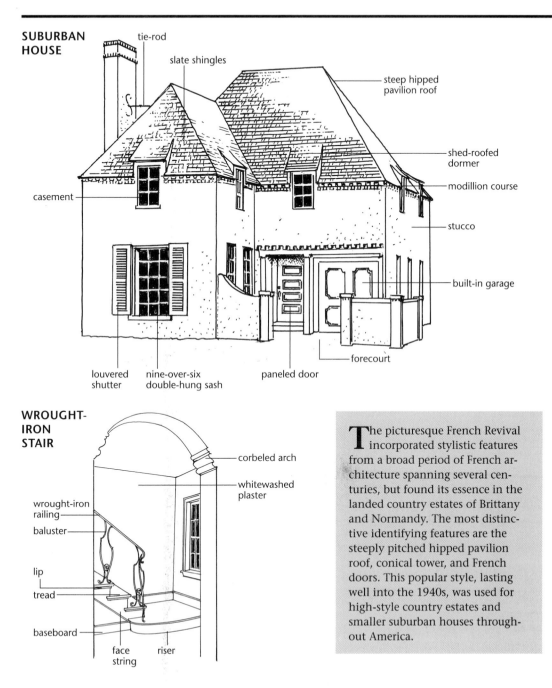

SUBURBAN HOUSE

tie-rod

slate shingles

steep hipped pavilion roof

shed-roofed dormer

modillion course

casement

stucco

built-in garage

louvered shutter

nine-over-six double-hung sash

paneled door

forecourt

WROUGHT-IRON STAIR

corbeled arch

whitewashed plaster

wrought-iron railing

baluster

lip

tread

baseboard

face string

riser

The picturesque French Revival incorporated stylistic features from a broad period of French architecture spanning several centuries, but found its essence in the landed country estates of Brittany and Normandy. The most distinctive identifying features are the steeply pitched hipped pavilion roof, conical tower, and French doors. This popular style, lasting well into the 1940s, was used for high-style country estates and smaller suburban houses throughout America.

French Revival

ESTATE HOUSE

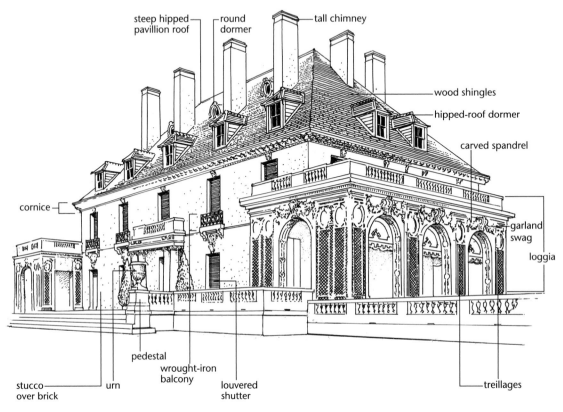

steep hipped pavillion roof — round dormer — tall chimney

wood shingles

hipped-roof dormer

carved spandrel

cornice

garland swag

loggia

pedestal

wrought-iron balcony

louvered shutter

treillages

stucco over brick — urn

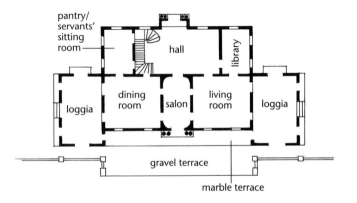

pantry/servants' sitting room

hall

library

loggia

dining room

salon

living room

loggia

gravel terrace

marble terrace

STABLE

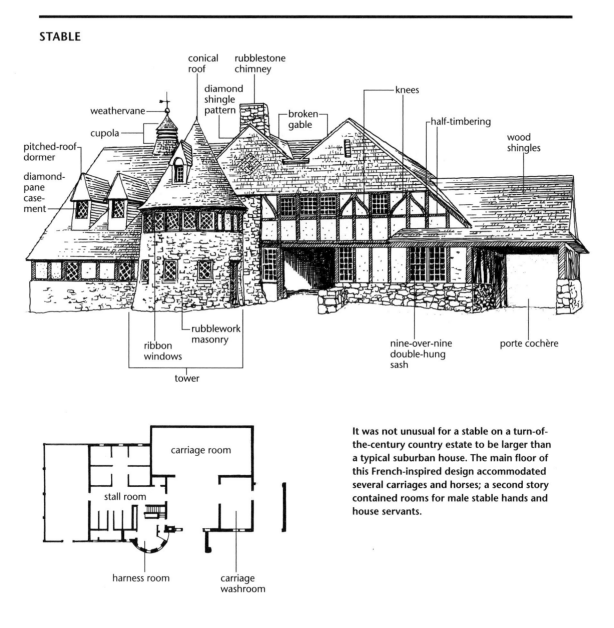

conical roof

rubblestone chimney

diamond shingle pattern

weathervane

cupola

pitched-roof-dormer

diamond-pane case-ment

broken gable

knees

half-timbering

wood shingles

ribbon windows

rubblework masonry

tower

nine-over-nine double-hung sash

porte cochère

carriage room

stall room

harness room

carriage washroom

It was not unusual for a stable on a turn-of-the-century country estate to be larger than a typical suburban house. The main floor of this French-inspired design accommodated several carriages and horses; a second story contained rooms for male stable hands and house servants.

Spanish Revival

Spanish-inspired houses began appearing at the turn of the century in the form of the Mission style, which reflected a loose adaptation of features often found on Spanish Colonial mission buildings, including the shaped parapet and quatrefoil window. In 1915 the California-Pacific Exposition opened in San Diego to inaugurate the Panama Canal. One of the great stars of the fair was the California pavilion, a romantic, slightly exotic building designed in a freely interpreted Spanish Colonial style by the fashionable architect Bertram Grosvenor Goodhue (1869–1924). Both the exposition and Goodhue did much to promote this more academic and sophisticated interpretation, which borrowed from a broad vocabulary of Moorish, Byzantine, and Renaissance detailing, often based on actual prototypes in Spain. In vogue into the 1930s, the Spanish Revival was found primarily in the Southwest, California—where it was a style of choice for Hollywood stars—and fashionable Florida resorts.

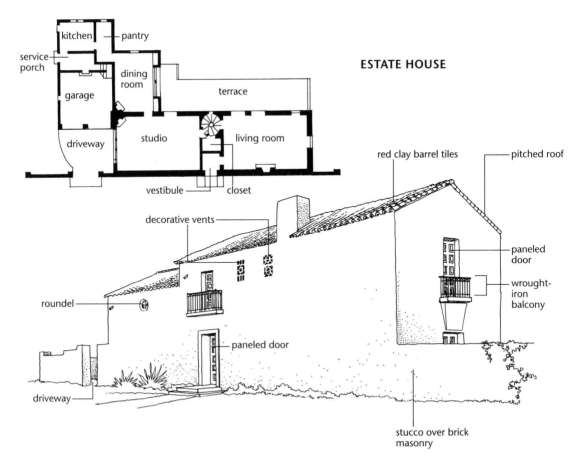

ESTATE HOUSE

Spanish Revival

SUBURBAN HOUSE

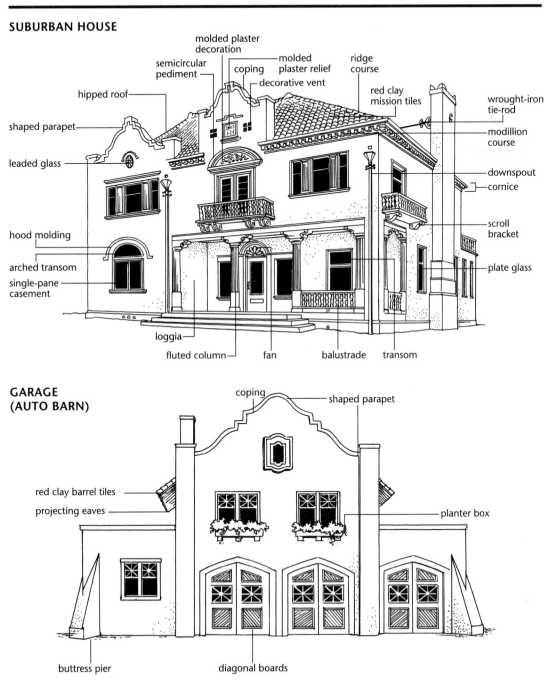

molded plaster decoration

semicircular pediment

coping

molded plaster relief

decorative vent

ridge course

red clay mission tiles

hipped roof

wrought-iron tie-rod

shaped parapet

modillion course

leaded glass

downspout

cornice

scroll bracket

hood molding

plate glass

arched transom

single-pane casement

loggia

fluted column

fan

balustrade

transom

GARAGE (AUTO BARN)

coping

shaped parapet

red clay barrel tiles

projecting eaves

planter box

buttress pier

diagonal boards

Classicism and the Revivals   197

Spanish Revival

STAIRCASE (INTERIOR)

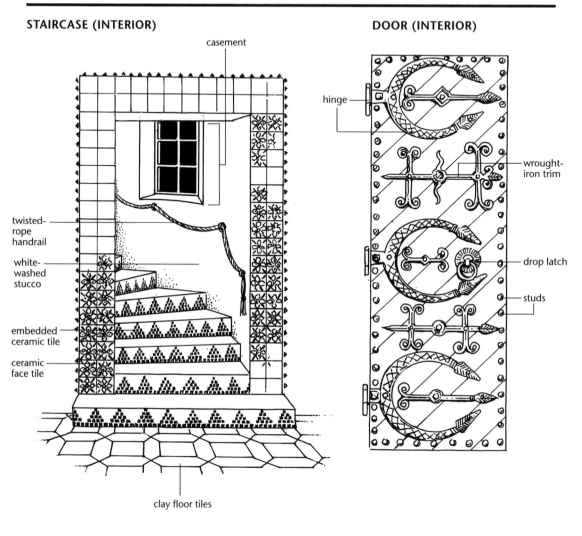

casement

twisted-
rope
handrail

white-
washed
stucco

embedded
ceramic tile

ceramic
face tile

clay floor tiles

DOOR (INTERIOR)

hinge

wrought-
iron trim

drop latch

studs

**WROUGHT-IRON
STRAP HINGES**

 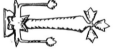 

PATIO

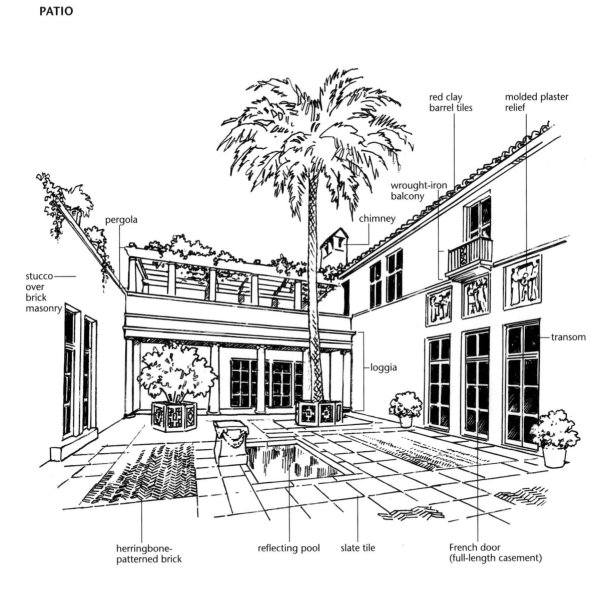

red clay
barrel tiles

molded plaster
relief

wrought-iron
balcony

pergola

chimney

stucco
over
brick
masonry

loggia

transom

herringbone-
patterned brick

reflecting pool

slate tile

French door
(full-length casement)

Tudor Revival

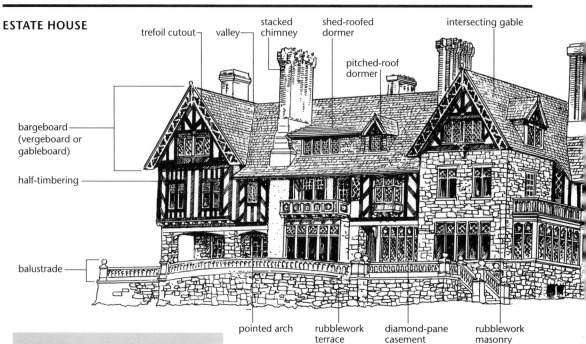

trefoil cutout — valley — stacked chimney — shed-roofed dormer — intersecting gable

pitched-roof dormer

bargeboard (vergeboard or gableboard)

half-timbering

balustrade

pointed arch — rubblework terrace — diamond-pane casement — rubblework masonry

The high-style Tudor Revival house of the late 19th and early 20th centuries derived primarily from English Renaissance buildings of the 16th and early 17th centuries, including those of the Elizabethan and Jacobean periods. These rambling, asymmetrically massed mansions typically featured steeply pitched roofs, one or more intersecting gables, decorative—rather than structural—half-timbering, and long rows of casement windows. By the early 20th century the Tudor Revival style was adapted to the middle-class suburban house and eventually became especially popular for the affordable small house of the 1920s and 1930s (page 212). There have been periodic revivals ever since.

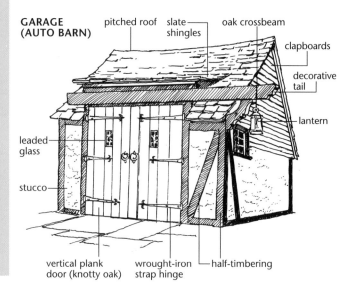

GARAGE (AUTO BARN)

pitched roof — slate shingles — oak crossbeam

clapboards

decorative tail

lantern

leaded glass

stucco

vertical plank door (knotty oak) — wrought-iron strap hinge — half-timbering

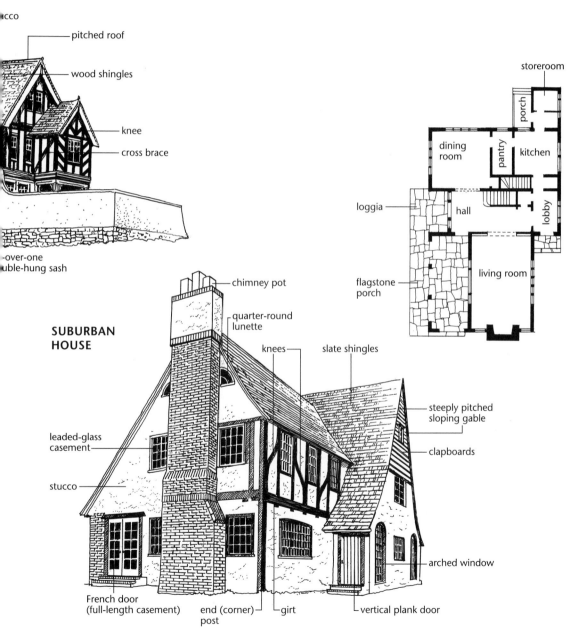

cco

pitched roof

wood shingles

knee

cross brace

-over-one
uble-hung sash

storeroom

porch

dining
room

pantry

kitchen

loggia

hall

lobby

flagstone
porch

living room

chimney pot

quarter-round
lunette

**SUBURBAN
HOUSE**

knees

slate shingles

steeply pitched
sloping gable

leaded-glass
casement

clapboards

stucco

arched window

French door
(full-length casement)

end (corner)
post

girt

vertical plank door

Chapter Nine
New American Visions

While period styles represented a major design current during the early 1900s, a few progressive minds began to establish influential standards of design wholly independent of historical European references. Among the strongest voices against the Classicism and formal composition of the Beaux Arts movement was that of Frank Lloyd Wright (1867–1959). Wright's work drew on many sources, including Japanese design, the contemporary English Arts and Crafts movement, and the Victorian preoccupation with the relationship of a building to its natural environment. Interpreted in the context of the flat Midwestern landscape—and Wright's own very personal design vocabulary—his Prairie style evolved as a truly original American art form.

The equally intelligent Craftsman designs of Charles Sumner Greene (1868–1957) and his brother Henry Mather Greene (1870–1954) were another important departure from the past. The fascination of these California architects with structural forms and the pure, simple beauty of wood and stone yielded superbly articulated buildings organically integrated with their sites.

Designed for an affluent clientele, the high-style Prairie and Craftsman houses had a relatively short life, over by the 1920s. But Wright and the Greene brothers were among the first American designers of their generation to emphasize comfort and convenience, and their concepts of human scale and sensible plans (alien to most Victorian architecture) helped shape a growing phenomenon of the time: the affordable small house for the middle class.

SUBURBAN HOUSE

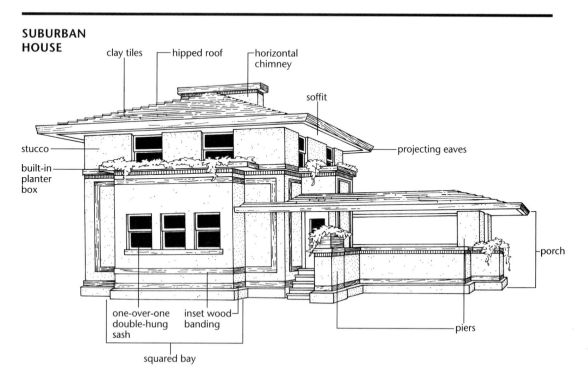

clay tiles — hipped roof — horizontal chimney

soffit

stucco

built-in planter box

projecting eaves

one-over-one double-hung sash

inset wood banding

porch

piers

squared bay

The Prairie School designs of Frank Lloyd Wright and his followers embodied Wright's belief that a building should appear to grow organically from its site. In Wright's mind, a design drew its beauty from within—from its own anatomy—rather than from applied decoration. The Prairie house was deliberate and composed, conceived as a practical, cohesive whole down to the landscaping, built-in furniture, and fixtures, which were treated with as much importance as the architectural elements. Its natural textures and horizontal profile, accented by broad, hovering roof planes and spreading terraces, were in concert with the flat landscape of the midwestern plains. Inside, the simplified open plan had a minimum of rooms, defined by screens and panels, radiating from a central living space.

The Prairie house, which ranged from modest designs to huge estates, reached its peak in Oak Park, Illinois, and other Midwest suburbs during the first two decades of the 20th century. Client interest in the large-scale version had faded by World War I, but the open floor plan, clean lines, and human scale associated with the style made a permanent mark on American architecture, particularly small-scale suburban house design.

Prairie School

LARGE SUBURBAN HOUSE

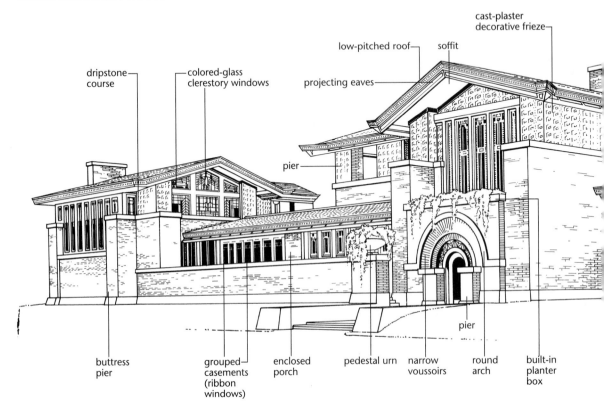

dripstone course

colored-glass clerestory windows

low-pitched roof

soffit

cast-plaster decorative frieze

projecting eaves

pier

buttress pier

grouped casements (ribbon windows)

enclosed porch

pedestal urn

narrow voussoirs

round arch

built-in planter box

pier

Prairie School

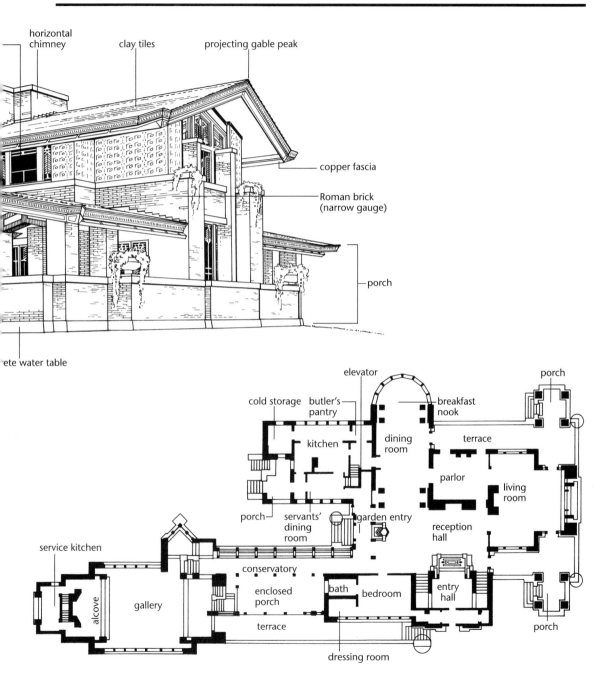

horizontal chimney

clay tiles

projecting gable peak

copper fascia

Roman brick
(narrow gauge)

porch

ete water table

elevator

cold storage

butler's
pantry

breakfast
nook

porch

kitchen

dining
room

terrace

parlor

living
room

porch

servants'
dining
room

garden entry

reception
hall

service kitchen

conservatory

enclosed
porch

bath

bedroom

entry
hall

alcove

gallery

terrace

porch

dressing room

Prairie School

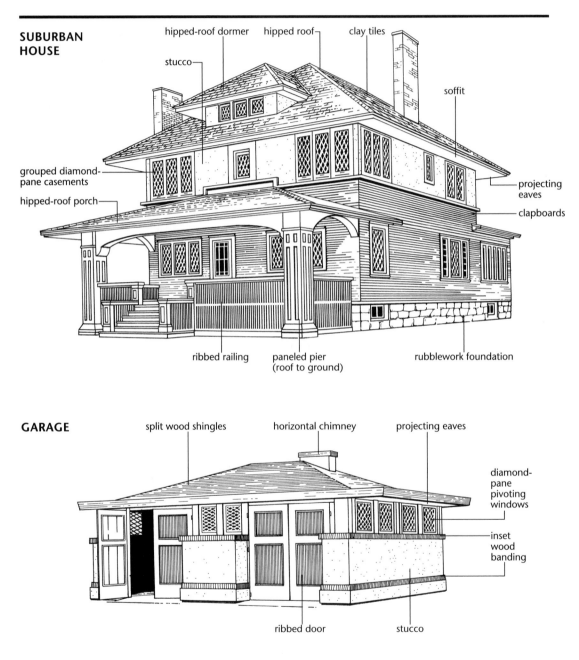

SUBURBAN HOUSE

hipped-roof dormer

hipped roof

clay tiles

stucco

soffit

grouped diamond-pane casements

hipped-roof porch

projecting eaves

clapboards

ribbed railing

paneled pier (roof to ground)

rubblework foundation

GARAGE

split wood shingles

horizontal chimney

projecting eaves

diamond-pane pivoting windows

inset wood banding

ribbed door

stucco

LIVING ROOM

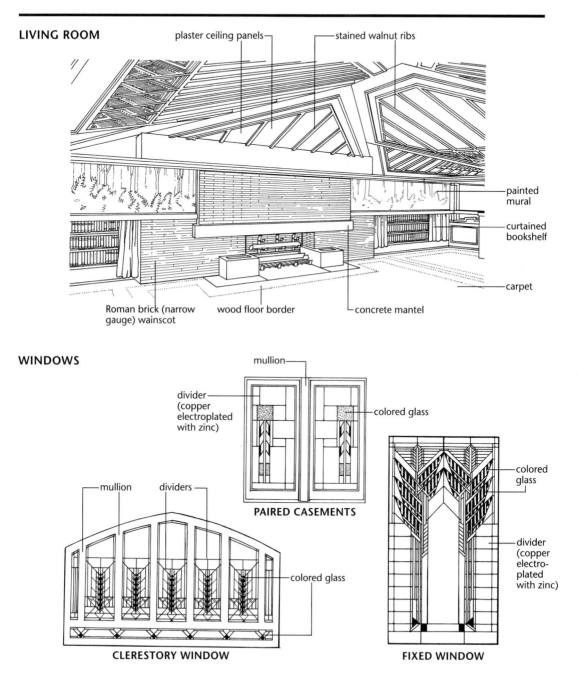

plaster ceiling panels

stained walnut ribs

painted mural

curtained bookshelf

carpet

Roman brick (narrow gauge) wainscot

wood floor border

concrete mantel

WINDOWS

mullion

divider (copper electroplated with zinc)

colored glass

PAIRED CASEMENTS

mullion

dividers

colored glass

CLERESTORY WINDOW

colored glass

divider (copper electroplated with zinc)

FIXED WINDOW

Craftsman

LARGE SUBURBAN HOUSE

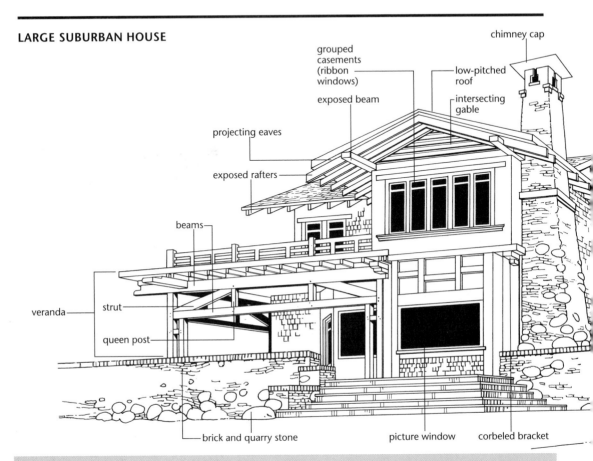

chimney cap

grouped casements (ribbon windows)

low-pitched roof

exposed beam

intersecting gable

projecting eaves

exposed rafters

beams

veranda

strut

queen post

brick and quarry stone

picture window

corbeled bracket

The Craftsman style represented an independent western movement in American architecture. Its guiding force was the English Arts and Crafts movement, which rejected the mass reproduction and mediocre design associated with the Industrial Revolution in favor of the beauty and "honesty" of traditional handcraftsmanship and natural materials.

In America these ideas were widely disseminated in the pages of the *Craftsman* magazine, published from 1901 to 1916 by the furniture maker and designer Gustav Stickley (1848–1942). The style was adapted for countless small houses and bungalows (see page 212) but found its most sophisticated expression in the California work of Pasadena architects Greene and Greene. Trained in the manual arts, these brothers were craftsmen who often became involved in the actual building of houses. Spanning the period of 1903 to 1928, their domestic work showed a love for material, technology, and craft—particularly the workmanship of Japanese architecture. Sheathed in dark shingles, the high-style Craftsman house was at one with its setting, the gardens and loggias treated as planned extensions of the architecture. Hand-polished woods such as oak, teak, and mahogany detailed each interior. Built-in features crafted of fine materials made each house a giant sculpture, with each detail part of the whole.

Craftsman

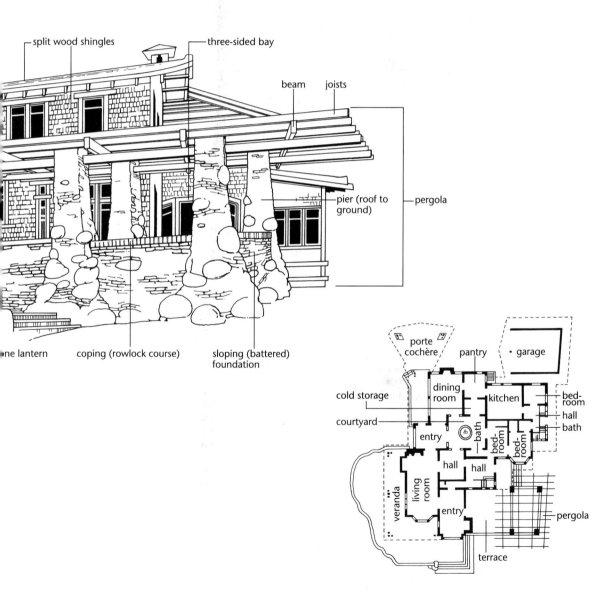

split wood shingles

three-sided bay

beam

joists

pier (roof to ground)

pergola

ne lantern

coping (rowlock course)

sloping (battered) foundation

porte cochère

pantry

garage

cold storage

dining room

kitchen

bedroom

hall

bath

courtyard

entry

bath

bedroom

bedroom

veranda

living room

hall

hall

entry

pergola

terrace

Craftsman

GARAGE

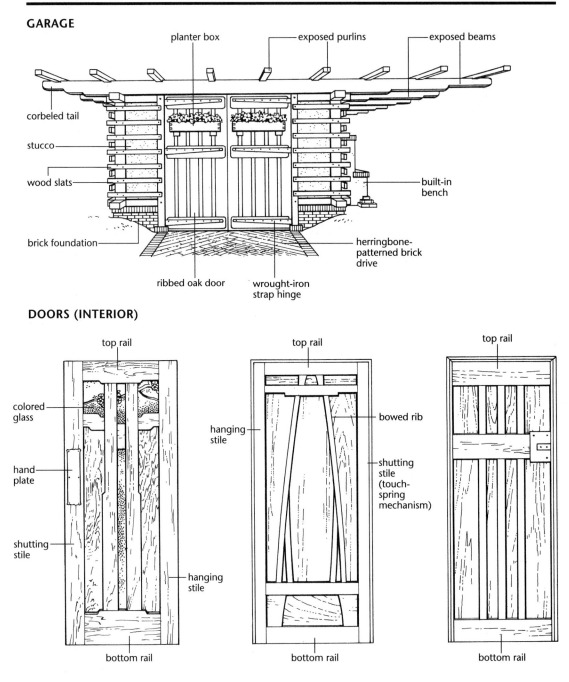

planter box — exposed purlins — exposed beams

corbeled tail

stucco

wood slats

built-in bench

brick foundation

herringbone-patterned brick drive

ribbed oak door   wrought-iron strap hinge

DOORS (INTERIOR)

top rail   top rail   top rail

colored glass

hand plate

shutting stile

hanging stile

bowed rib

hanging stile

shutting stile (touch-spring mechanism)

bottom rail   bottom rail   bottom rail

Craftsman

ENTRANCE HALL

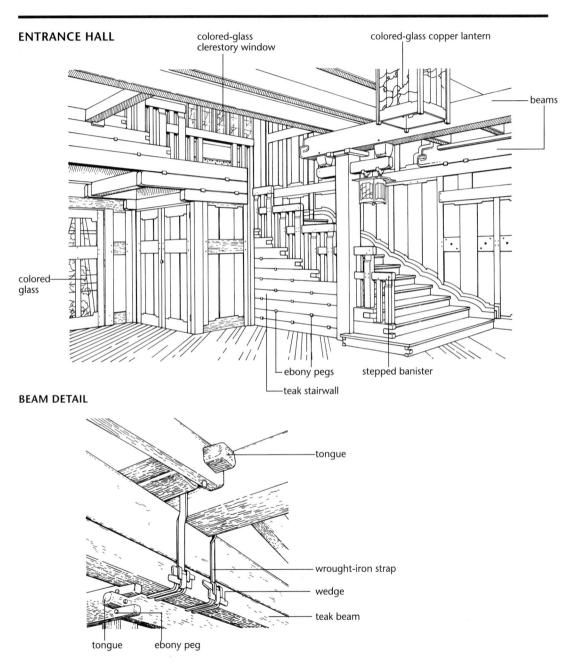

colored-glass clerestory window

colored-glass copper lantern

beams

colored glass

ebony pegs

teak stairwall

stepped banister

BEAM DETAIL

tongue

wrought-iron strap

wedge

teak beam

tongue

ebony peg

Bungalows and Small Houses

CRAFTSMAN BUNGALOW

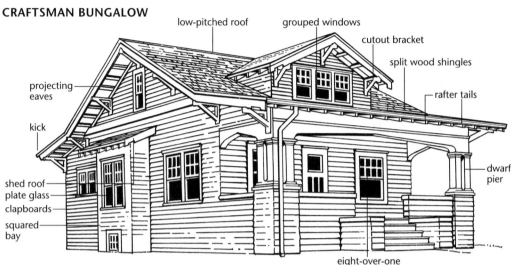

low-pitched roof

grouped windows

cutout bracket

split wood shingles

projecting eaves

rafter tails

kick

shed roof

plate glass

clapboards

squared bay

dwarf pier

eight-over-one double-hung sash

The first thirty years of the 1900s were a building boom for the small single- and two-family house, along with the detached "auto barn," or garage. This growth was spurred by a social movement to improve housing, as well as another development on the American scene: the suburb. In 1900 there were 8,000 cars on the road; just fifteen years later the number was well over two million. This automobility, along with improved railroads, created a demand for affordable housing within reach of the city.

Magazines led the way. Among the most influential was *Ladies Home Journal*, which around 1900 published designs for small model homes—often in chalet and period styles— complete plans for prefabricated frames, specifications for fireproofing, and such novel conveniences as electricity, plumbing, and gas ranges. The *Craftsman* (see page 208) was responsible for the widespread popularity of the Craftsman bungalow, a typically snug one-and-a-half-story home with a wide overhanging roof, deep porch, and simple interior with built-in cupboards and cozy inglenooks. For a few dollars a reader could purchase working plans for a house costing as little as $1,000 to build. Ready-to-build houses could also be bought by mail order from enterprises such as Sears, Roebuck, which would deliver the crated materials, fixtures, and assembly instructions for an entire house to the nearest railroad station.

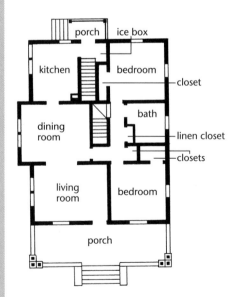

porch

ice box

kitchen

bedroom

closet

bath

dining room

linen closet

closets

living room

bedroom

porch

Bungalows and Small Houses

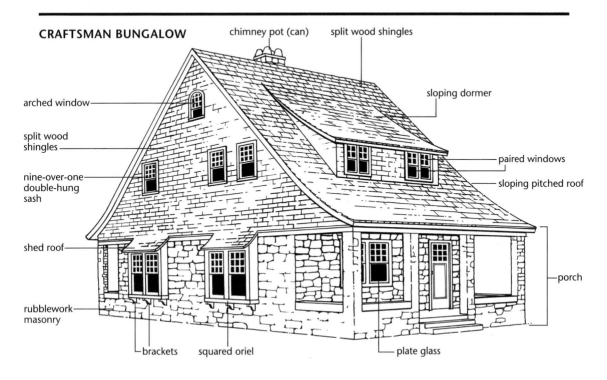

CRAFTSMAN BUNGALOW

chimney pot (can)

split wood shingles

sloping dormer

arched window

split wood shingles

nine-over-one double-hung sash

shed roof

rubblework masonry

brackets

squared oriel

paired windows

sloping pitched roof

porch

plate glass

FIRST FLOOR

porch — pantry — porch

kitchen

dining room

inglenook

living room

hall

vestibule

porch

SECOND FLOOR

bedroom

bath

closets

linen closet

closet

bedroom

bedroom

Bungalows and Small Houses

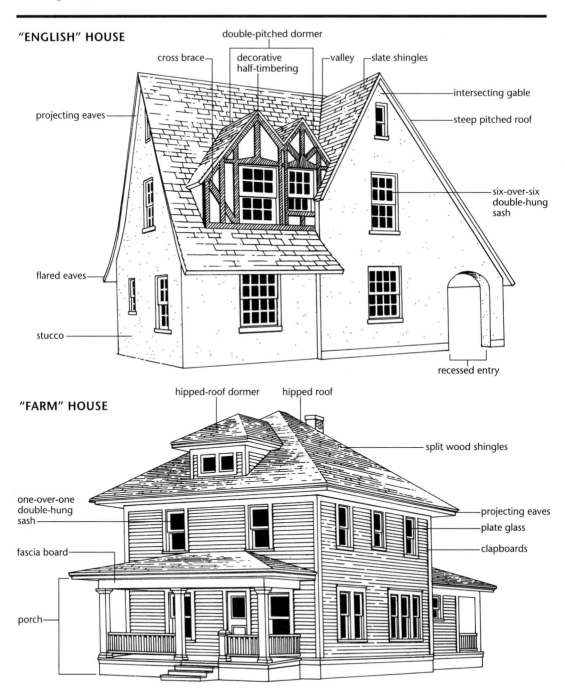

"ENGLISH" HOUSE

double-pitched dormer

cross brace

decorative half-timbering

valley

slate shingles

intersecting gable

steep pitched roof

projecting eaves

six-over-six double-hung sash

flared eaves

stucco

recessed entry

"FARM" HOUSE

hipped-roof dormer

hipped roof

split wood shingles

one-over-one double-hung sash

projecting eaves

plate glass

fascia board

clapboards

porch

Anatomy of a Steel Frame

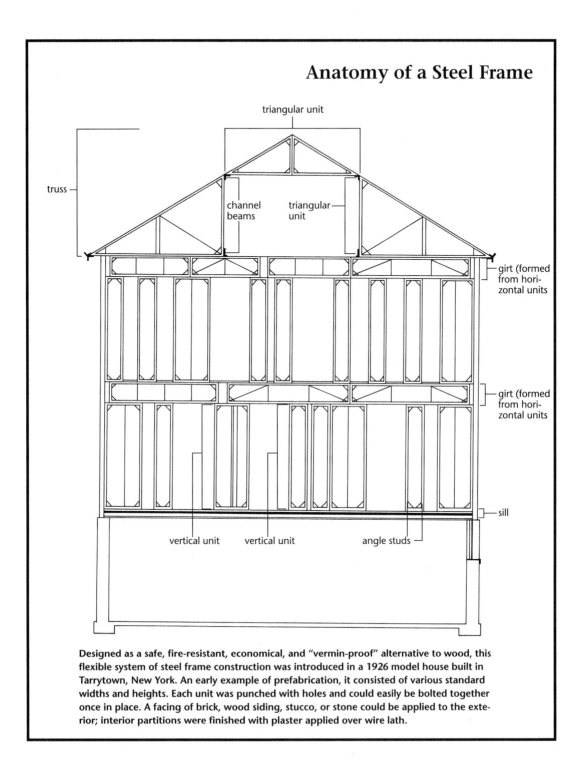

triangular unit

truss

channel beams

triangular unit

girt (formed from horizontal units

girt (formed from horizontal units

sill

vertical unit   vertical unit   angle studs

Designed as a safe, fire-resistant, economical, and "vermin-proof" alternative to wood, this flexible system of steel frame construction was introduced in a 1926 model house built in Tarrytown, New York. An early example of prefabrication, it consisted of various standard widths and heights. Each unit was punched with holes and could easily be bolted together once in place. A facing of brick, wood siding, stucco, or stone could be applied to the exterior; interior partitions were finished with plaster applied over wire lath.

Bungalows and Small Houses

"SPANISH" HOUSE

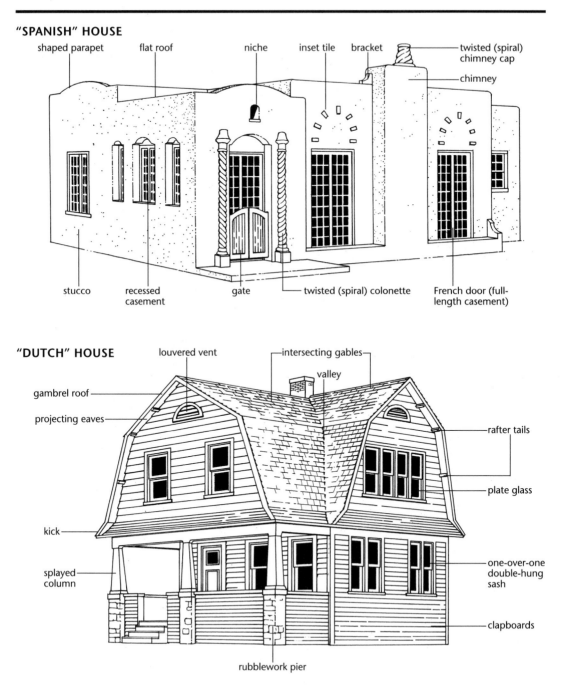

shaped parapet · flat roof · niche · inset tile · bracket · twisted (spiral) chimney cap · chimney

stucco · recessed casement · gate · twisted (spiral) colonette · French door (full-length casement)

"DUTCH" HOUSE

louvered vent · intersecting gables · valley

gambrel roof · projecting eaves · rafter tails · plate glass

kick · one-over-one double-hung sash

splayed column · clapboards

rubblework pier

Bungalows and Small Houses

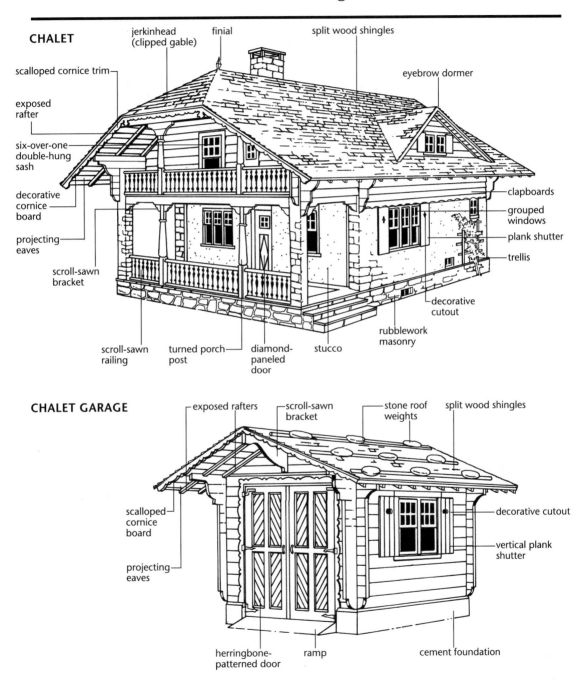

CHALET

jerkinhead (clipped gable)

finial

split wood shingles

scalloped cornice trim

eyebrow dormer

exposed rafter

six-over-one double-hung sash

decorative cornice board

clapboards

grouped windows

plank shutter

projecting eaves

trellis

scroll-sawn bracket

decorative cutout

scroll-sawn railing

turned porch post

diamond-paneled door

stucco

rubblework masonry

CHALET GARAGE

exposed rafters

scroll-sawn bracket

stone roof weights

split wood shingles

scalloped cornice board

decorative cutout

vertical plank shutter

projecting eaves

herringbone-patterned door

ramp

cement foundation

Bungalows and Small Houses

TWO-FAMILY HOUSE

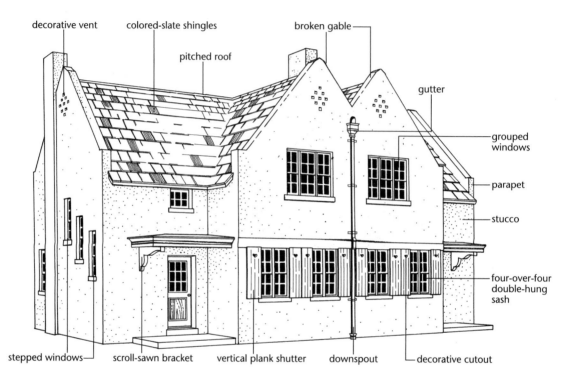

decorative vent   colored-slate shingles   broken gable

pitched roof

gutter

grouped windows

parapet

stucco

four-over-four double-hung sash

stepped windows   scroll-sawn bracket   vertical plank shutter   downspout   decorative cutout

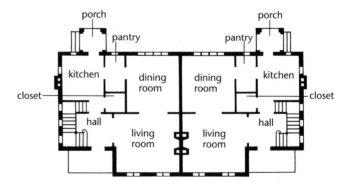

porch   porch

pantry   pantry

closet   kitchen   dining room   dining room   kitchen   closet

hall   living room   living room   hall

Anatomy of Fireproof Construction

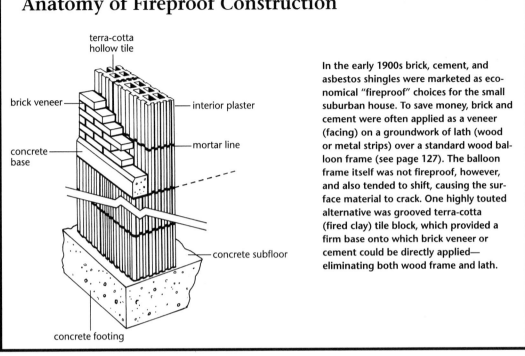

terra-cotta
hollow tile

brick veneer

interior plaster

concrete
base

mortar line

concrete subfloor

concrete footing

In the early 1900s brick, cement, and asbestos shingles were marketed as economical "fireproof" choices for the small suburban house. To save money, brick and cement were often applied as a veneer (facing) on a groundwork of lath (wood or metal strips) over a standard wood balloon frame (see page 127). The balloon frame itself was not fireproof, however, and also tended to shift, causing the surface material to crack. One highly touted alternative was grooved terra-cotta (fired clay) tile block, which provided a firm base onto which brick veneer or cement could be directly applied— eliminating both wood frame and lath.

FIREPROOF HOUSE

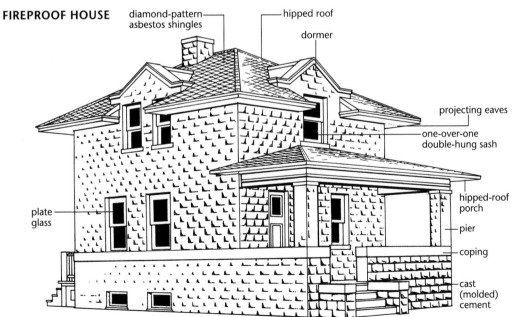

diamond-pattern asbestos shingles

hipped roof

dormer

projecting eaves

one-over-one
double-hung sash

plate
glass

hipped-roof
porch

pier

coping

cast
(molded)
cement

Bungalows and Small Houses

INGLENOOK

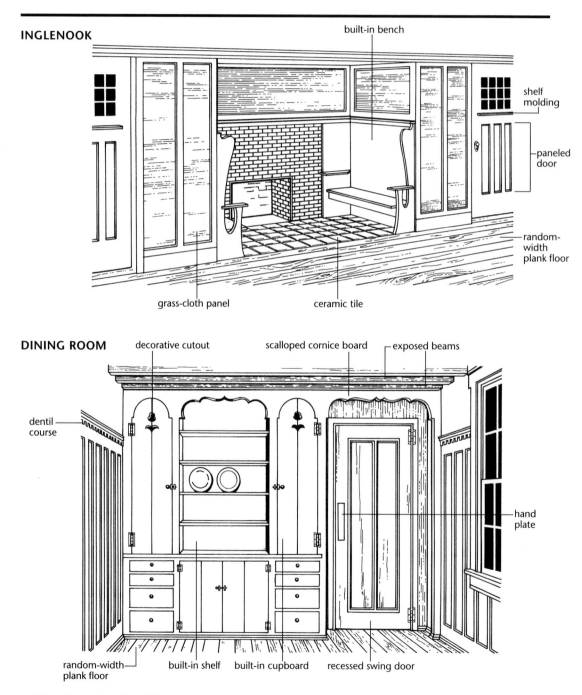

built-in bench

shelf molding

paneled door

random-width plank floor

grass-cloth panel

ceramic tile

DINING ROOM

decorative cutout

scalloped cornice board

exposed beams

dentil course

hand plate

random-width plank floor

built-in shelf

built-in cupboard

recessed swing door

OAK DOORS (INTERIOR)

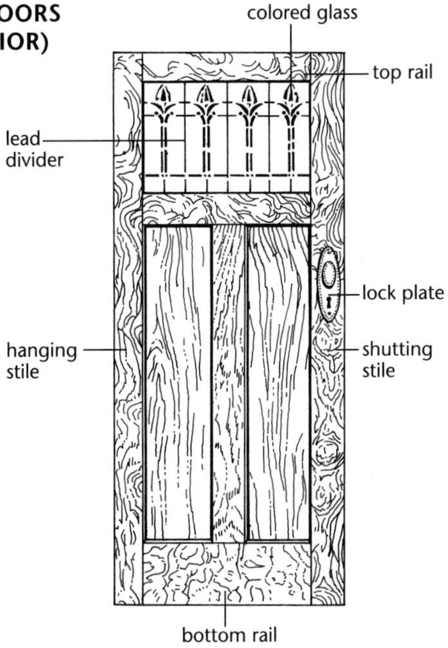

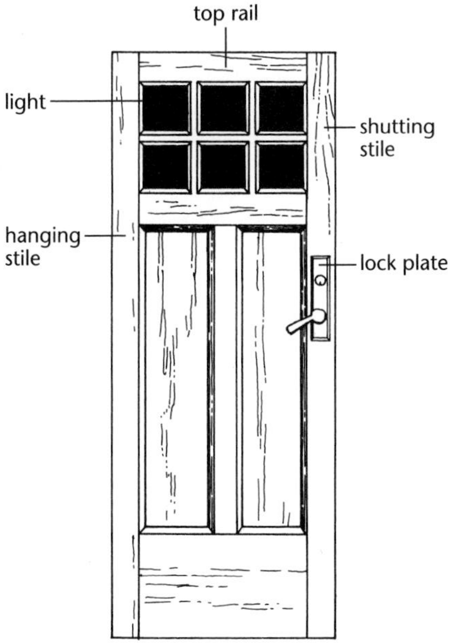

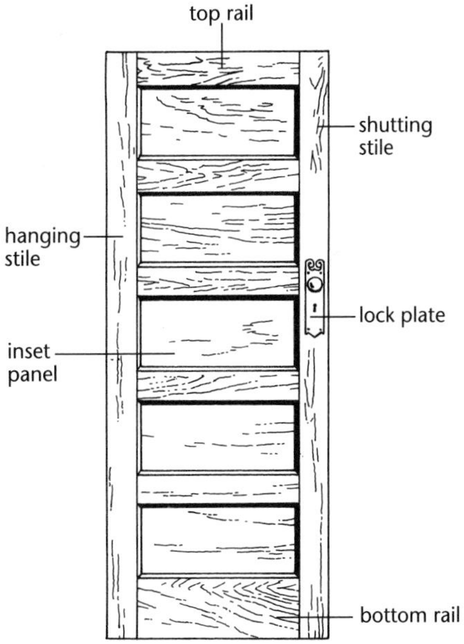

colored glass

top rail

lead divider

lock plate

hanging stile

shutting stile

bottom rail

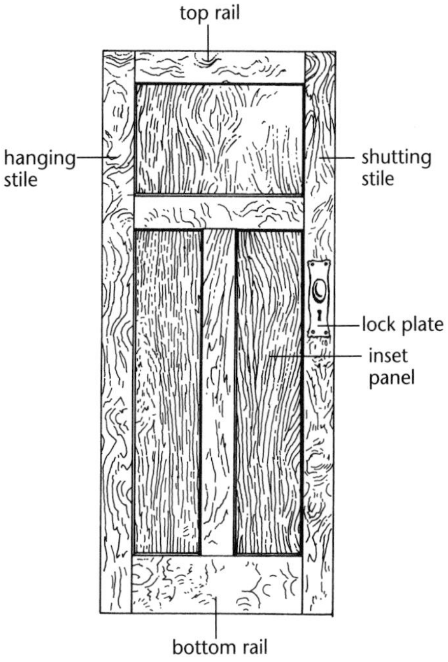

top rail

hanging stile

shutting stile

lock plate

inset panel

bottom rail

top rail

light

shutting stile

hanging stile

lock plate

top rail

shutting stile

hanging stile

lock plate

inset panel

bottom rail

Chapter Ten
Early Modernism

The period between World War I and World War II was one of strong contrasts. With the acceleration of industrialized technology came the wide availability of new materials such as plywood, reinforced concrete, steel, and chrome; mechanized building processes; and the prefabrication of standardized, interchangeable building elements. For the most part, however, the architectural taste of the mainstream remained stubbornly grounded in the predictable period revivals, which offered a comforting nostalgia in the face of the machine age. Modern European-based influences, such as Art Deco, only had a limited impact on single-family house design.

In the 1920s the modern movement began to gain momentum in the United States with the arrival of the Austrian architects Rudolph Schindler (1887–1953) and Richard Neutra (1892–1970) and the Swiss William Lescaze (1896–1969). They were joined in the 1930s by several Bauhaus architects, such as Ludwig Mies van der Rohe (1886–1969) and Walter Gropius (1883–1969), who were driven out of Europe by the Nazis. The work of these innovators represented the early tenets of the International Style, rooted in the cubic architecture of the Dutch De Stijl movement and the idealized industrial aesthetic of the Bauhaus, the German school of architecture Gropius had founded in 1919.

The International Style fully embraced the industrial ideal, advocating a clean break with the past. Progressive thinking, however, was slow to find a footing in America, and the geometrically precise aesthetic of early Modernism never had the same widespread acceptance for residential architecture as the familiar bungalows and cozy Dutch, Tudor, and Colonial houses of suburbia.

Early Modernism

CIRCULAR HOUSE

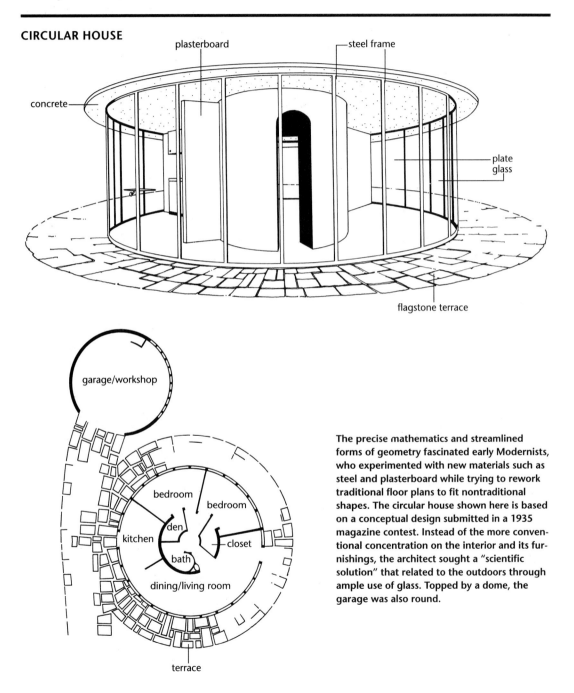

plasterboard

steel frame

concrete

plate glass

flagstone terrace

garage/workshop

bedroom

bedroom

kitchen

den

closet

bath

dining/living room

terrace

The precise mathematics and streamlined forms of geometry fascinated early Modernists, who experimented with new materials such as steel and plasterboard while trying to rework traditional floor plans to fit nontraditional shapes. The circular house shown here is based on a conceptual design submitted in a 1935 magazine contest. Instead of the more conventional concentration on the interior and its furnishings, the architect sought a "scientific solution" that related to the outdoors through ample use of glass. Topped by a dome, the garage was also round.

International Style

SUBURBAN HOUSE

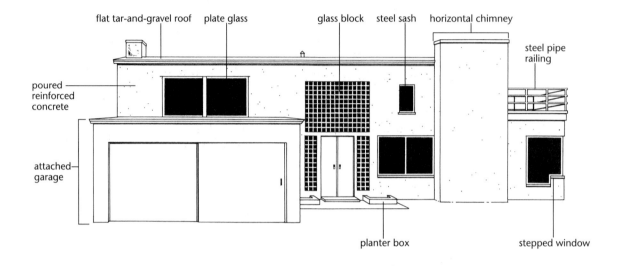

flat tar-and-gravel roof   plate glass

glass block   steel sash   horizontal chimney

steel pipe railing

poured reinforced concrete

attached garage

planter box

stepped window

In 1932 Alfred Barr, Jr., the director of the Museum of Modern Art in New York, mounted a groundbreaking show called "Modern Architecture: International Exhibition," organized by the American architect Philip Johnson (b. 1906) and architectural historian Henry-Russell Hitchcock (1903–87). That exhibition gave the Modernist movement in Europe and the United States its name.

The phrase "less is more" is often invoked to explain the International style, which rejected all historical stylistic references in favor of clean, volumetric forms completely devoid of applied pattern, texture, and "superfluous" ornament. This mode of building, in which each element was defined as clearly as possible, was dependent on industrial technology. The use of steel and concrete as structural elements made the load-bearing wall unnecessary and encouraged the use of large expanses of glass. Filled with light, interiors were opened up and fitted with simple, often built-in furniture to keep the space flowing and free of clutter.

DINING AREA

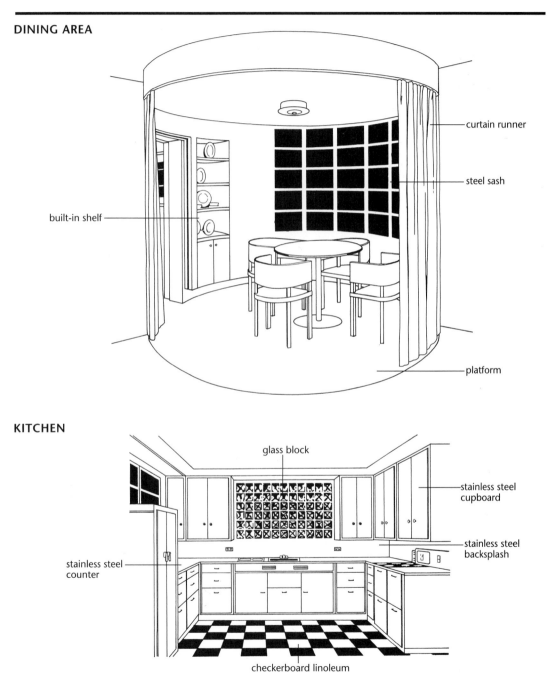

curtain runner

steel sash

built-in shelf

platform

KITCHEN

glass block

stainless steel cupboard

stainless steel backsplash

stainless steel counter

checkerboard linoleum

Moderne

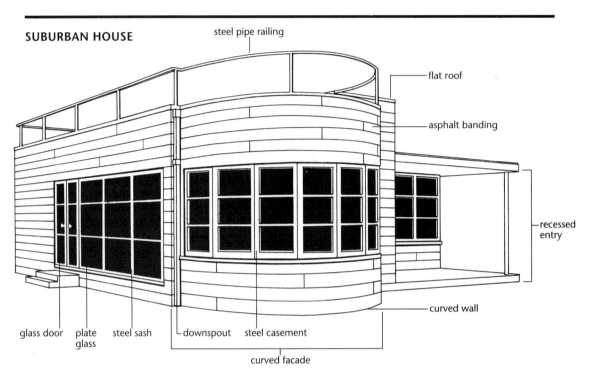

steel pipe railing

flat roof

asphalt banding

recessed entry

curved wall

glass door · plate glass · steel sash · downspout · steel casement

curved facade

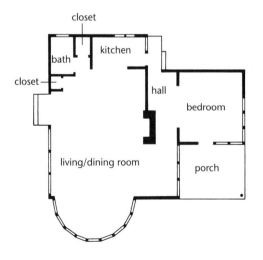

closet
bath
kitchen
closet
hall
bedroom
living/dining room
porch

Making a short appearance in America in the 1930s, the smooth-surfaced, flat-roofed Moderne-style house was an essay in streamlined geometry, stripped of ornament except for an occasional frieze of horizontal grooves designed as "speed lines." Such streamlining was also reflected in curving wall planes. It expressed not only economy of line, but also a fascination with the aerodynamic speed and romance of the locomotive, the airplane, and the ocean liner (whose portholes often showed up as windows). In domestic architecture, the Moderne style was used primarily for small, single-family houses. These were found in the residential areas of small cities, in suburbs, and in seaside communities.

Moderne

SEASIDE HOUSE

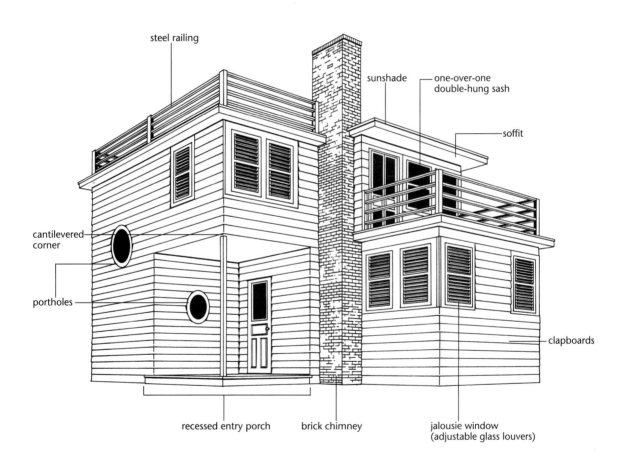

steel railing

sunshade

one-over-one
double-hung sash

soffit

cantilevered
corner

portholes

clapboards

recessed entry porch

brick chimney

jalousie window
(adjustable glass louvers)

Art Deco

DOORS

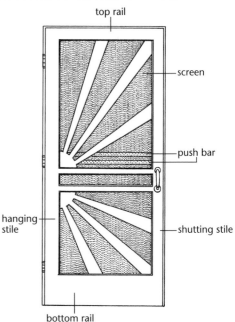

lock plate

aluminum grille

kick plate

top rail

screen

push bar

hanging stile

shutting stile

bottom rail

The term "Art Deco" derives from the title of a 1925 Paris design fair, called the *Exposition Internationale des Arts Décoratifs et Industriels Modernes* (*Arts Deco*, for short), where numerous rooms in the style were on display. Art Deco had begun to appear in Europe before World War I. It was a curious blend of Modernism, history, and fantasy, influenced by the speed-infused aesthetic of the Italian Futurists and the mystical images of Mayan, Assyrian, and Moorish cultures. These, in turn, were expressed by the richest of materials: marble, colored terrazzo, chrome, and ebony.

Adopted in America primarily in the 1930s, the Art Deco style was seldom used for single-family houses, but reached its apogee in New York, Los Angeles, and Miami, primarily in apartment buildings and city skyscrapers, which seemed best suited to this style of applied, concentrated decoration. Doorways, in particular, showed off the stylized forms and tropical motifs.

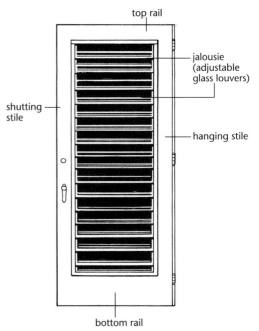

top rail

jalousie (adjustable glass louvers)

shutting stile

hanging stile

bottom rail

A-Frame

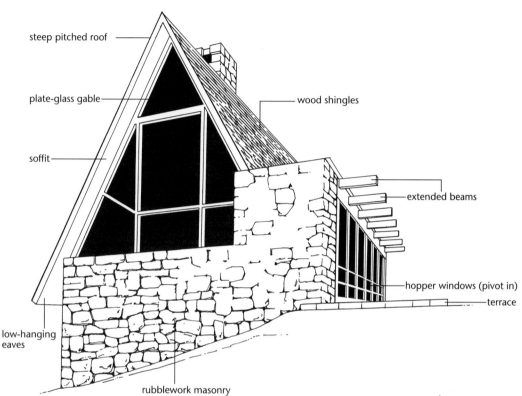

steep pitched roof

plate-glass gable

soffit

wood shingles

extended beams

hopper windows (pivot in)

terrace

low-hanging eaves

rubblework masonry

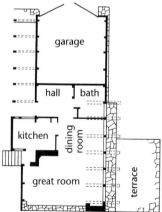

garage

hall   bath

kitchen

dining room

great room

terrace

In 1934 the architect Rudolph Schindler designed a modern weekend house for a client, Gisela Bennati, in Lake Arrowhead, California. A planned community, Lake Arrowhead required all new houses to be designed in the Norman Revival style (see page 193). Schindler responded rather sarcastically with a design dominated by a "Norman" roof that fell from the ridge all the way to the ground. Challenged by a dubious jury, the architect countered with photographs of steep-roofed houses, and as none of the panelists had ever been to France, he handily won the argument.

The result was the first A-frame built in America. True to the Modernist credo, Schindler sheathed the interior in one of the latest industrial products—plywood—and opened up the gable ends with large panes of glass. The open plan incorporated one large living/dining area and a built-in garage.

Chapter Eleven
The Postwar Era

The decades immediately following World War II constituted a boom era of unparalleled prosperity. This was, indeed, the dawn of the "affluent society," and no one was quicker to capitalize on it than the leaders of the housing industry. "DREAMS CAN COME TRUE!" promised the banner headline of the 1945 issue of the *Small Homes Annual*. The editors went on to assure their readers that the new stock plans offered on their pages were not for the cold, boxlike houses of the "modernistic" era. "They will be functional," they said, "but the primary function of a house is to be a *home*."

The house designs of the postwar era placed a new emphasis on comfort, efficiency, and informal "one-story living." The single-story house permitted shorter plumbing lines and heating ducts, eliminated annoying and hazardous stairs, and, most significant, allowed easy access to the yard or garden and the all-important patio barbecue.

As labor, land, and material prices climbed in the 1950s and 1960s, the search for more space at less cost eliminated halls and yielded the multi-use living/dining room, family room/kitchen, and guest room/study, as well as built-in storage units and furniture, the freestanding fireplace, the "conversation pit," and the carport. Experiments in open planning coincided with new developments in mass-produced materials, including reinforced concrete, long-span steel beams, particleboard, laminated wood, and plywood. The idea that technology and advanced engineering could solve any problem was wholeheartedly embraced, producing experiments in virtually every kind of construction.

TWO-FAMILY HOUSE

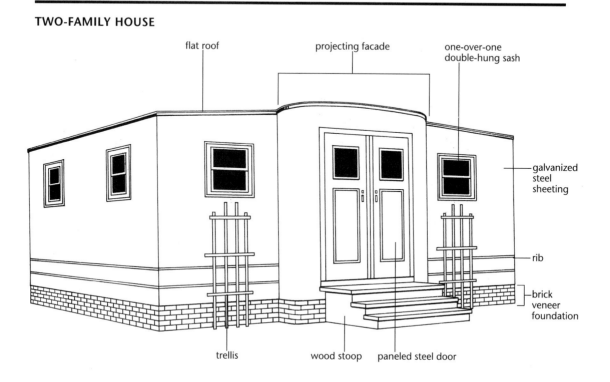

flat roof

projecting facade

one-over-one
double-hung sash

galvanized
steel
sheeting

rib

brick
veneer
foundation

trellis

wood stoop

paneled steel door

After World War II, a severe housing shortage in America resulted in a market for pre-fabricated industrial homes that could be arranged in temporary settlements just outside existing developments. Not only were these cheap, but they could also be put up miraculously fast. The parts for the steel-sheathed "Palace" on this page, for example, were transported by truck from factory to building site. Within three hours of delivery, claimed the advertisement, the house, complete with furniture, conventional plumbing, heating, wiring, and kitchen appliances, was ready for two families. The prefab Quonset hut (see page 232) had few amenities and only a chemical toilet, but manufacturers claimed it was immune to sagging, warping, rotting, fire, and termites.

Prefab Housing

QUONSET HUT

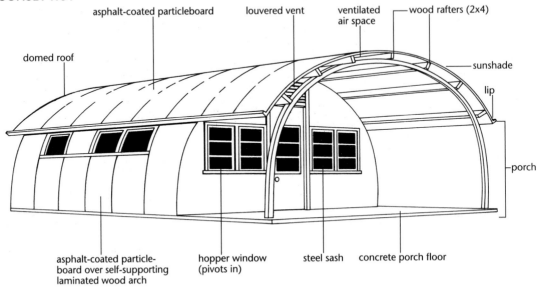

asphalt-coated particleboard · louvered vent · ventilated air space · wood rafters (2x4)

domed roof · sunshade · lip · porch

asphalt-coated particle-board over self-supporting laminated wood arch · hopper window (pivots in) · steel sash · concrete porch floor

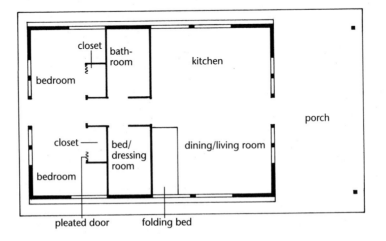

closet · bathroom · kitchen

bedroom

porch

closet · bed/dressing room · dining/living room

bedroom

pleated door · folding bed

Prefab Housing

DYMAXION DEPLOYMENT UNIT

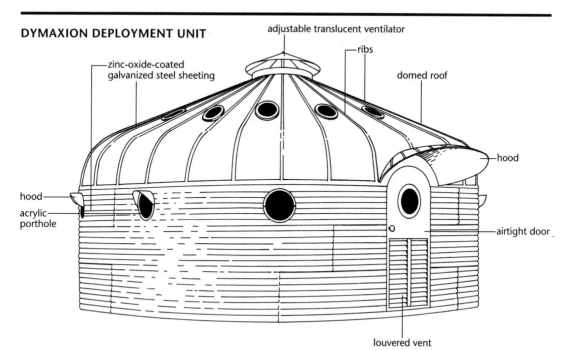

- adjustable translucent ventilator
- ribs
- domed roof
- zinc-oxide-coated galvanized steel sheeting
- hood
- hood
- acrylic porthole
- airtight door
- louvered vent

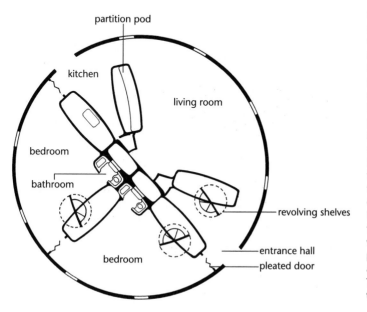

- partition pod
- kitchen
- living room
- bedroom
- bathroom
- revolving shelves
- bedroom
- entrance hall
- pleated door

In 1941 architect R. Buckminster Fuller (1895–1983) offered a new, improved version of a model house he had designed in 1927. Fuller claimed that the Dymaxion (from "dynamism," "maximum," and "ions") Deployment Unit II could house a small family at a cost of less than a dollar per square foot. The prefab Dymaxion house was built in reverse of the usual practice of ground up. First, the metal dome was assembled on the ground and raised on a temporary pole; the wall sections were then applied from the top down. The corrugated, galvanized steel shell was laminated inside with fiberglass insulation and the round portholes filled with plastic—the first time this high-priority World War II material was used anywhere other than in an airplane. The Dymaxion came complete with all the materials and a tool kit.

Prefab Housing

MOBILE HOME

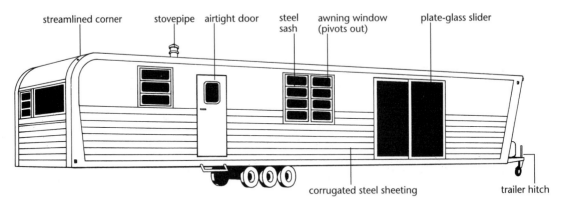

streamlined corner   stovepipe   airtight door   steel sash   awning window (pivots out)   plate-glass slider

corrugated steel sheeting   trailer hitch

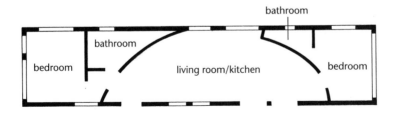

bathroom

bedroom   bathroom   living room/kitchen   bedroom

The first mass-produced mobile home, credited to the Covered Wagon Company of Detroit, appeared in America around 1933. This novel trailer had an inauspicious start, originally used as cheap, temporary housing in empty lots that were once called the "tin-can camps of Depression and wartime migrants." Trailer parks were not taken seriously until World War II, when such encampments were used to house thousands of workers in and around war-production centers. The trailer park, where people would often live in their mobile homes for years on end, gained a better reputation in the 1950s, when increasing numbers of professionals and retirees settled into these semipermanent communities. One other reason for respect: models over twenty-five feet long now had bathrooms. By the end of the 1950s, fully furnished models, with at least three rooms and a bath, sold for between $3,500 and $13,000.

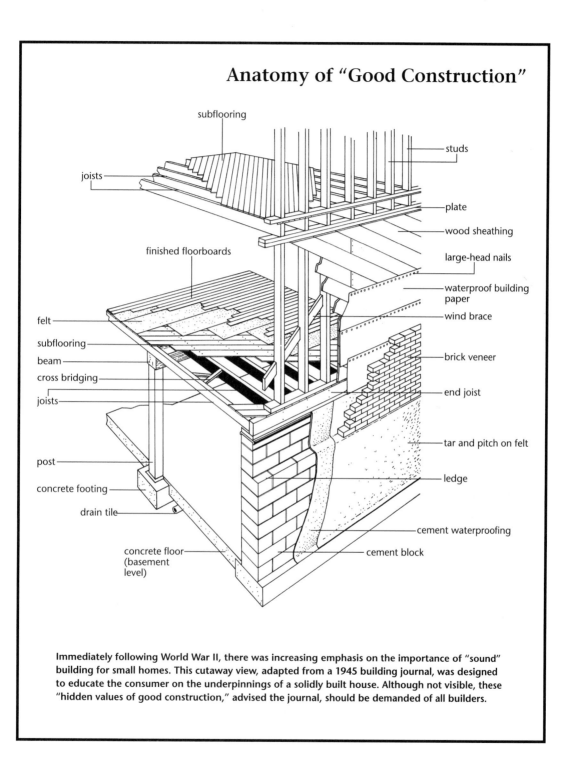

Anatomy of "Good Construction"

subflooring

joists

studs

plate

wood sheathing

finished floorboards

large-head nails

waterproof building paper

wind brace

felt

brick veneer

subflooring

beam

cross bridging

end joist

joists

tar and pitch on felt

post

ledge

concrete footing

drain tile

cement waterproofing

concrete floor (basement level)

cement block

Immediately following World War II, there was increasing emphasis on the importance of "sound" building for small homes. This cutaway view, adapted from a 1945 building journal, was designed to educate the consumer on the underpinnings of a solidly built house. Although not visible, these "hidden values of good construction," advised the journal, should be demanded of all builders.

Ranch House

The ranch house was perhaps the ultimate symbol of the postwar American dream: a safe, affordable home promising efficiency and casual living. California architects introduced the "close-to-the-ground" ranch in the 1930s, evidently finding inspiration in the one-story plan of the Spanish rancho of the Southwest. By the late 1940s, this new house type had caught on across the country and still remains popular.

With its open kitchen/living area, the ranch was specifically geared to casual entertaining. Another key selling point was the desirable indoor/outdoor living promised by the one-story layout, which featured sliding glass doors, picture windows, and terraces and patios secluded in a rear yard. "The ability to move in and out of your house freely, without the hindrance of steps," boasted *Sunset* magazine's 1946 edition of *Western Ranch Houses*, "is one of the things that makes living in it pleasant and informal."

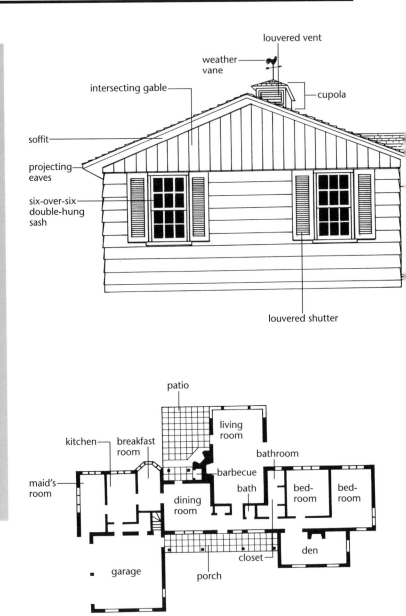

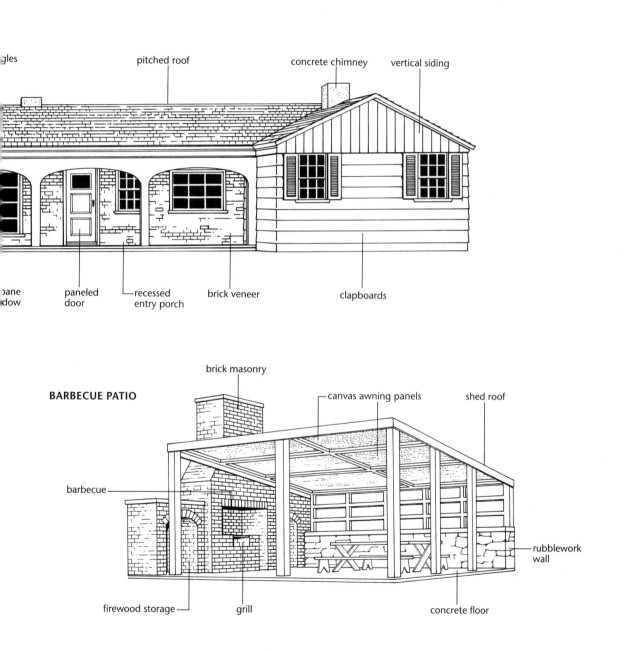

gles

pitched roof

concrete chimney

vertical siding

pane dow

paneled door

recessed entry porch

brick veneer

clapboards

BARBECUE PATIO

brick masonry

canvas awning panels

shed roof

barbecue

rubblework wall

firewood storage

grill

concrete floor

Ranch House

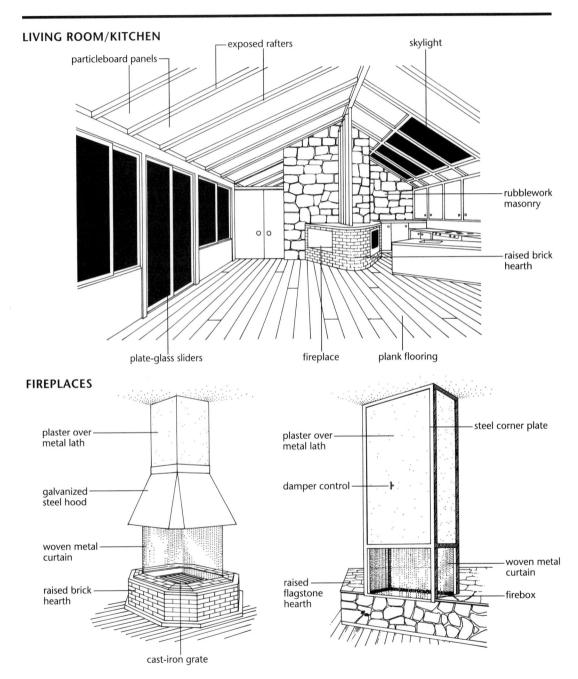

LIVING ROOM/KITCHEN

particleboard panels

exposed rafters

skylight

rubblework masonry

raised brick hearth

plate-glass sliders

fireplace

plank flooring

FIREPLACES

plaster over metal lath

galvanized steel hood

woven metal curtain

raised brick hearth

cast-iron grate

plaster over metal lath

damper control

raised flagstone hearth

steel corner plate

woven metal curtain

firebox

The Economical Small House

SMALL SUBURBAN HOUSE

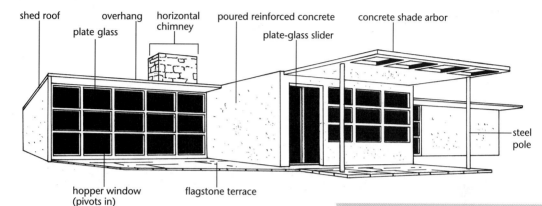

shed roof overhang horizontal chimney poured reinforced concrete concrete shade arbor

plate glass plate-glass slider

steel pole

hopper window (pivots in) flagstone terrace

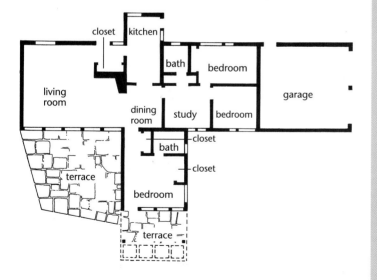

closet kitchen

bath bedroom

living room garage

dining room study bedroom

closet

bath

closet

terrace

bedroom

terrace

Frequently built from mail-order plans, the economical small house of the postwar era offered a cheap alternative to the ranch house. Prospective buyers could leaf through plan books and magazines; choose a model named the "Monarch," the "Tarry," or perhaps the "Alpine;" and for the price of a stamp and a few dollars become the proud owners of a complete set of working blueprints and specifications.

Houses built from stock plans were touted as "pretested," offering a fine "custom" design without the considerable cost of hiring a professional architect. To keep prices down, the plan companies specified inexpensive factory-made plywood or prefab wood siding and stucco. The convenient one-story plan proliferated, but there was also the new split-level, or "hi-ranch design" (see page 242). This boasted vinyl tile floors, interior walls of gypsum (plasterboard), and a lower level often designed to be left unfinished until the space was needed.

The Economical Small House

SMALL SUBURBAN HOUSE

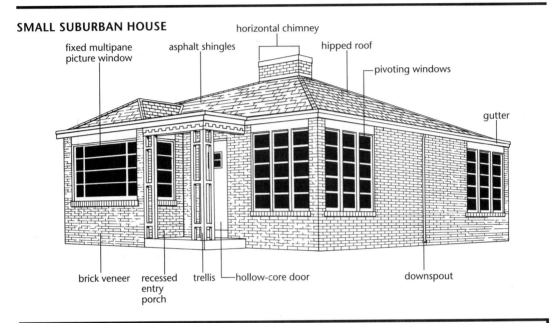

fixed multipane picture window
horizontal chimney
asphalt shingles
hipped roof
pivoting windows
gutter
brick veneer
recessed entry porch
trellis
hollow-core door
downspout

Anatomy of Brick Veneer

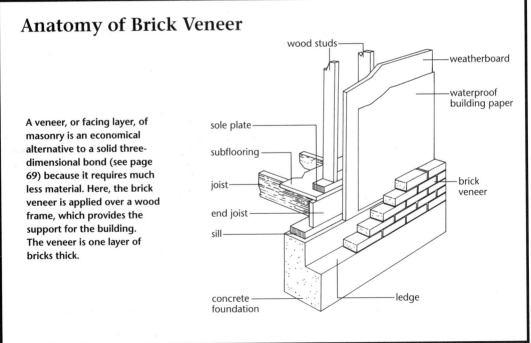

A veneer, or facing layer, of masonry is an economical alternative to a solid three-dimensional bond (see page 69) because it requires much less material. Here, the brick veneer is applied over a wood frame, which provides the support for the building. The veneer is one layer of bricks thick.

wood studs
weatherboard
waterproof building paper
sole plate
subflooring
joist
brick veneer
end joist
sill
concrete foundation
ledge

The Economical Small House

SMALL SUBURBAN HOUSE

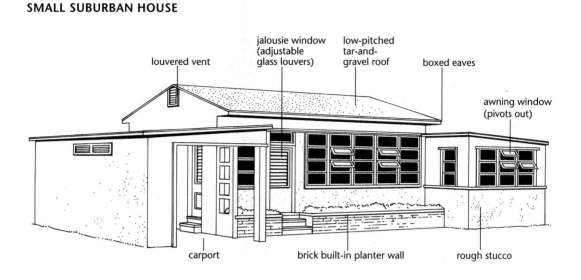

louvered vent

jalousie window (adjustable glass louvers)

low-pitched tar-and-gravel roof

boxed eaves

awning window (pivots out)

carport

brick built-in planter wall

rough stucco

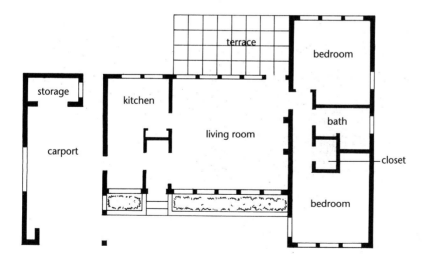

storage

carport

kitchen

terrace

bedroom

living room

bath

closet

bedroom

The Economical Small House

SPLIT-LEVEL HOUSE

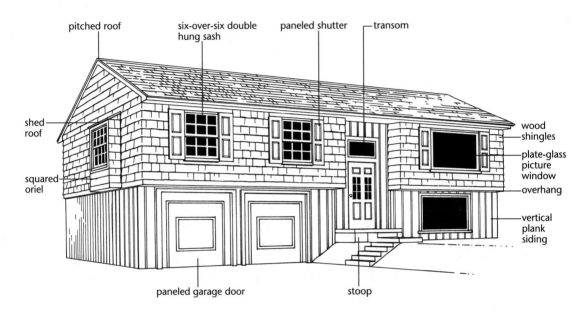

pitched roof

six-over-six double hung sash

paneled shutter

transom

shed roof

squared oriel

wood shingles

plate-glass picture window

overhang

vertical plank siding

paneled garage door

stoop

MAIN FLOOR

patio

bath

bedroom

bath-room

kitchen

bedroom

bedroom

living/ dining room

The Traditional House

REGENCY-STYLE HOUSE

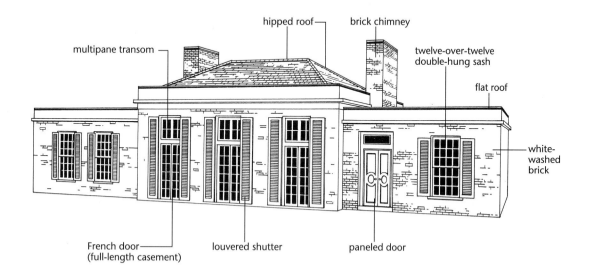

hipped roof — brick chimney

multipane transom

twelve-over-twelve
double-hung sash

flat roof

white-
washed
brick

French door
(full-length casement)

louvered shutter

paneled door

Although new ideas meant new designs in the postwar era, traditional styles never lost their popularity. The low-slung Regency-style house, above, with its floor-to-ceiling windows, was especially well suited to comfortable one-story living. As always, Colonial-style houses were in demand, especially reproductions of houses from Williamsburg, the restored capital of 18th-century Virginia that had been opened as the country's first outdoor museum in 1926.

All designs, of course, were freely updated for "modern" living. "If cooking's going to be fun," wrote one designer of a small traditional house in 1954, "we might as well make a family room out of the kitchen."

The Traditional House

WILLIAMSBURG-STYLE HOUSE

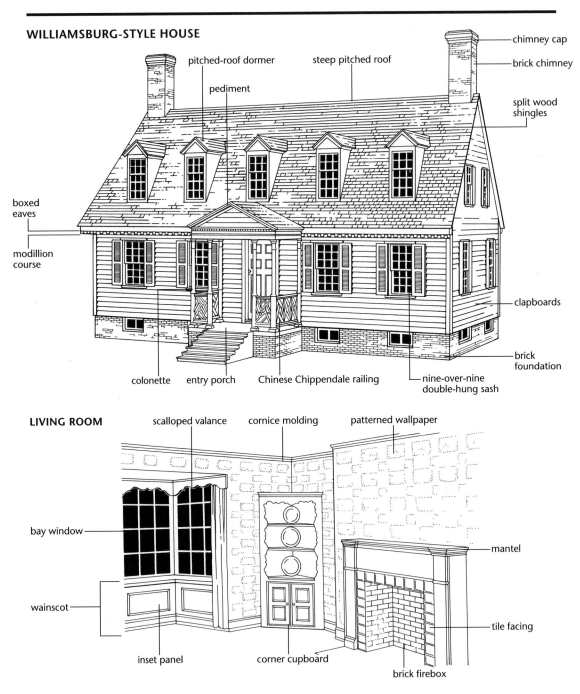

chimney cap

brick chimney

split wood shingles

pitched-roof dormer

steep pitched roof

pediment

boxed eaves

modillion course

clapboards

colonette

entry porch

Chinese Chippendale railing

brick foundation

nine-over-nine double-hung sash

LIVING ROOM

scalloped valance

cornice molding

patterned wallpaper

bay window

mantel

wainscot

tile facing

inset panel

corner cupboard

brick firebox

The Traditional House

COLONIAL-STYLE HOUSE

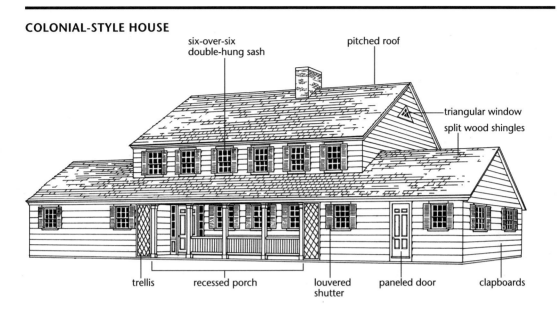

six-over-six double-hung sash

pitched roof

triangular window

split wood shingles

trellis

recessed porch

louvered shutter

paneled door

clapboards

KITCHEN

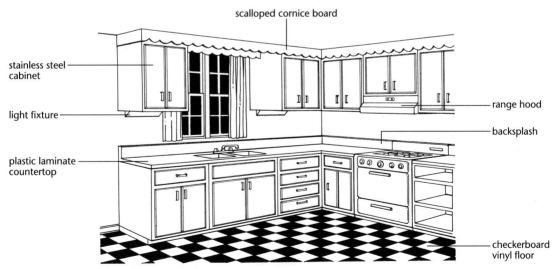

scalloped cornice board

stainless steel cabinet

light fixture

plastic laminate countertop

range hood

backsplash

checkerboard vinyl floor

Anatomy of a Platform Frame

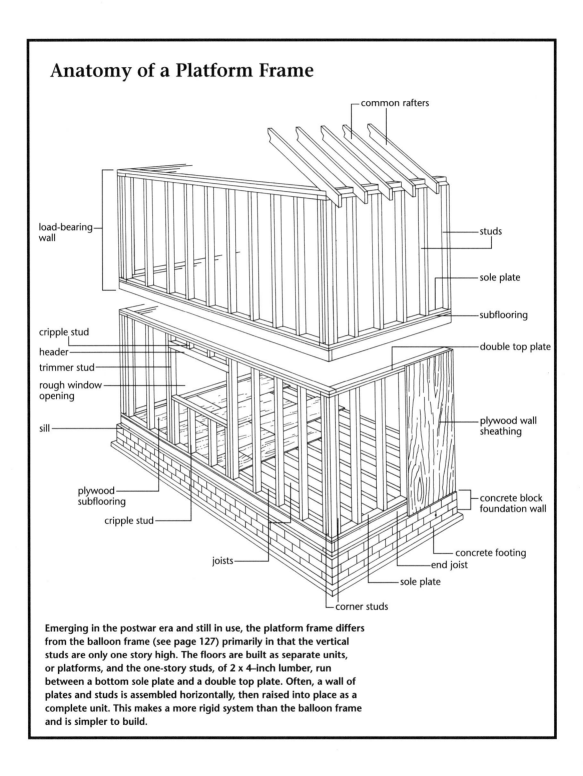

common rafters

load-bearing wall

studs

sole plate

subflooring

cripple stud

header

trimmer stud

rough window opening

sill

double top plate

plywood wall sheathing

plywood subflooring

cripple stud

joists

concrete block foundation wall

concrete footing

end joist

sole plate

corner studs

Emerging in the postwar era and still in use, the platform frame differs from the balloon frame (see page 127) primarily in that the vertical studs are only one story high. The floors are built as separate units, or platforms, and the one-story studs, of 2 x 4–inch lumber, run between a bottom sole plate and a double top plate. Often, a wall of plates and studs is assembled horizontally, then raised into place as a complete unit. This makes a more rigid system than the balloon frame and is simpler to build.

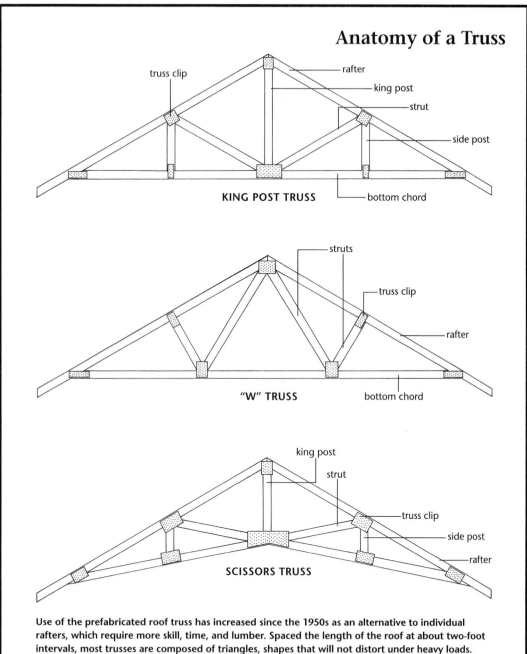

Anatomy of a Truss

KING POST TRUSS

- truss clip
- rafter
- king post
- strut
- side post
- bottom chord

"W" TRUSS

- struts
- truss clip
- rafter
- bottom chord

SCISSORS TRUSS

- king post
- strut
- truss clip
- side post
- rafter

Use of the prefabricated roof truss has increased since the 1950s as an alternative to individual rafters, which require more skill, time, and lumber. Spaced the length of the roof at about two-foot intervals, most trusses are composed of triangles, shapes that will not distort under heavy loads. The three variations above commonly used for pitched roofs, look similar, but the web pattern in each actually distributes force quite differently; thus, each is rated for different loads and spans.

The Futuristic Home

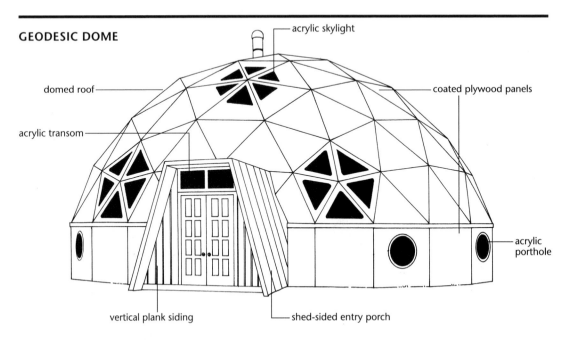

GEODESIC DOME

acrylic skylight

domed roof

coated plywood panels

acrylic transom

acrylic porthole

vertical plank siding

shed-sided entry porch

While tradition held through the 1950s and 1960s, innovative designers were always looking for new expressions. As the space age unfolded, visions of the ultra-modern future captured the American imagination, sometimes inspiring house designs that would have looked more at home on other planets than on Earth. New building methods made virtually any structural feat possible, and bizarre shapes were no problem. Most fell by the wayside, but the geodesic dome (above), patented by Buckminster Fuller in 1954, caught on in the 1960s, and by the next decade more than 80,000 sets of plans for dome homes had been sold.

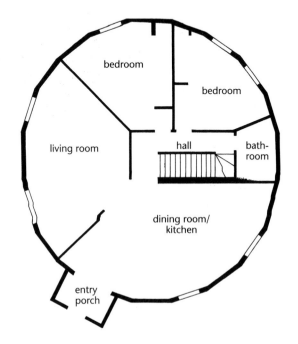

bedroom

bedroom

living room

hall

bathroom

dining room/ kitchen

entry porch

The Futuristic Home

BUBBLE HOUSE

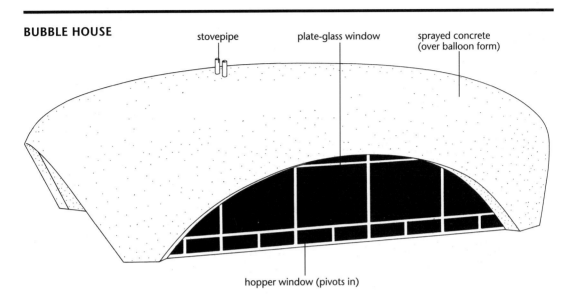

stovepipe

plate-glass window

sprayed concrete
(over balloon form)

hopper window (pivots in)

The bubble house was based on a construction technique known as Airform, patented by California architect Wallace Neff around 1940 and used sporadically in the 1950s. After the foundation was poured, a balloon was stretched over a steel cable, inflated, coated with reinforcing, then sprayed with concrete. A compressor kept the balloon full until the concrete had set, and then the balloon was deflated and removed.

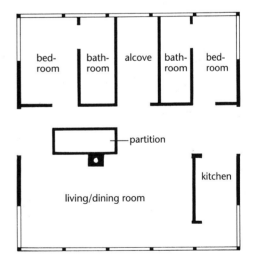

bed-
room

bath-
room

alcove

bath-
room

bed-
room

partition

kitchen

living/dining room

The Futuristic Home

EARTH-SHELTERED HOUSE

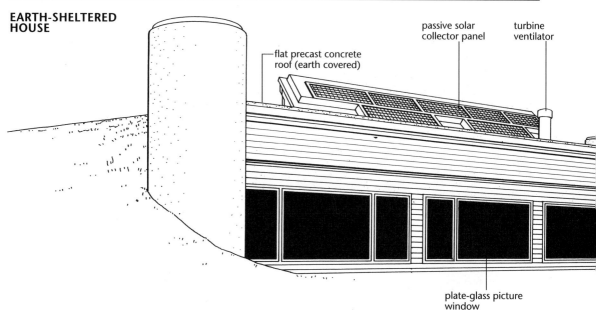

passive solar collector panel

turbine ventilator

flat precast concrete roof (earth covered)

plate-glass picture window

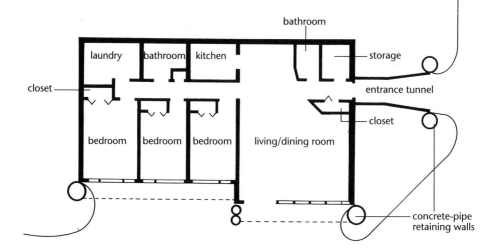

bathroom

laundry   bathroom   kitchen

storage

closet

entrance tunnel

bedroom   bedroom   bedroom

living/dining room

closet

concrete-pipe retaining walls

The Futuristic Home

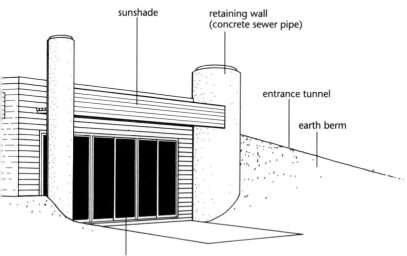

sunshade

retaining wall
(concrete sewer pipe)

entrance tunnel

earth berm

plate-glass slider

CONSTRUCTION DETAIL

(FRONT)

metal flashing

plywood curb

fiberglass insulation

steel truss

sun-shade

roll-up sunshade

concrete-pipe retaining wall

earth

drainage layer (sand or gravel)

plywood support fin

rigid insulation

concrete plank

concrete block

(BACK)

waterproofing

heat duct

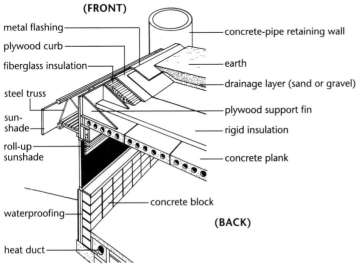

The concept of the quiet, energy-efficient, earth-sheltered house, in which the roof and at least three sides of the structure are covered with soil, was developed in the early 1960s as an outgrowth of atomic fallout shelters, and its popularity grew in the next decades with increased awareness of environmental concerns. The primary building material is typically concrete, which acts as a thermal mass. The insulating soil helps warm the structure in cool weather and draws heat out in warm months. Solar panels collect and store natural energy, while south-facing windows capture low-angle winter sunlight.

Chapter Twelve
Contemporary Trends

America's era of post–World War II affluence had come to a definite end by the 1970s. One major reason was the Vietnam War; as military activity increased overseas and energy costs skyrocketed at home, the United States went into a deep economic recession. Many small architectural firms closed, and those that survived increasingly sought economical alternative designs, developing solar technology in tandem with the growing interest in environmentalism, and turning to adaptive redesign of old buildings for new uses.

At an individual level, architects in the 1960s and 1970s were still exploring Modernist expressions. Dissatisfaction was growing, however, as it became increasingly apparent that an abstract approach often failed to take into account the needs and effects of specific sites, climates, and materials. In 1975 an exhibition of project drawings from the Ecole des Beaux-Arts mounted by the Museum of Modern Art in New York recognized and confirmed the interest in a return to architectural ornament and traditional academic solutions to building problems.

This trend had already become evident in Postmodern architecture, which emerged in the 1960s in reaction to the stark aesthetic of the International style. Mies van der Rohe reportedly had declared "Less is more" in the 1920s, but forty years later the Philadelphia architect Robert Venturi (b. 1925) countered with "Less is a bore." To the Postmodernist eyes of Venturi and many others, ornament and historical references set a mood, providing wit and a sense of scale and interest, and also humanized a building. Neither movement is dead. The tension between respect for the lessons of history and the quest for originality and modern, independent expression continues today.

252

SEASIDE HOUSE

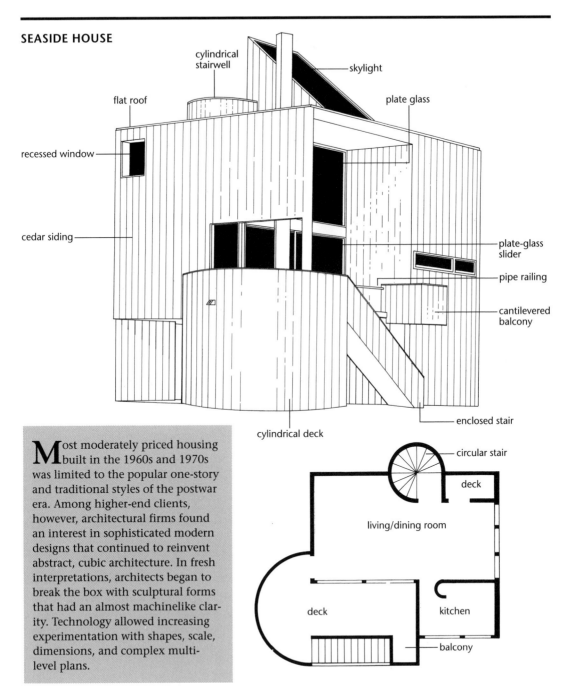

cylindrical stairwell

skylight

flat roof

plate glass

recessed window

cedar siding

plate-glass slider

pipe railing

cantilevered balcony

enclosed stair

cylindrical deck

circular stair

deck

living/dining room

deck

kitchen

balcony

Most moderately priced housing built in the 1960s and 1970s was limited to the popular one-story and traditional styles of the postwar era. Among higher-end clients, however, architectural firms found an interest in sophisticated modern designs that continued to reinvent abstract, cubic architecture. In fresh interpretations, architects began to break the box with sculptural forms that had an almost machinelike clarity. Technology allowed increasing experimentation with shapes, scale, dimensions, and complex multilevel plans.

Modernism

SEASIDE HOUSE

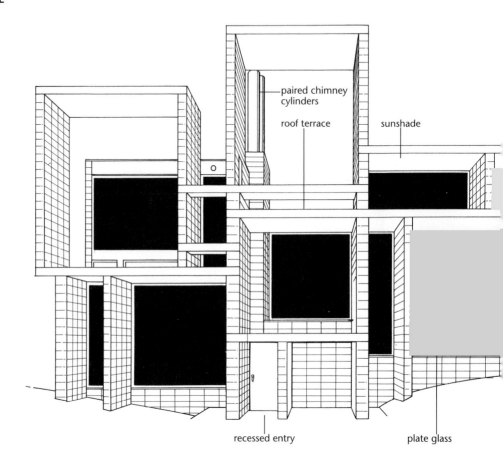

paired chimney
cylinders

roof terrace

sunshade

recessed entry

plate glass

Modernism

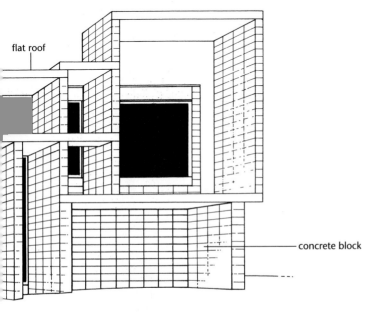

flat roof

concrete block

FIRST FLOOR

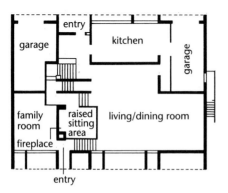

entry

garage

kitchen

garage

family room

raised sitting area

living/dining room

fireplace

entry

SECOND FLOOR

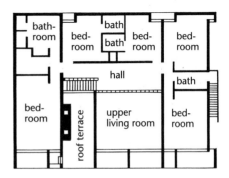

bath-room

bedroom

bath

bath

bedroom

bedroom

bedroom

hall

bath

roof terrace

upper living room

bedroom

Modernism

SOLAR HOUSE

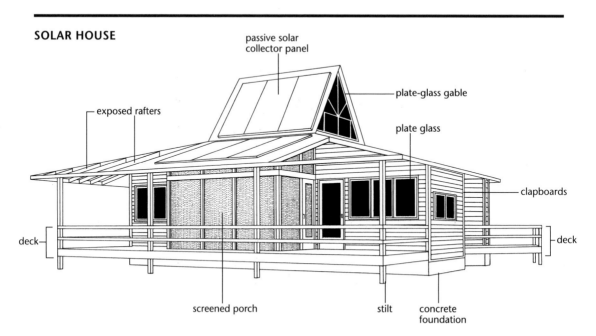

passive solar collector panel

plate-glass gable

exposed rafters

plate glass

clapboards

deck

deck

screened porch

stilt

concrete foundation

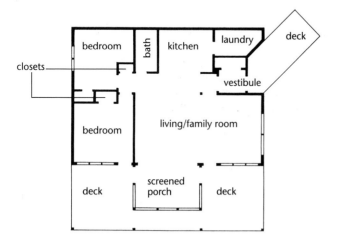

bedroom

bath

kitchen

laundry

deck

closets

vestibule

bedroom

living/family room

deck

screened porch

deck

SOLAR HOUSE

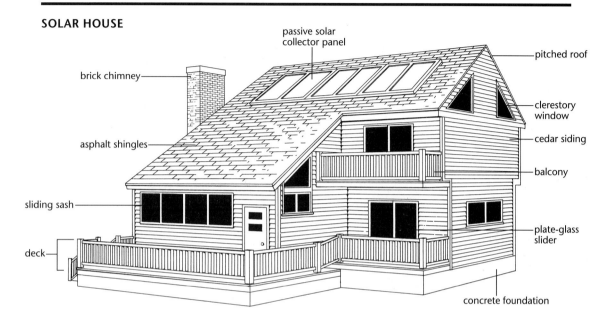

passive solar collector panel

pitched roof

brick chimney

clerestory window

cedar siding

asphalt shingles

balcony

sliding sash

plate-glass slider

deck

concrete foundation

entry

closet | bath

kitchen

bedroom

dining room

living room

deck

deck

Modernism

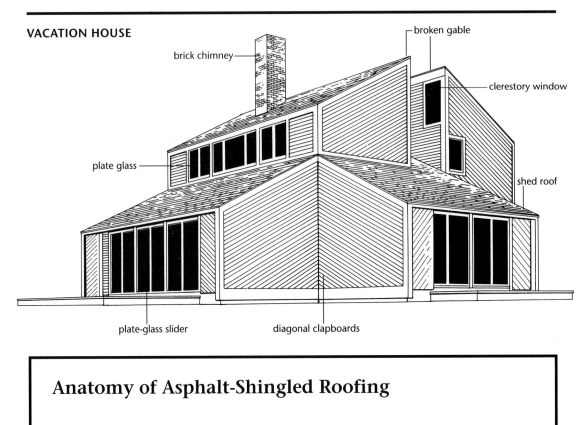

brick chimney

broken gable

clerestory window

plate glass

shed roof

plate-glass slider

diagonal clapboards

Anatomy of Asphalt-Shingled Roofing

Because it is inexpensive and waterproof, asphalt is a commonly used roofing material. As opposed to individual wood shingles, or shakes, asphalt shingles are typically made as butt strips with three tabs at the lower edge. When overlapped, the tabs appear as individual shingles.

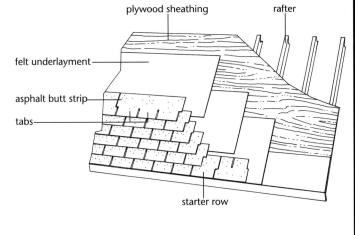

plywood sheathing

rafter

felt underlayment

asphalt butt strip

tabs

starter row

SEASIDE HOUSE

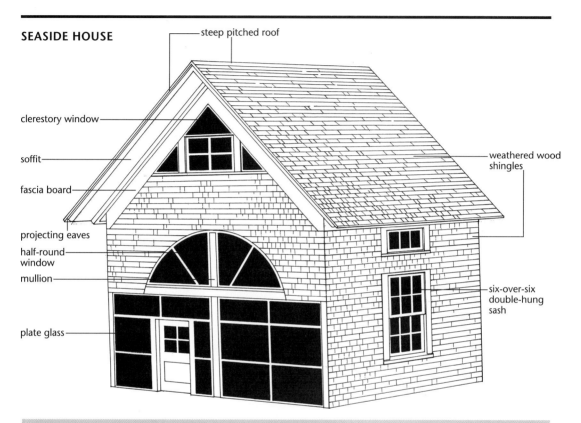

steep pitched roof

clerestory window

soffit

fascia board

projecting eaves

half-round window

mullion

plate glass

weathered wood shingles

six-over-six double-hung sash

Postmodernism is a contextual architecture in which a house design is developed with specific regard to the site, the design of neighboring structures, and climatic conditions. Designs often draw on local building types, such as the Florida Cracker House (see pages 112–113) as well as colonial architectural and American vernacular modes such as the Shingle and Stick styles. This interest coincided with a growing preservation movement in America, which gained momentum with the National Historic Preservation Act of 1966.

In contrast to previous revival movements, Postmodernism has a sense of humor and an attitude —a certain chip on its shoulder that gives the style its edge. Turned out in Pompeiian colors, designs might make liberal use of such traditional Classical vocabulary as the pediment and the Palladian window, but the familiar forms are deliberately exaggerated, overblown, flattened, or designed to look broken or eroded. This is a style of applied ornament in which decoration does not require a specific purpose. Designers have been criticized for rummaging among various styles and combining elements in an indiscriminate and superficial pastiche. At its best, however, Postmodernism is stark and original and represents a return to "humanized" design.

The movement reached its height of popularity in the 1970s and 1980s. Its playful qualities made it particularly well suited to beach houses.

Postmodernism

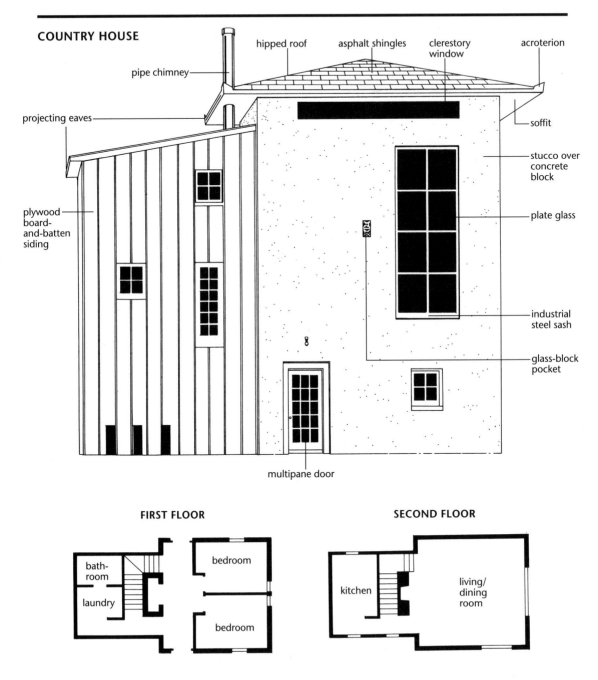

COUNTRY HOUSE

pipe chimney

hipped roof

asphalt shingles

clerestory window

acroterion

projecting eaves

soffit

stucco over concrete block

plate glass

plywood board-and-batten siding

industrial steel sash

glass-block pocket

multipane door

FIRST FLOOR

bathroom

laundry

bedroom

bedroom

SECOND FLOOR

kitchen

living/ dining room

SEASIDE HOUSE

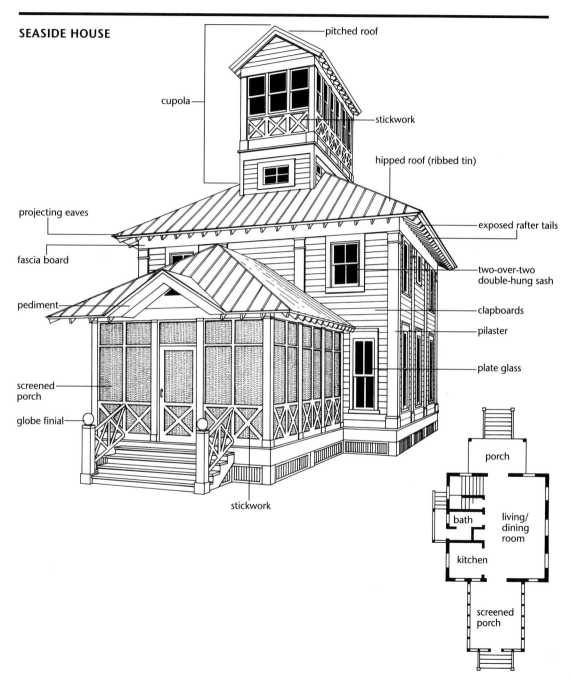

pitched roof

cupola

stickwork

hipped roof (ribbed tin)

projecting eaves

exposed rafter tails

fascia board

two-over-two
double-hung sash

pediment

clapboards

pilaster

plate glass

screened
porch

globe finial

stickwork

porch

bath

living/
dining
room

kitchen

screened
porch

Postmodernism

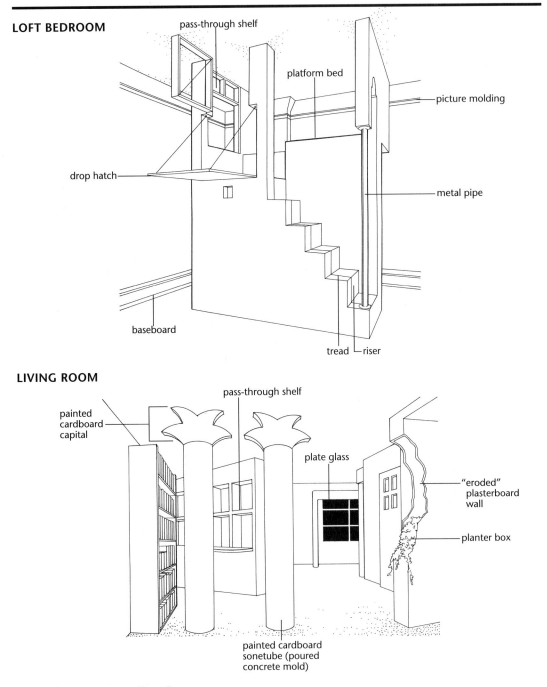

LOFT BEDROOM

pass-through shelf

platform bed

picture molding

drop hatch

metal pipe

baseboard

tread — riser

LIVING ROOM

pass-through shelf

painted cardboard capital

plate glass

"eroded" plasterboard wall

planter box

painted cardboard sonetube (poured concrete mold)

FIREPLACES

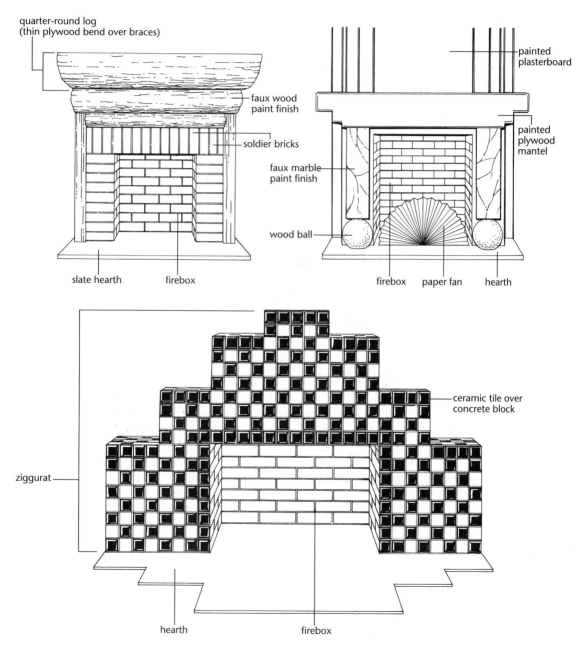

quarter-round log
(thin plywood bend over braces)

faux wood
paint finish

soldier bricks

slate hearth   firebox

painted
plasterboard

painted
plywood
mantel

faux marble
paint finish

wood ball

firebox   paper fan   hearth

ziggurat

ceramic tile over
concrete block

hearth   firebox

Bibliography

BOOKS

Ahrens, Donna; Tom Ellison; and Ray Sterling. *Earth-Sheltered Homes.* New York: Van Nostrand Reinhold, 1981.

Andrews, Ralph. *Curtis' Western Indians.* New York: Bonanza Books, 1952.

Andrews, Wayne. *Architecture, Ambition, and Americans.* New York: Free Press, 1978.

The Architectural Treasures of Early America. Harrisburg, Pa.: National Historical Society, 1987.

Barber, George Franklin. *George F. Barber's Cottage Souvenir Number Two.* Watkins Glen, N.Y.: American Life, 1982.

Barns, Cass. *The Sod House.* Lincoln: University of Nebraska Press, 1930.

Bealer, Alex. *The Log Cabin: Homes of the American Wilderness.* Barre, Mass.: Barre Publications, 1978.

Benjamin, Asher. *The American Builder's Companion.* New York: Dover Publications, 1969. Reprint of 6th edition (R. P. & C. Williams, 1827).

———. *The Architect, or Practical House Carpenter (1830).* New York: Dover Publications, 1988. Reprint of 1830 edition.

The Book of a Hundred Houses. New York: Duffield, 1906.

The Book of Little Houses. New York: MacMillan, 1915.

Brown, Henry Collins. *Book of Home-Building and Decoration.* Garden City, N.Y.: Doubleday, Page, 1912.

Bunting, Bainbridge. *Early Architecture of New Mexico.* Albuquerque: University of New Mexico Press, 1976.

———. *Taos Adobes.* Albuquerque: University of New Mexico Press, 1992.

Caemmerer, Alex. *The Houses of Key West.* Sarasota, Fla.: Pineapple Press, 1992.

Comstock, William T. *Victorian Domestic Architectural Plans and Details.* New York: Dover Publications, 1987. Reprint of *Modern Architectural Designs and Details* (New York: Architectural Publisher, 1881).

Cummings, Abbott Lowell. *The Framed Houses of Massachusetts Bay, 1625–1725.* Cambridge, Mass., and London: Belknap Press of Harvard University Press, 1979.

Davidson, Marshall. *The American Heritage History of Notable American Houses.* New York: American Heritage Publishing, 1971.

Dickinson, Duo. *The Small House.* New York: McGraw-Hill, 1986.

Downing, A. J. *The Architecture of Country Houses.* New York: Da Capo Press, 1969. Reprint of 1850 edition (New York: D. Appleton).

Downing, Antoinette, and Vincent Scully, Jr. *The Architectural Heritage of Newport, Rhode Island.* New York: American Legacy Press, 1982.

Driver, Harold. *Indians of North America.* Chicago: University of Chicago Press, 1925.

Ehrsam, Fritz. *The Swiss Chalet in America.* Reading, Pa., 1916.

Fink, Augusta. *Adobes in the Sun.* San Francisco: Chronicle Books, 1972.

500 Small Houses of the Twenties. New York: Dover Publications, 1990. Reprint of *The Books of a Thousand Homes,* vol. 1. New York: Home Owners Service Institute, 1923.

Fleming, John; Hugh Honor; and Nicholaus Pevsner. *A Dictionary of Architecture.* Middlesex, England: Penguin Books, 1966.

Foley, Mary Mix. *The American House.* New York: Harper & Row, 1980.

Ford, James, and Katherine Ford. *The Modern House in America.* New York: Architectural Book Publishing, 1940.

Forman, Henry. *Early Manor and Plantation Houses of Maryland.* Eastern Maryland: Private printing, n.d.

Fowler, Orson S. *The Octagon House.* New York: Dover Publications, 1973. Reprint of *A Home for All* (1853).

Gamble, Robert. *The Alabama Catalogue: Historic American Buildings Survey.* Tuscaloosa: University of Alabama Press, 1987.

Gillon, Edmund V., Jr. *Pictorial Archive of Early Illustrations and Views of American Architecture.* New York: Dover Publications, 1971.

Glassie, Henry. *Pattern in the Material Folk Culture of the Eastern United States.* Philadelphia: University of Pennsylvania Press, 1968.

Gordon-Van Tine Co. *117 House Designs of the Twenties.* New York: Dover Publications, 1992. Reprint of *Gordon-Van Tine Homes* (Davenport, Iowa: Gordon-Van Tine Co., 1923).

Great Georgian Houses of America, vols. 1–2. New York: Kalkhoff Press, 1933, 1937.

Greene and Greene. The Architecture and Related Designs of Charles Sumner Greene and Henry Mather Greene: 1894–1934. Los Angeles: Los Angeles Municipal Art Gallery, 1977.

Grow, Lawrence. *Classic Old House Plans.* Pittstown, N.J.: Main Street Press, 1978, 1984.

——— and Dina Von Zweck. *American Victorian.* New York: Harper & Row, 1984.

Haase, Ronald. *Classic Cracker.* Sarasota, Fla.: Pineapple Press, 1992.

Hamlin, Talbot. *Greek Revival Architecture in America.* New York: Oxford University Press, 1944.

Handlin, David. *The American Home.* Boston: Little, Brown, 1979.

Hannaford, Donald, and Revel Edwards. *Spanish Colonial or Adobe Architecture of California 1800–1850.* New York: Architectural Book Publishing, 1931.

Harris, Cyril. M.,ed. *Illustrated Dictionary of Historic Architecture.* New York: Dover Publications, 1977.

Hatton, Hap. *Tropical Splendor.* New York: Knopf, 1987.

Historic American Buildings Survey in Indiana. Bloomington: Indiana University Press, 1983.

Historic American Buildings Survey: New York. New York: Garland Publications, 1979.

Historic American Buildings Survey: Northern Illinois, 1833–1872. Washington, D.C.: National Park Service, 1936–37.

Historic American Buildings Survey: Texas Catalogue. San Antonio: Trinity University Press, 1974.

Hitchcock, Henry-Russell. *Architecture: Nineteenth and Twentieth Centuries.* Middlesex, England: Penguin Books, 1958.

Hofsinde, Robert. *Indians at Home.* New York: William Morrow, 1964.

House and Garden's Book of Houses. New York: Condé Nast, 1920.

Hubka, Thomas. *Big House, Little House, Back House, Barn.* Hanover, N.H.: University Press of New England, 1984.

Jensen, Robert. *Ornamentalism: The New Decorativeness in Architecture and Design.* New York: Clarkson Potter, 1982.

Jordy, William. *American Buildings and Their Architects: Progressive and Academic Ideals at the Turn of the Twentieth Century.* Garden City, N.Y.: Anchor Books, 1976.

Kauffman, Henry. *Architecture of the Pennsylvania Dutch Country 1700–1900.* Elverson, Pa.: Old Springfield Shoppe, 1992.

Keefe, Charles, ed. *The American House.* New York: U.P.C. Book Company, 1922.

Kelly, J. Frederick. *Early Domestic Architecture of Connecticut.* New York: Dover Publications, 1963.

Lafever, Minard. *The Beauties of Modern Architecture.* New York: Da Capo Press, 1968. Reprint of 3rd edition (New York: D. Appleton, 1839).

Lancaster, Clay. *The American Bungalow.* New York: Abbeville Press, 1985.

———. *Antebellum Architecture of Kentucky.* Lexington: University Press of Kentucky, 1991.

Lavine, Sigmund. *The Houses the Indians Built.* New York: Dodd, Mead, 1975.

Lewis, Arnold. *American Country Houses of the Gilded Age.* New York: Dover Publications, 1982. Reprint of George William Sheldon's *Artistic Country-Seats* (New York: D. Appleton, 1886–87).

Lockwood, Charles. *Bricks and Brownstone: The New York Row House, 1783–1929.* New York: McGraw-Hill, 1972.

Makinson, Randell. *Greene and Greene.* Salt Lake City: Peregrine Smith, 1979.

Manucy, Albert. *The Houses of St. Augustine.* Gainsville: University Press of Florida, 1978. Reprint of 1962 edition, sponsored by St. Augustine Historical Society.

Mayhew, Edgar, and Minor Meyers, Jr. *A Documentary History of American Interiors from the Colonial Era to 1915.* New York: Charles Scribner's Sons, 1980.

McCalester, Virginia, and Lee McCalester. *A Field Guide to American Houses.* New York: Alfred A. Knopf, 1984.

McCoy, Esther. *Five California Architects.* New York: Reinhold Publishing, 1961.

McDermott, John, ed. *The French in the Mississippi Valley.* Champaign: University of Illinois Press, 1965.

McKee, Harley. *Introduction to Early American Masonry.* Washington, D.C.: National Trust for Historic Preservation and Columbia University, 1973.

Metz, Don, ed. *The Compact House Book.* Pownal, Vt.: Garden Way Publishing, 1983.

Mohney, David, and Keller Esterling, eds. *Seaside: Making a Town in America*. New York: Princeton Architectural Press, 1991.

A Monograph of the Works of McKim, Mead & White, 1879–1915. New York: Da Capo Press, 1985. Reprint of 1925 edition (New York: Architectural Book Publishing).

Monteil, W. L. *Kentucky Folk Architecture*. Lexington: University Press of Kentucky, 1976.

Morgan, Lewis. *Houses and House-Life of the American Aborigines*. Chicago: University of Chicago Press, 1915.

Morrison, Hugh. *Early American Architecture from the First Colonial Settlements to the National Period*. New York: Oxford University Press, 1952.

Nabokov, Peter, and Robert Easton. *Native American Architecture*. New York: Oxford University Press, 1989.

The Natco Double House. Boston: Rogers & Manson, 1914.

New England Begins: The Seventeenth Century, vol. 2. Boston: Museum of Fine Arts, 1982.

New Orleans Architecture, vols. 4 and 6. Gretna, La.: Pelican Publishing, 1974.

New York City Landmarks Preservation Commission. *Guide to New York City Landmarks*. Washington, D.C.: Preservation Press, 1992.

Newcomb, Rexford. *Old Kentucky Architecture*. New York: W. Helburn, 1940.

Newport Mansions: The Gilded Age. Little Compton, R.I.: Foremost Publishers, 1982.

Nichols, Frederick. *The Architecture of Georgia*. Savannah: Beehive Press, 1976.

Noble, Allen. *Wood, Brick and Stone: The North American Settlement Landscape*, vol. 1: *Houses*. Amherst: University of Massachusetts Press, 1984.

Oringderff, Barbara. *True Sod: Sod Houses of Kansas*. North Neton, Kans.: Mennonite Press, 1976.

Patterson, Augusta Owen. *American Homes of Today*. New York: MacMillan, 1924.

Perrin, Richard. *The Architecture of Wisconsin*. Madison: State Historical Society of Wisconsin, 1967.

Pierson, William H., Jr. *American Buildings and Their Architects: The Colonial and Neo-Classical Styles*. Garden City, N.Y.: Anchor Books, 1976.

———. *American Buildings and Their Architects: Technology and the Picturesque; the Corporate and the Early Gothic Styles*. Garden City, N.Y.: Doubleday, 1978.

Pomada, Elizabeth, and Michael Larson. *Painted Ladies*. New York: E. P. Dutton, 1978.

Radford's Artistic Homes. Chicago: Radford Architectural Company, 1908.

Rawson, Richard. *The Old House Book of Barn Plans*. New York: Sterling Publishing, 1990.

Rifkind, Carole. *A Field Guide to American Architecture*. New York: New American Library, 1980.

Roth, Leland. *A Concise History of American Architecture*. New York: Harper & Row, 1979.

Schwartz, Marvin. *The Jan Martense Schenck House*. Brooklyn: Brooklyn Institute of Arts and Sciences, 1964.

Scully, Vincent, Jr. *American Architecture and Urbanism*. New York: Holt, Rinehart & Winston, 1969.

———. *The Shingle Style and the Stick Style*. New Haven: Yale University Press, 1955, 1971.

Seale, William. *Recreating the Historic House Interior*. Nashville: American Association for State and Local History, 1979.

Selected Houses from PA. New York: Reinhold Publishing, n.d.

Sexton, R. W. *Spanish Influence on American Architecture and Decoration*. New York: Brentano's, 1927.

Shephard, Augustus. *Camps in the Woods*. New York: Architectural Book Publishing, 1931.

Silver, Nathan. *Lost New York*. Boston: Houghton Mifflin, 1967.

Sloan, Samuel. *Sloan's Victorian Buildings*. New York: Dover Publications, 1980. Reprint of *The Model Architect* (Philadelphia: E. S. Jones, 1852).

Stotz, Charles. *The Early Architecture of Western Pennsylvania*. W. Helburn, 1936.

Stoudt, John. *Early Pennsylvania Arts and Crafts*. New York: A. S. Barnes, 1964.

Swank, Scott. *Arts of the Pennsylvania Germans*. New York: W. W. Norton, 1983.

Twenty-five Years of Record Houses. New York: McGraw-Hill, 1981.

Upton, Dell, ed. *America's Architectural Roots*. Washington, D.C.: Preservation Press, 1986.

——— and John Michael Vlach, eds. *Common Places: Readings in American Vernacular Architecture*. Athens, Ga.: University of Georgia Press, 1986.

Walker, Lester. *American Shelter*. Woodstock, N.Y.: Overlook Press, 1981.

Warren, Nancy Hunter. *New Mexico Style*. Santa Fe: Museum of New Mexico Press, 1986.

Wells, Sharon, and Lawson Little. *Portraits: Wooden Houses of Key West*. Key West: Historic Key West Preservation Board, 1979.

White, Jon. *Everyday Life of the North American Indians*. New York: Dorset Press, 1979.

Wicks, William. *Log Cabins: How to Build and Furnish Them*. New York: Forest & Stream Publishing, 1889.

Wills, Royal Barry. *Living on the Level: One-Story Houses*. Cambridge, Mass.: Houghton Mifflin, 1954.

———. *More Houses for Good Living*. New York: Architectural Book Publishing, 1968.

Wilson, Samuel. *The Architecture of Colonial Louisiana: Collected Essays*. Lafayette, La.: Center for Louisiana Studies, University of Southwestern Louisiana, 1987.

———. *Gulf Coast Architecture*. Department of State, Historic Pensacola Preservation Board.

Woodbridge, Sally. *California Architecture: Historic American Buildings Survey*. San Francisco: Chronicle Books, 1988.

Wright, Frank Lloyd. *Drawings and Plans of Frank Lloyd Wright*. New York: Dover Publications, 1983. Reprint of *Ausgefuhrte Bauten und Entwurfe von Frank Lloyd Wright* (Berlin: Ernst Wasmuth, 1910).

Wright, Richardson, ed. *House and Garden's Book of Houses*. New York: Condé Nast, 1915.

ARTICLES

Boyd, Elizabeth. "Fireplaces and Stoves in Colonial New Mexico." *El Palacio*, vol. 65, no. 6, 1958.

Bucher, Robert. "The Continental Log House." *Pennsylvania Folklife*, vol. 12, no. 4, Summer 1962.

———. "The Swiss Bank House in America." *Pennsylvania Folklife*, vol. 18, 1969.

Bushnell, David., Jr. "Native Villages and Village Sites East of the Mississippi." *Bureau of American Ethnology Bulletin*, no. 69. Washington, D.C.: Government Printing Office, Smithsonian Institute, 1919.

Gulliford, Andrew. "Sod Houses." *Fine Homebuilding*, Feb.–March 1986.

Landau, Sarah Bradford. "Richard Morris Hunt, the Continental Picturesque, and the 'Stick Style.'" *Journal of the Society of Architectural Historians*, Oct. 1983.

Long, Amos, Jr. "Bake-Ovens in the Pennsylvania Folk Culture." *Pennsylvania Folklife*, Dec. 1964.

Noble, Allen. "Pioneer Settlement on the Plains: Sod Dugouts and Sod Houses." *Pioneer America Society Transactions*, 1981.

Peterson, Charles. "Early St. Genevieve and Its Houses." *Missouri Historical Review*, vol. 35, Jan. 1941.

———. "French Houses of the Illinois Country." *Missouriana*, Aug.–Sept. 1938.

Weaver, William Woys. "The Pennsylvania German House." *Winterthur Portfolio*, vol. 21, no. 4, Winter 1986.

PERIODICALS

American Architect, vols. 1–3, 5, 7–8 (1919–27).

Amercian Architect and Building News, vols. 1–152 (1876–1938).

American Homes and Gardens, vols. 1–12, (1905–15).

The Architectural Forum (1935–38).

Architectural Record (1892–1945).

The Architectural Review and American Builder's Journal, vols. 1, 3 (1868–70).

The Craftsman (Feb. 1905).

The House Beautiful, vols. 16–81 (1904–76).

House and Garden, vols. 3–145 (1903–45).

Whitehead, Russell F., ed. *The White Pine Series of Architectural Monographs*, vols. 9 (no. 3)–17 (no. 6). St. Paul, Minn.: White Pine Bureau, 1921–31.

Credits

ABBREVIATIONS AND NOTATIONS

AIA (adapted from photos and measured drawings, The White Pine Monograph Series, Collected and Edited by Russell F. Whitehead, The George P. Lindsay Collection, The American Institute of Architects Library and Archives, Washington, D.C.); AMNH (adapted from photo, American Museum of Natural History); BL (adapted from photo, Bancroft Library, University of California, Berkeley); HABS (adapted from drawings, Historic American Buildings Survey); MAI (adapted from photo, Museum of the American Indian); NTHP (adapted from building, National Trust for Historic Preservation); SI (adapted from photo, Smithsonian Institute); SPNEA (adapted from building or object, Society for the Preservation of New England Antiquities); UA (adapted from photo, University of Arizona).

CHAPTER 1 15 Engraving, Village of Pomeiooc, 1590, Smithsonian Institute. 16 (top, center) MAI; (bottom) BL, in *Native American Architecture* by Peter Nabokov & Robert Easton (New York: Oxford University Press, 1989). 17 (top) adapted from *Houses and House-Life of the American Aborigines* by Lewis Morgan (Chicago: University of Chicago Press, 1915); (center) adapted from *Indians at Home* by Robert Hosfinde (New York: William Morrow, 1964); (bottom) adapted from photo (Edward S. Curtis) in *Curtis' Western Indians* by Ralph Andrews (New York: Bonanza Books, 1952). 20 (center left) adapted from *Indians of North America* by Harold Driver (Chicago: University of Chicago Press, 1961); (bottom) adapted from engraving "Cherokee Settlement of Toqua," SI, in *Native American Architecture*. 21 (top, bottom) MAI. 22 (top) adapted from *Houses and House-Life of the American Aborigines*; (bottom left) AMNH, in *Native American Architecture*; (bottom right) adapted from *Indians of North America*. 23 (top) MAI; (center left) adapted from *Everyday Life of the North American Indians* by Jon Manchip White (New York: Dorset Press, 1979); (center right) adapted from photo (S. McAlister) in *Native American Architecture*; (bottom) adapted from *The Houses the Indians Built* by Sigmund Lavine (New York: Dodd, Mead, 1975). 24 (top) UA, (center) AMNH, both in *Native American Architecture*; (bottom) adapted from *The Houses the Indians Built*.

CHAPTER 2 28 (bottom), 29 adapted from *The Houses of St. Augustine* by Albert Manucy (Gainsville: University Press of Florida, 1962). 30 (bottom) adapted from *Early Architecture of New Mexico* by Bainbridge Bunting (Albuquerque: University of New Mexico Press, 1976). 31 (top) interior, El Rancho de las Golondrinas, La Cienega, N.M. 32 adapted from photos in *New Mexico Style* by Nancy Hunter Warren (Santa Fe: Museum of New Mexico Press, 1986). 36 DeWint House, Rockland County, N.Y., 1700, HABS (Daniel Hopping). 37 (top) door, Bennett House, Brooklyn, 1766, HABS (Carl Stove); (bottom left) door, Jackson Jones Homestead, Wantaugh, N.Y., HABS (Charles Hoffman); (bottom right) door, DuMond House, Hurley, N.Y., HABS (A. Schrowang). 38 adapted from drawing (Ian Smith), based on Schenck House, Brooklyn, c. 1670, in *The Jan Martense Schenck House* by Marvin Schwartz (Brooklyn: Brooklyn Institute of Arts and Sciences, 1964). 39 (bottom right) plan, Nicolas Haring Barn, Rockleigh, N.J., HABS. 43 Schaeffer House, Schaefferstown, Pa., c. 1736. 44 section view based on research by Albert T. Gamon. 45 Fort Zeller, Newmanville, Pa., 1745. 46–47 Oley Forge Ironmaster's Mansion, Oley, Pa., adapted from measured drawings by

Kenneth LeVan. 48 Peter Wentz Farmstead, Worcester, Pa., 1758. 49 bakehouse, Christian Herr House, Lampeter Township, Pa. 50–51 (bottom) plan, David Stauffer Barn, Butler County, Pa., HABS. 52–53, 56, 57 (bottom) based on research by Charles E. Peterson. 55 (bottom) plan, Riverlake Plantation, Pointe Coupee Parish, La., c. 1820, HABS (Sid Gray). 57 (top) Roque House, Nachitoches, La., mid-1700s, adapted from photo (J. Alphonse Prudhomme) in *America's Architectural Roots*, ed. Dell Upton (Washington, D.C.: Preservation Press, 1986). 58, 60, 61 Oakland Plantation, Nachitoches, La., HABS (Cynthia Steward, Jeffrey Solak). 59 Saribault Cabin, Murphy's Landing State Park, Minn., adapted from photos (Jim Mone) in *The Log Cabin: Homes of the American Wilderness* by Alex Bealer (Barre, Mass.: Barre Publications, 1978).

CHAPTER 3 65 (bottom left) c. 1675, SPNEA. 66 Eleazer Arnold House, Lincoln, R.I., c. 1687, SPNEA. 67 (bottom) based on research by William McMillen. 68 Lynnhaven, Virginia Beach, Va., 1725. 70–71 (top) Bond Castle, Calvert County, Md., c. 1650; (bottom left) Fairfield, Carter's Creek, Va., 1692. 73 (top left) door, White-Ellery House, Gloucester, Mass.; (center) door, Corwin House, Salem, Mass., c. 1675; (bottom right) window, Plymouth County, Mass., c. 1650; all adapted from *The Framed Houses of Massachusetts Bay* by Abbot Lowell Cummings (Cambridge, Mass.: Belknap Press of Harvard University Press, 1979). (top right) door, Salem, Mass., c. 1650–1700; (bottom left) window, Barnstable, Mass., c. 1700–30; both adapted from *New England Begins* (Boston: Museum of Fine Arts, 1982). (center left) window, Buttolph-Williams House, Weathersfield, Ct., c. 1693. 74 Sparrow-Leach House, Plymouth, Mass., c. 1679, adapted from drawings (Robert St. George & Robert Trent) in *New England Begins*. 75 Cushing Barn, Hingham, Mass., c. 1695, adapted from drawings (Robert St. George & Robert F. Trent) in *Common Places*, ed. Dell Upton & John Michael Vlach (Athens, Ga.: University of Georgia Press, 1986).

CHAPTER 4 77 Meason House, Philadelphia, 1802, adapted from measured drawings (Raymond Celli) in *The Early Architecture of Western Pennsylvania* by Charles Stotz (New York: W. Helburn, 1936). 78–79 Blandfield, Tappahannock, Va., 1769–73, HABS. 81 Gadsden House, Charleston, S.C., c. 1800, HABS. 82, 85 (top left), 87 (top left), 89 (bottom), Cowles House, Farmington, Ct., 1761, adapted from *Great Georgian Houses of America*, vol. 1 (New York: Kalkhoff Press, 1933). 83 (top) adapted from *Early Domestic Architecture of Connecticut* by J. Frederick Kelly (New York: Dover Publications, 1963). 84 (top) Deane-Barstow House, East Taunton, Mass., c. 1800, AIA (Kenneth Clark); (bottom) Roberts House, Washington County, Pa., adapted from measured drawings (C. A. McGrill) in *The Early Architecture of Western Pennsylvania*. 85 (top right) John Imlay House, Allentown, N.J., c. 1792, AIA (Kenneth Clark). 87 (top right) AIA. 88 (bottom right) John Stuart House, Charleston, S.C., c. 1770, adapted from measured drawings (H. J. Pringle) in *Great Georgian Houses of America*; (bottom left) Colross House, Alexandria, Va., 1799, AIA (Kenneth Clark). 89 (top) AIA (Kenneth Clark); (center) Beverly, Pocomoke River, Md., AIA.

CHAPTER 5 91 William Waln House, Philadelphia, 1805–8, arch. Benjamin Henry Latrobe. 92 (bottom left) plan, Harrison Gray Otis House, Boston, 1806, arch. Charles Bulfinch, adapted from *The American Heritage History of Notable American Houses* by Marshall Davidson (New York: American Heritage Publishing, 1971). 93 (top) Brewton-Sawter House, Charleston, S.C., AIA (Kenneth Clark);

(bottom) Thomas Bennet House, AIA (A.T. S. Stoney); 94 No. 55 Beacon Street, Boston, 1807, AIA (Kenneth Clark). 95 (top) William Blacklock House, Charleston, S.C., c. 1800; (bottom) Mount Nebo, Baldwin County, Ga., HABS (J. B. Richardson). 96 Smith House, Wiscasset, Me., c. 1792, AIA (Kenneth Clark). 97 Vreeland House, Nordhoff, N.J., 1818, AIA (Kenneth Clark). 99 (top) door, Rose Hill, Lexington, Ky., HABS; (center) door, Charleston, S.C., AIA (Kenneth Clark). 100 Brevoort House, N.Y.C., 1834, attributed to archs. Ithiel Town & A. J. Davis. 101 (top) Joseph Bowers House, Northampton, Mass., c. 1830, arch. Ithiel Town; (bottom) interior, Gordon-Banks House, Ga., adapted from *The Architecture of Georgia* by Frederick Nichols (Savannah: Beehive Press, 1976). 102 (top) Rattle and Snap, Columbia, Tenn., 1845; (bottom left) plan, adapted from *Greek Revival Architecture in America* by Talbot Hamlin (New York: Oxford University Press, 1944); (bottom right) fireplace adapted from *The Architect, or Practical House Carpenter* by Asher Benjamin (New York: Dover Publications, 1988; reprint of 1830 ed.). 103 (top) Rutledge House, Troup County, Ga., 1852; (bottom) fireplace adapted from *The Beauties of Modern Architecture* by Minard Lafever (New York: Da Capo Press, 1968; reprint of 3rd ed. [New York: D. Appleton, 1839]). 104 based on Le Petit Salon, Vieux Carré, New Orleans, 1838. 105 (top right) door, Hendrix House, Riceville, Pa., adapted from photos and measured drawings (Robert Schmertz) in *The Early Architecture of Western Pennsylvania* by Charles Stotz (New York: W. Helburn, 1936); (bottom left) door, Diamond Point, Harrodsburg, Ky., adapted from *Old Kentucky Architecture* by Rexford Newcomb (New York: W. Helburn, 1940); (bottom right) door, Curtis-Devon House, Mt. Vernon, Ohio, HABS (R. W. Frend & H. C. Summersett). 106 (top) Dunton House, Belvidere, Ill., HABS (Bertha Whitman); (bottom) Starr Street House, New London, Ct., 1825. 107 Alsop House, Middletown, Ct., 1838, adapted from *Great Georgian Houses of America*, vol. 2 (New York: Kalkhoff Press, 1933).

CHAPTER 6 109 Poole Cottage, Gloucester, Mass., AIA (Frank Brown). 110–11 Sawyer-Blackwell Farm, Sweden, Me., adapted from *Big House, Little House, Back House, Barn* by Thomas Hubka (Hanover, N.H.: University Press of New England, 1984). 112 Whiddon Cabin, Forest Capital Museum, Perry, Fla.; (bottom) adapted from *Classic Cracker* by Ronald Haase (Sarasota, Fla.: Pineapple Press, 1992). 113 adapted from *Classic Cracker*. 114–15 adapted from *New Orleans Architecture* (Gretna, La.: Pelican Publishing, 1974). 118 (top, bottom) adapted from photos in *True Sod* by Barbara Oringderff (North Neton, Kans.: Mennonite Press, 1976). 120 David Crenshaw House, Fayette County, Ky., adapted from *Antebellum Architecture of Kentucky* by Clay Lancaster (Lexington: University Press of Kentucky, 1991); 121 John Bowman II House, Mercer County, Ky., adapted from *Antebellum Architecture of Kentucky*; 124 Krause House, Kirchhayne, Wis. 125 Klein-Naegelin House, New Braunfels, Tex., c. 1846, HABS (Richard Werner & Glen Wilson). 126 Long S Box and Strip House, Martin County, Tex., HABS (Joseph Ruscin). 128–29 Estudillo House, San Diego, c. 1825, HABS (Richard Wilkinson). 130 Guadalupe Rancho Adobe, Guadalupe, Cal., HABS (Arthur Fox). 131 Larkin House, Monterey, Cal., c. 1840, HABS (Richard Berteaux). 132 Trescony Barn, Rancho San Lucas, Cal., adapted from photos (Morley Baer) in *Adobes in the Sun* by Augusta Fink (San Francisco: Chronicle Books, 1972). 133 adapted from photos in *New Mexico Style* by Nancy Hunter Warren (Santa Fe: Museum of New Mexico Press, 1986).

CHAPTER 7 136 Belmead, Powhatan County, Va., c. 1845, arch. A. J. Davis. **137** (bottom) Lyndhurst, Tarrytown, N.Y., 1838, arch. A. J. Davis., NTHP. **138** Bowen House, Woodstock, Ct., 1846, arch. Joseph Wells, SPNEA. **139** Wayside Cottage, adapted from *Sloan's Victorian Houses* by Samuel Sloan (New York: Dover Publications, 1980; reprint of *The Model Architect* [Philadelphia: E. S. Jones, 1852]). **140** *Sloan's Victorian Houses.* **141** (top left, center) adapted from *The Architecture of Country Houses* by A. J. Downing (New York: Dover Publications, 1969; reprint of 1850 edition [New York: D. Appleton]); (bottom right) Green-Meldrim House, Savannah, c. 1850. **142–44** adapted from *Sloan's Victorian Houses.* **146** Benjamin Petty House, Clayton, Ala., c. 1860, HABS (Waid, Holmes & Assoc.). **147** adapted from *The American Agriculturalist,* 1885; in *The Old House Book of Barns* by Richard Rawson (New York: Sterling Publishing, 1990). **148–49** John Anderton House and Stable, Chicopee Falls, Mass., c. 1879. **150, 152** Seabright, N.J., house, c. 1875, arch. R. H. Robertson. **153** Samuel Pratt House, Newport, R.I., c. 1872; plan (Warren Oakley) adapted from *The Architectural Heritage of Newport, Rhode Island* by Antoinette Downing & Vincent Scully, Jr. (New York: American Legacy Press, 1982). **154, 156** San Francisco house, adapted from photos (Morley Baer) in *Painted Ladies* by Elizabeth Pomada & Michael Larsen (New York: E. P. Dutton, 1978). **155** Smythe House, Washington, D.C., c. 1883, arch. W. Claude Frederic. **157** c. 1875, archs. A. Kimbel & J. Cabus. **158** Short Hills, N.J., house, c. 1880, archs. Lamb & Wheeler, adapted from *Victorian Domestic Architectural Plans and Details* by William T. Comstock (New York: Dover Publications, 1987; reprint of *Modern Architectural Designs and Detail* [New York: Architectural Publisher, 1881]). **159** Eldridge Johnson House, 1882, Cape May, N.J., HABS (Benson). **161** (bottom), **162** adapted from *George F. Barber's Cottage Souvenir Number Two* by George F. Barber (Watkins Glen, N.Y.: American Life, 1982). **163** Short Hills, N.J., house, c. 1882, archs. Lamb & Rich. **164** Dudley House, Waverly, Mass., 1908, arch. William Northrop. **163** (top) L. W. Bacon House, Norwich, Ct., 1882, arch. Stephen Farle; (bottom) Williams Stable, Cohasset, Mass., c. 1901, arch. J. A. Schweinfurth. **166–67** Carroll Street houses, Brooklyn, 1888, arch. C. P. H. Gilbert, adapted from measured drawing (Robert Hartman & Harry Hansen) in *Guide to New York City Landmarks* by New York City Landmarks Preservation Commission (Washington, D.C.: Preservation Press., 1992). **168** Sylvester Everett House, Cleveland, 1883, arch. Charles Schweinfurth, adapted from *American Country Houses of the Gilded Age* by Arnold Lewis (New York: Dover Publications, 1982; reprint of George William Sheldon's *Artistic Country-Seats* [New York: D. Appleton, 1886–87]). **169** Sturtevant Stable, Brookline, Mass., c. 1901, arch. W. G. Preston. **170–71** Read Lodge, Adirondacks, N.Y., 1905, archs. Davis, McGrath & Sherwood. **172** Courtesy Adirondack Museum, Blue Mountain Lake, N.Y. **173** Edward Mallinckrodt Boathouse, arch. Augustus Shephard. **174** 1889, arch. William S. Wicks. **175** (bottom left) Grace Church Rectory, N.Y.C., c. 1845, adapted from photo (Robert Mayer) in *Bricks and Brownstone: The New York Row House, 1783–1929* by Charles Lockwood (New York: McGraw-Hill, 1972); (bottom right) Wheelwright House, Woods Hole, Mass., 1888.

CHAPTER 8 177 (bottom) Biltmore, Asheville, N.C., 1895, arch. Richard Morris Hunt. **178** Burrage House, Boston, 1899, arch. Charles Brigham. **179** H. A. C. Taylor House, N.Y.C., 1896, archs. McKim, Mead & White., adapted from *A Monograph of the Works of McKim, Mead & White, 1879–1915* (New York:

Da Capo Press, 1985; reprint of 1925 ed. [New York: Architectural Book Publishing]). **180** Pulitzer House, N.Y.C., 1903, archs. McKim, Mead & White, adapted from *A Monograph of the Works of McKim, Mead & White.* **182** (top) Charles Garret House, Norristown, Pa., 1913, arch. Gordon McCririe; (bottom) archs. Taylor & Levi; both adapted from *House and Garden's Book of Houses* (New York: Condé Nast, 1920). **183** 4 East 74th St., N.Y.C., 1900, arch. Alexander Welch. **184** The Elms, Newport, R.I., 1901, arch. Horace Trumbauer. **185** J. R. De Lamar House, N.Y.C., 1903, arch. C. P. H. Gilbert. **186–87** William Evans House, Greenwich, Ct., archs. J. E. R. Carpenter & Walter D. Blair Assoc. **188** Arthur Keith House, Washington Heights, D.C., 1899, arch. Waddy B. Wood. **189** (top, bottom left) Andrew Stout House, Redbank, N.J., arch. John Russell Pope. **190–91** (top) Frederick Coffin House, Brookline, Mass., 1900, arch. J. A. Scweinfurth. **191** (bottom) Marshall Morgan House, Philadelphia, 1912, archs. Thomas, Churchman & Molitor. **192** (top, center) Lathrop Brown House, St. James, N.Y., 1922, archs. Peabody, Wilson & Brown; (bottom) George Herron House, Portland, Ore., arch. Harold Doty, adapted from *Architectural Record,* Feb. 1927. **193** (top) adapted from *House Beautiful,* Feb. 1920; (bottom) Frenaye House, Llewellyn Park, N.J., 1935, archs. Howard & Frenaye. **194** Gambrill House, Newport, R.I., archs. Carrere & Hastings. **195** Weston Stable, Dalton, Mass., 1902, arch. J. Vance. **196** George Washington Smith House, Santa Barbara, Cal., c. 1899, arch. George Washington Smith. **197** (top) Edward Hosmer House, Pasadena, Cal., 1986, archs. Greene & Greene, adapted from *Greene and Greene* by Randell Makinson (Salt Lake City: Peregrine Smith, 1979); (bottom) Lewis Garage, Racine, Wis., archs. Guilbert & Funston. **198** (left) George Washington Smith House; (top right) door, des. Samuel Yellin; hinges, des. P. A. Fiebiger; all adapted from *Spanish Influence on American Architecture and Decoration* by R. W. Sexton (New York: Brentano's, 1927). **199** "El Fureidis," 1903, arch. Bertram Goodhue. **200** (top) Brookline, Mass., house, 1912, archs. Allen & Collens; (bottom) garage, arch. Bernhardt Muller, adapted from *Pencil Points,* March 1936. **201** Edith Bogue House, Montclair, N.J., arch. Clifford Wendehack, adapted from *Architectural Record,* Feb. 1924.

CHAPTER 9 203 arch. Frank Lloyd Wright, adapted from *Drawings and Plans of Frank Lloyd Wright* (New York: Dover Publications, 1983). **204–5** Susan Lawrence Dana House, Springfield, Ill. (Dana-Thomas House State Historic Site), 1902–4, arch. Frank Lloyd Wright, HABS (James Hollis). **206** (top) Frank Hall House, Oak Park, Ill., 1904, arch. Eben Roberts. **207** (top) Avery Coonley House, Riverside, Ill., 1908, arch. Frank Lloyd Wright, adapted from *Drawings and Plans of Frank Lloyd Wright;* (bottom center) Amberg House, Grand Rapids, Mich., 1913, arch. R. V. Von Holst; (bottom right) Dana-Thomas House. **208–9** Theodore M. Irwin House, Pasadena, Cal., 1906, archs. Greene & Greene. **209** (bottom) plan adapted from *The American Bungalow* by Clay Lancaster (New York: Abbeville Press, 1985). **210** (top) garage, James A. Culbertson House, Pasadena, Cal., 1906; (bottom left), door, Mary E. Cole House, Pasadena, 1907; (bottom center, right) Charles Sumner Greene House, Pasadena, 1901; all, archs. Greene & Greene. **211** (top) Blacker House; Pasadena, Cal., 1907, archs. Greene & Greene. **212** "Very Popular 4-Bedroom Bungalow," adapted from *117 House Designs of the Twenties* (New York: Dover Publications, 1992; reprint of *Gordon-Van Tine Homes* [Davenport, Ill.: Gordon-Van Tine, 1923]). **213** "Homelike Cottage," 1905, des. Gustav Stickley. **214, 216** adapted from *500 Small Houses of the Twenties* (New York: Dover

Publications, 1990; reprint of *The Books of a Thousand Homes,* vol. 1 ([New York: Home Owners Service Institute, 1923]). **215** adapted from *American Architect,* May 1926. **217** adapted from *The Swiss Chalet in America* by Fritz Ehrsam (Reading, Pa., 1916). **218** "The Natco Double House," arch. George Frech. **220** (top) des. Gustav Stickley, 1903; (bottom) "Modern Home Interiors," National Lumber Manufacturers Association, 1929. **221** (top left, top right, bottom right) adapted from "The Door Beautiful," Morgan Co., Oshkosh, Wis., 1911; (bottom left) des. Gustav Stickley.

CHAPTER 10 223 adapted from design by arch. Arne Kartwold, Berkeley, Cal., in *Architectural Forum,* April 1935. **225** (top) adapted from "Demonstration House for Yonkers Better Housing Committee," in *Architectural Forum,* June 1935; (bottom) adapted from design by Charles Porter, in *Architectural Forum,* April 1935. **229** Bennati House, Lake Arrowhead, Cal., 1934, arch. Rudolph Schindler, adapted from *Five California Architects* by Esther McCoy (New York: Reinhold Publishing, 1961).

CHAPTER 11 231 based on "The Palace," Travel Coach Corp., Flint, Mich., 1943. **232** adapted from "Victory House," in *Architectural Forum,* April 1943. **233** based on Dymaxion II, c. 1941, arch. R. Buckminster Fuller. **235** adapted from *The Small Homes Annual* (Washington, D.C.: Home-builders' Research Institute, 1945). **238** (bottom left) fireplace, arch. Arthur Deam; (bottom right) fireplace, archs. Leinweber, Yamasaki, & Helmuth; both adapted from *Selected Houses from PA* (New York: Reinhold Publishing, n.d.). **239** adapted from *Living on the Level* by Royal Barry Wills (Cambridge, Mass.: Houghton Mifflin, 1954). **241** based on "The Alpine," 1946, American Plan Service, Miami, Fla. **243** adapted from *More Houses for Good Living* by Royal Barry Wills (New York: Architectural Book Publishing, 1968). **245** arch. Aymar Embury, adapted from *Life Houses,* 1938. **249** Hobe Sound, Fla., house, 1956, arch. Eliot Noyes, adapted from *Twenty-five Years of Record Houses* (New York: McGraw-Hill, 1981). **250–51** Minnesota Housing Agency Demonstration House, Camden State Park, Minn., 1980, arch. Peter Pfister, adapted from *Earth-Sheltered Homes* by Donna Ahrens et al. (New York: Van Nostrand Reinhold, 1981).

CHAPTER 12 253 based on Gwathmey Residence, Amagansett, N.Y., 1966–67, arch. Charles Gwathmey. **254–55** (top) based on design by arch. Paul Rudolph, 1963. **256** based on design by arch. Bob Giddings, adapted from *The Compact House Book,* ed. Don Metz (Pownal, Vt.: Garden Way Publishing, 1983). **258** (top) based on design by archs. Willis Mills, Jr., & Timothy Martin, 1971, adapted from *Twenty-five Years of Record Houses* (New York: McGraw-Hill, 1981). **259** based on Coxe-Hayden House, Block Island, R.I., 1981, archs. Venturi, Scott Brown & Assoc. **260** based on Reid House, Johns Island, S.C., 1987, archs. Clark & Menefee. **261** Cooper House, Seaside, Fla., based on design by Don & Libby Cooper, archs. Cooper Johnson Smith. **262** based on designs by arch. Wayne Berg. **263** (top) based on designs by Huck Snyder; (bottom) based on design by arch. Mike Jackson.

Index